Best of the Best from the

East Coast

Cookbook

Selected Recipes from the Favorite Cookbooks of
Maryland, Delaware, New Jersey, Washington DC,
Virginia, and North Carolina

The U.S. Capitol in Washington DC is among the most symbolically important buildings in the nation. It has housed the meeting chambers of the House of Representatives and the Senate for two centuries, and stands today as a monument to the American people and their government.

Best of the Best from the
East Coast
Cookbook

**Selected Recipes from the Favorite Cookbooks of
Maryland, Delaware, New Jersey, Washington DC,
Virginia, and North Carolina**

EDITED BY

Gwen McKee

AND

Barbara Moseley

Illustrated by Tupper England

QUAIL RIDGE PRESS
Preserving America's Food Heritage

Library of Congress Cataloging-in-Publication Data

Best of the best from the East Coast cookbook : selected recipes from the
favorite cookbooks of Maryland, Delaware, New Jersey, Washington,
DC, Virginia, and North Carolina / edited by Gwen McKee and Barbara
Moseley ; illustrated by Tupper England. — 1st ed.
  p. cm. — (Best of the best cookbook series)
  Includes index.
  ISBN-13: 978-1-934193-24-2
  ISBN-10: 1-934193-24-0
   1. Cookery, American. 2. Cookery—Atlantic States. I. McKee,
Gwen. II. Moseley, Barbara. III. Title: East Coast cookbook.
  TX715.B485646 2009
  641.5973–dc22   2008043529

ISBN-13: 978-1-934193-24-2 • ISBN-10: 1-934193-24-0

Book design by Cynthia Clark • Cover photo by Greg Campbell
Printed in Canada

First edition, February 2009

On the cover: Best Maryland Crab Cakes, page 184; Washington Red Skins, page 112;
and Cheese Bread, page 44.

QUAIL RIDGE PRESS
P. O. Box 123 • Brandon, MS 39043
info@quailridge.com• www.quailridge.com

Contents

PHOTO BY GWEN MCKEE.

The Concord Point Lighthouse in Havre de Grace, Maryland, is the oldest continuously operated lighthouse on the East Coast.

Quest for the Best
Regional Cooking

It seems that everywhere Barbara and I travel, we find that people love to talk about food. Invariably they mention specific dishes that have been an important part of their family's heritage and tradition, and do so with exuberance and pride.

"My mother always serves her fabulous cornbread dressing with our Thanksgiving turkey, and it is simply 'the best.'"

"Aunt Susan's famous pecan pie is always the first to go."

"No family occasion would be complete without Uncle Joe's chicken salad sandwiches."

Well, we heard, we researched, and we captured these bragged-about recipes so that people all over the country . . . and the world . . . could enjoy them.

My co-editor Barbara Moseley and I have been searching for the country's best recipes for three decades, and home cooks everywhere have learned to trust and rely on our cookbooks to bring them fabulous meals their friends and family will love! We always choose recipes based first and foremost on taste. In addition, the ingredients have to be readily available, and the recipes simple, with easy-to-follow instructions and never-fail results.

While touring the country and tasting the local fare, we delight in finding the little secrets that make the big difference. We have eaten buffalo in Wyoming, halibut in Alaska, lobster in Maine, gumbo in Louisiana, each prepared in a variety of creative ways. Finding out about conch in Florida and boysenberries in Oregon and poi in Hawaii . . . . No matter where we venture, this part of our job is always fun, often surprising, and definitely inspiring!

We found many similarities in cooking in this grouping of the states of Virginia, North Carolina, New Jersey, Maryland, and Delaware, and the District of Columbia. Truly we enjoyed the farms, the food, the flowers, as well as the history of the

early beginnings of our country. From this region we call the "East Coast," you'll find an abundance of fresh veggie recipes from their fertile gardens, a bounty of seafood recipes from shoreline catches, a variety of barbecue dishes, and so much more.

Discover and enjoy the tantalizing cuisine of the East Coast.

Gwen McKee

Gwen McKee and Barbara Moseley, editors of
Best of the Best State Cookbook Series

Beverages and Appetizers

PHOTO © LEN KAUFMAN / VIRGINIA TOURISM CORPORATION.

Susan Constant was the largest of three ships led by Captain Christopher Newport on the 1607 voyage that resulted in the founding of the first permanent English settlement in North America, Jamestown, in the new colony of Virginia. Replicas of the ship and her sisters, *Godspeed* and *Discovery,* are docked at Jamestown.

Wedding Punch

5 cups sugar
5 cups water
2 (3-ounce) packages strawberry
 Kool-Aid
1 (6-ounce) can frozen orange
 juice concentrate

1 (6-ounce) can frozen lemonade
 concentrate
1 (46-ounce) can pineapple juice
2 quarts ginger ale

Combine sugar and water in saucepan. Heat to boiling, stirring until sugar is dissolved. Add Kool-Aid to mixture while hot. Allow to cool. Add remaining ingredients along with enough water and ice to make 3 gallons.

Mennonite Country-Style Recipes (Virginia)

Champagne Nectar Punch

2 (12-ounce) cans apricot nectar
1 (6-ounce) can frozen orange
 juice concentrate
3 cups water

¼ cup lemon juice
⅛ teaspoon salt
3 (⅘-quart) bottles champagne,
 chilled

Mix all ingredients except champagne; chill. Add champagne just before serving. Makes about 42 servings in champagne glasses.

What's New in Wedding Food (North Carolina)

Fruit Fizz Punch

2 quarts boiling water
3 family-size tea bags
1 (6-ounce) can frozen
 orange juice concentrate
1 (6-ounce) can frozen
 grape juice concentrate

1 (6-ounce) can frozen
 lemonade concentrate
1 (32-ounce) bottle ginger ale
Ice

In large pitcher, pour water over tea bags. Steep 4 minutes. Remove tea bags. Allow to cool. In punch bowl, combine tea, juices, and lemonade. Before serving, add ginger ale and ice. Makes 20 (5-ounce) servings.

*Davie County Extension and Community Association Cookbook
(North Carolina)*

Lockhouse Punch

1 cup sugar
2 cinnamon sticks
1 whole nutmeg
4 whole allspice

2 cups apple cider, or apple juice
6 cups orange juice
2 cups vodka (optional)

Mix all ingredients except vodka in a crockpot and stir well. Cover and cook on low setting for 4–10 hours. Cook on high setting for 2–3 hours. Just before serving, you may add 2 cups vodka. This is the punch served at the Lockhouse during the Candlelight Tour (without the vodka).

Cooking Along the Susquehanna (Maryland)

Julie's Mint Tea

2 family-size tea bags (or
   4 regular)
Fresh mint
2 quarts boiling water

1⅓ cups sugar
½ cup lemon juice
¾ cup orange juice
2 cups ginger ale

Put tea bags and mint in a large container. Pour 2 quarts boiling water over. Cool. Add remaining ingredients and serve over ice. Makes about 3 quarts.

From Ham to Jam (Virginia)

Spiced Tea

½ cup unsweetened lemon-
   flavored instant iced tea
¼ cup sugar
¼ cup orange-flavored
   breakfast drink (dry)

¼ teaspoon ground cinnamon
¼ teaspoon ground cloves
⅛ teaspoon ground ginger
12 cups boiling water

Mix all ingredients, except water. Store in tightly covered container at room temperature up to 1 week. Pour boiling water over tea mixture; stir until dissolved. Makes 16 servings.

A Heavenly Taste You Can't Miss (North Carolina)

Cranberry Ice and Pineapple Shrubs

In colonial Virginia, shrubs were popular fruit juice concoctions spiked with alcohol and vinegar. Shrubs have evolved into nonalcoholic fruit juice beverages served over crushed ice, frozen fruit ice, or sorbet. Make the cranberry ice a day ahead and serve this recipe in a punch bowl or individual glasses.

FOR THE CRANBERRY ICE:

1 (16-ounce) can whole-berry cranberries

2 cups sweetened cranberry juice, or cranberry juice cocktail

Place the cranberries and cranberry juice in a blender and purée. Pour into ice cube trays for individual shrubs, or into a 1-quart container for a punch bowl presentation, and freeze.

FOR THE SHRUBS:

24 ounces soda water
1 quart pineapple juice, preferably fresh, chilled

2 limes, thinly sliced, for garnish

For a punch bowl presentation, pour soda water and pineapple juice over cranberry ice and garnish with lime slices.

   For individual shrubs, pour 2 ounces soda water into each glass and top off with pineapple juice, leaving enough room for 1–2 cubes cranberry ice. Add cranberry ice to each glass and garnish with lime slices. Allow cranberry ice to melt and soften a few minutes prior to serving. Serves 10–12.

Holiday Fare (Virginia)

One day, Elizabeth Lee, one of the few cranberry growers living in New Egypt, New Jersey, decided to boil some damaged berries instead of throwing them away. She liked the tasty jelly so much she started a business selling "Bog Sweet Cranberry Sauce." That was the beginning of the Ocean Spray company that still sells cranberry products today.

Wassail

½ cup sugar
½ cup water
12 whole cloves
2 cinnamon sticks

1½ quarts orange juice
2 cups grapefruit juice
1 quart apple or cider juice
1 orange

Combine sugar, water, and spices in deep saucepan; simmer 10 minutes. Strain this mixture, then add orange juice, grapefruit juice, and cider. Reheat and serve hot from punch bowl. For garnish, slice orange and float on top. Serves 16.

Hint: Use a star-shaped cookie cutter to cut each orange slice and float in punch bowl.

Discovery Tour 2006 Cookbook (Virginia)

Old Virginia Mint Julep

Steep fresh mint in best brandy; make a syrup of sugar and water (use this sparingly); fill a tumbler (cut-glass) to one-third of brandy; put in 3 teaspoonfuls of syrup; fill glass with pounded ice; stick 5 or 6 sprigs of mint on top and 2 or 3 strawberries. If old whiskey is used instead of brandy, more is required to make it strong enough. For an extra fillip, dash the julep with rum.

Chesapeake Bay Country (Virginia)

Bourbon Slush

4 tea bags
2 cups boiling water
2 cups sugar
7 cups water
1 (12-ounce) can frozen orange
   juice concentrate

1 (6-ounce) can frozen lemonade
   concentrate
1 cup bourbon

Steep tea bags in boiling water for 2–3 minutes. Remove tea bags and stir in sugar until melted. Add all remaining ingredients and stir well. Pour into 2–3 freezing cartons. Remove from mold and thaw 20–30 minutes before serving from punch bowl. Yields 20 (5-ounce) servings.

The Enlightened Titan (Virginia)

Raspberry Cordial

To each quart of ripe red raspberries, put one quart of best French brandy; let it remain about a week, then strain it through a sieve or bag, pressing out all the liquid. When you have got as much as you want, reduce the strength to your taste with water, and put a pound of powdered loaf sugar to each gallon; let it stand till refined. Strawberry cordial is made the same way. It destroys the flavor of these fruits to put them on the fire.

The Virginia House-wife (Virginia)

Grandmother's Eggnog

6 eggs	**2 cups whipping cream**
4 tablespoons sugar	**½ teaspoon salt**
5 tablespoons bourbon	**Nutmeg to taste**
1 tablespoon rum	**1 teaspoon vanilla**

Separate eggs, keeping whites cold until used. Beat yolks until light. Add sugar, a little at a time, beating well as you add it. Then add whiskeys a teaspoon at a time. (It is important to add whiskey slowly so egg yolks get well cooked and won't have a raw taste.) Whip cream and add to mixture. Then add the well-beaten egg whites, salt, a grating or so of nutmeg, and vanilla. Allow to ripen at least 12 hours, which improves the taste. Keep in cool place till ready to use, and mix well before serving. (It was once thought whiskey "cooked" eggs in the way vinegar cooks raw fish in seviche.)

Korner's Folly Cookbook (North Carolina)

One of Virginia's nicknames is "Mother of Presidents" because no other state has produced more U.S. presidents than Virginia. The eight presidents who were born in Virginia are: George Washington (1789–1797), Thomas Jefferson (1801–1809), James Madison (1809–1817), James Monroe (1817–1825), William H. Harrison (1841), John Tyler (1841–1845), Zachary Taylor (1849–1850), and Woodrow Wilson (1913–1921). This list includes six of the first ten presidents of the United States.

Homemade Irish Cream

A Bailey's Irish Cream substitute.

1 cup Irish whiskey
1 (14-ounce) can sweetened
  condensed milk
4 eggs, slightly beaten
2 tablespoons vanilla extract

2 tablespoons chocolate extract
1 tablespoon coconut extract
1 tablespoon powdered espresso or
  coffee

Blend all ingredients together in blender or food processor. Refrigerate 12–16 hours before serving to allow flavors to mellow. Serve over ice in Old Fashion glasses. Serves 4–6.

Note: In places where Bailey's Irish Cream is expensive, like in the states, or people don't have it with them, this recipe is fantastic and even richer than Bailey's. Try it out and I think you'll agree.

Sip to Shore (North Carolina)

Banana or Chocolate Milk Shakes

1 banana, peeled and sliced, or
  6 chocolate sandwich cookies
1 tablespoon vanilla ice cream

1 tablespoon honey
⅔ cup cold milk
⅓ cup plain yogurt

For banana shake, put all ingredients, except chocolate cookies, in blender, put lid on, and whiz it for about 1 minute. The milk shake should be evenly mixed and creamy. Pour and serve immediately.

For chocolate shake, eliminate bananas and substitute chocolate cookies; proceed as above.

Taste & See (Virginia)

Hot Crab Dip

2 (8-ounce) packages cream
  cheese, softened
1 (8-ounce) carton sour cream
4 tablespoons mayonnaise
½ teaspoon lemon juice
1 teaspoon dry mustard
⅛ teaspoon garlic salt
1 teaspoon Worcestershire
  (optional)

½ teaspoon horseradish (optional)
1 pound backfin crabmeat
1 cup shredded sharp Cheddar
  cheese, divided
Paprika
Assorted crackers

Preheat oven to 325°. Blend all ingredients except crabmeat, ½ cup cheese, and paprika in a blender or mixer. Fold in crabmeat and pour into baking dish. Bake for 45 minutes. Remove from oven and top with remaining cheese. Sprinkle with paprika. Serve with crackers. Yields 5½ cups.

Let Us Keep the Feast in Historic Beaufort (North Carolina)

Creamed Crab

1 pound fresh crabmeat
¼ cup margarine
¼ cup all-purpose flour
2 cups milk or half-and-half

Salt and pepper to taste
Worcestershire to taste
Herbed toast points

Remove and discard cartilage from crabmeat; set aside. Melt margarine in a large saucepan over low heat. Add flour; stir in milk, crabmeat, and seasonings. Transfer to a chafing dish. Serve over herbed toast points. Yields 8–10 servings.

Seafood Sorcery (North Carolina)

King Charles II regarded the Virginians "the best of his distant children" and elevated Virginia to the position "of dominion" along with England, Scotland, Ireland, and France. Thus one of the state's nicknames is the "Old Dominion."

Chafing Dish Crab Dip

Easy, and can be made ahead. Perfect for a party!

1 pound fresh backfin crabmeat,
   picked
1 (8-ounce) package cream
   cheese, softened
2 tablespoons milk
1 medium onion, chopped
2 tablespoons horseradish
Dash hot pepper sauce

Salt and white pepper to taste
4 tablespoons mayonnaise
3 tablespoons sherry/wine
Pinch seafood seasoning
Dash paprika
Toasted almonds
Crackers

Combine all ingredients except almonds and crackers. Bake at 375°
for 10–15 minutes. Sprinkle with toasted almonds, and serve in chafing dish with crackers. Serves 10–12.

Of Tide & Thyme (Maryland)

Hot Virginia Dip

Everybody's favorite!

1 cup pecans, chopped
2 teaspoons butter
2 (8-ounce) packages cream
   cheese, softened
4 tablespoons milk

5 ounces dried beef, minced
1 teaspoon garlic salt
1 cup sour cream
4 teaspoons minced onion

Sauté pecans in butter. Reserve. Mix all ingredients thoroughly.
Place in 1½-quart baking dish, top with pecans. Chill until serving
time. Bake at 350° for 20 minutes. Serve hot with crackers or small
bread sticks.

Virginia Hospitality (Virginia)

Reuben Dip

½ pound corned beef, chopped
½ cup sauerkraut, drained
   thoroughly, chopped
¼ pound Velveeta cheese,
   cubed

¼ pound Swiss cheese, grated
1½ tablespoons Dijon mustard
¾ cup mayonnaise

Mix all ingredients and bake uncovered in a 350° oven for 35 minutes.

The Fine Art of Dining (Virginia)

Layered Bruschetta Dip

1 (8-ounce) package cream
  cheese, softened
2 cloves garlic, minced

2 small tomatoes, chopped
⅓ cup sliced green onions
⅓ cup shredded Cheddar cheese

Mix cream cheese and garlic; spread onto bottom of 8- or 9-inch pie plate. Top with tomatoes, green onions, and cheese. Cover and refrigerate until ready to serve. Serve with favorite crackers.

Delightfully Seasoned Recipes (Virginia)

Game Day Dip

1 (8-ounce) package cream
  cheese, softened
1 (8-ounce) carton sour cream
2 cups shredded Cheddar
  cheese
½ cup chopped country ham

⅓ cup chopped green onions
⅓ cup chopped green bell pepper
¼ teaspoon Worcestershire
Paprika
Crackers or corn chips

Beat cream cheese at medium speed until smooth. Add sour cream. Stir in cheese, ham, onion, pepper, and Worcestershire. Spoon into oven-proof dish. Bake at 350° for 30 minutes. Sprinkle with paprika. Serve with crackers or corn chips.

Making Time (North Carolina)

Halftime Hot and Spicy Corn Dip

1 (8-ounce) package cream
  cheese
2 tablespoons butter or
  margarine
1 tablespoon garlic salt
2 tablespoons milk

2 tablespoons finely chopped
  jalapeño pepper
1 (8-ounce) can shoepeg corn,
  drained
1 large bag blue corn tortilla chips

Cook first 3 ingredients in a saucepan over medium heat until creamy and bubbly. Add milk, jalapeño, and corn; cook, stirring often, until thoroughly heated. Spoon into a serving dish. Serve with blue corn tortilla chips. Serves 8–10.

What Can I Bring? (Virginia)

Apple Dip

1 (8-ounce) package cream
  cheese, softened
½ cup packed brown sugar
¼ cup white sugar

1 (7½-ounce) bag bits-of-brickle
  (Heath)
Apple slices
Sprite or ginger ale

Mix cheese and sugars. Fold in brickle; mix well and refrigerate. Set out one hour before serving. Soak apple slices in Sprite or ginger ale to keep them from darkening. Drain before serving.

Just Like Mama's (Virginia)

Tarheel Crocks

½ pound sharp New York cheese
  (black rind), grated
2 hard-cooked eggs, mashed
¾ cup mayonnaise
1 teaspoon Worcestershire

8 stuffed green olives, chopped
½ teaspoon salt
¼ teaspoon paprika
1 teaspoon minced fresh parsley
¾ teaspoon grated onion

Combine all ingredients and blend together by hand. (Do not use a food processor, as it will purée the chopped ingredients.) Put in a crock and chill until ready to serve. Serve with crackers, Melba toast, or dark bread rounds. Yields 1 large or 2 small cheese crocks.

Even More Special (North Carolina)

How did North Carolina get the nickname the Tar Heel State? The story goes that during one of the fiercest battles of the War Between the States, the column supporting the North Carolina troops was driven from the field. After the battle, the North Carolinians, who had successfully fought it out alone, were greeted from the passing derelict regiment with the question, "Any more tar down in the Old North State, boys?" The answer: "No, not a bit; old Jeff's bought it all up. He's going to put it on you-un's heels to make you stick better in the next fight." General Lee, upon hearing of the incident, said, "God bless the 'Tar Heel' boys." And from that the nickname "stuck."

Pepper Jelly Dip

1 cup chopped pecans
1 cup shredded sharp Cheddar
  cheese

2 spring onions, chopped
1 (10-ounce) jar pepper jelly
Crackers

Mix ingredients together. Serve with your favorite crackers. Serves 8.

A Taste of the Outer Banks III (North Carolina)

Hot Pepper Jelly Appetizers

2 cups shredded Cheddar cheese
6 tablespoons (¾ stick) butter,
  chilled, chopped

1 cup flour
½ cup hot pepper jelly

Combine Cheddar cheese, butter, and flour in a food processor and process until mixture resembles coarse meal. Process for an additional 5–6 seconds or until mixture forms a ball. Chill, wrapped in plastic wrap, for 30 minutes. Shape into 2-inch balls. Arrange 1 inch apart on an ungreased baking sheet. Bake at 400° for 5 minutes.

Make a small indention on the top of each ball. Spoon one teaspoon of the hot pepper jelly into each indention. Bake for 5 minutes longer or until golden brown. Cool on the baking sheet for 2 minutes; remove to a wire rack to cool completely. Yields 24.

Beyond Peanut Butter and Jelly (New Jersey)

Sun-Dried Tomato Spread

3 ounces sun-dried tomatoes
2 large garlic cloves
1 teaspoon dried basil
½ teaspoon salt
½ cup olive oil

2 parsley sprigs
¼ teaspoon red pepper
1 green onion, chopped
6 ounces cream cheese
2 ounces butter, softened

Cover dried tomatoes with boiling water and let stand for 20 minutes to rehydrate. Drain. Combine all but cream cheese and butter in processor, then let marinate for 2 hours.

Combine cream cheese and butter. Whip until smooth. In small bowl lined with plastic wrap, layer cheese, tomato, cheese, tomato, and cheese. This keeps for several days in refrigerator. Serve with Cayenne Toast.

CAYENNE TOAST:
½ teaspoon sugar
½ teaspoon pepper
½ cup olive oil
½ teaspoon cayenne pepper

½ teaspoon salt
½ teaspoon paprika
½ teaspoon garlic powder
1 loaf French bread

Whisk ingredients (except bread) together. Cut bread into ¼-inch slices. Spread oil mixture on each slice with a pastry brush. Bake on ungreased sheet in a 200° oven for 1 hour.

Steppingstone Cookery (Maryland)

Layered Pesto Spread

1 cup whole fresh basil leaves,
    plus extra for garnish
⅓ cup grated Parmesan cheese
    (1⅓ ounces)

2 tablespoons olive oil
½ cup pine nuts
1 (8-ounce) container whipped
    cream cheese

Line a small bowl with plastic wrap. Chop 1 cup of basil in a food processor. Blend in Parmesan cheese and olive oil. Stir in the pine nuts by hand. Layer whipped cream cheese and basil pesto alternately in lined bowl, beginning and ending with cream cheese. Refrigerate for 60 minutes. Invert onto a serving plate and remove plastic wrap. Garnish with extra basil leaves and serve with crackers. Yields 1½ cups.

Note: This can be refrigerated in a tightly sealed container for up to 2 weeks.

Breakfast at Nine, Tea at Four (New Jersey)

Pecan Crusted Artichoke and Cheese Spread

4 tablespoons butter, divided
1 medium onion, diced
2 garlic cloves, minced
1 cup chopped frozen spinach, thawed, drained
½ cup mayonnaise
1 (14-ounce) jar artichoke hearts, drained and chopped

1 (8-ounce) package cream cheese, cut in cubes
¾ cup grated Parmesan cheese
1 (8-ounce) package 4-cheese blend shredded cheese
⅔ cup chopped pecans
½ cup herb stuffing mix
Pita chips or sturdy crackers

Melt 3 tablespoons butter in a large skillet; add onion and garlic; sauté until tender. Add spinach, and cook over medium heat, stirring often, for about 3 minutes. Add mayonnaise, artichoke hearts, cream cheese, Parmesan cheese, and shredded cheese, stirring until cheese melts. Spoon into a greased 2-quart baking dish. Bake at 350° for 20 minutes. Combine remaining 1 tablespoon butter, pecans, and stuffing mix, tossing until blended. Sprinkle over top, and bake 15 minutes more. Serve with pita bread chips or crackers.

Angel Food (North Carolina)

Cream Cheese with Jezebel Sauce

Great replacement for pepper jelly. Also a wonderful gift idea. May also be served with roast beef or pork.

1 (18-ounce) jar pineapple preserves
1 (18-ounce) jar apple jelly
1 (5-ounce) jar prepared horseradish

1 (1-ounce) can dry mustard
1 tablespoon cracked peppercorns
1 package cream cheese (any size)

In a bowl, combine preserves, jelly, horseradish, mustard, and peppercorns, mixing well. Pour into airtight containers. Cover and store in refrigerator. Serve over cream cheese as a spread accompanied with crackers. Yields approximately 4 cups of sauce.

Virginia Seasons (Virginia)

Brie with Brown Sugar

Very attractive.

1 small round of Brie
3 tablespoons butter
3 tablespoons brown sugar

3 tablespoons chopped nuts
  (pecans or walnuts)
1 tablespoon honey

Microwave Brie on HIGH for 15 seconds. Place on serving dish. Combine butter, brown sugar, nuts, and honey in a small microwave container. Microwave on HIGH for 15 seconds. Spread on top of Brie. Serve with sliced apples and plain crackers. Yields 8 servings.

Virginia Fare (Virginia)

Chesapeake Bay Virginia Crab Puffs

1 pound fresh or 1 (14.5-ounce)
  can crabmeat
1 cup mayonnaise
½ cup grated onion

1 cup shredded Cheddar cheese
1 tablespoon lemon juice
Pinch of salt
1 package hot dog buns

In a large bowl, combine all ingredients except hot dog buns. Cut rounds from buns using a small cookie cutter or rim of a juice glass, cutting 3 from each half of buns. Spread crab mixture evenly on top of rounds. Broil or bake at 400° about 5 minutes. Makes 48 puffs.

Note: Puffs may be baked and frozen for later use. Before serving, reheat at 400° about 10 minutes.

Virginia Cook Book (Virginia)

There are a number of different types of crabmeat to choose from when preparing recipes. "Lump" is the largest pieces of meat from the crab's body; it is the most expensive form of crabmeat. "Backfin" is white body meat in lump and large flakes and is best for dishes where appearance is important. "Special," flakes of white body meat other than lump, is good for casseroles and crabcakes. "Claw" is small, brownish meat from the claws; as the least expensive type of crab meat, it is good for appetizers, soups, and dips.

Crab-Potato Nibblers

1 (2-serving size) package instant
  mashed potatoes
1 teaspoon minced onion
1¼ teaspoons Worcestershire
⅛ teaspoon garlic powder

Dash of pepper
8 ounces crabmeat
1 egg, slightly beaten
½ cup fine bread crumbs

Prepare potatoes as directed except use 2 tablespoons less milk than specified. Add minced onion to amount of water specified in directions. Stir in Worcestershire, garlic powder, and pepper. Add crabmeat. Shape into bite-size balls. Dip into beaten egg; roll in bread crumbs. Fry in deep fat at 375° about 1 minute, until golden brown. Drain; serve hot. Yields 36 nibblers.

Island Born and Bred (North Carolina)

Crab Tassies

These tarts have a rich crab filling.

½ cup butter, softened
3 ounces cream cheese, softened
1 cup flour
¼ teaspoon salt
1 pound crabmeat
½ cup mayonnaise
1 tablespoon lemon juice

¼ cup finely chopped celery
2 small scallions, finely chopped
½ cup grated Swiss cheese
½ teaspoon Worcestershire
¼ teaspoon seasoned salt
Dash of Tabasco

Cream butter and cream cheese. Stir in flour and salt. Roll into 24 small balls and chill 1 hour. Press into tiny muffin tins, about 1¾ inches in diameter.

Mix crab with remaining ingredients. Spoon into unbaked shells and bake at 350° until golden, approximately 30 minutes. Yields 24.

Capital Classics (Washington, DC)

Cheesy Crab Hors D'Oeuvres

1 (8-ounce) package cream
  cheese, softened
1 teaspoon milk
1 tablespoon instant minced
  onion
¼ cup grated Parmesan cheese

½ teaspoon horseradish
1 cup (8 ounces) crabmeat
Salt and pepper to taste
1 (2-ounce) package slivered
  almonds (optional)

Blend together cream cheese, milk, onion, Parmesan cheese, and horseradish. Gently mix in crabmeat. Add salt and pepper. Put in shallow 1-quart baking dish, sprinkle almonds over top, if desired. Bake at 350° until lightly browned on top, about 20 minutes. Serve hot on crackers or as a dip.

Note: Can be served without cooking. Simply add milk to proper consistency for use as a spread or dip. Keep refrigerated until served.

The Rappahannock Seafood Cookbook (Virginia)

Shrimp Stuffed Celery

Good quickie hors d'oeuvre. Also good when serving several hors d'oeuvres.

1 (4½-ounce) can shrimp
  washed, drained, broken
1 teaspoon dried chives
3 tablespoons finely chopped
  onion
5 black olives, pitted, finely
  chopped

2 tablespoons slivered almonds
Dash of lemon juice
Enough mayonnaise for
  consistency
Celery stalks, cut in 3-inch
  pieces

Mix all ingredients thoroughly. Stuff celery and arrange on platter.

Sip to Shore (North Carolina)

Shrimp Spread

1 (8-ounce) package cream
  cheese, softened
½ cup sour cream
¼ cup good mayonnaise
1 cup seafood cocktail sauce
1 (8-ounce) package shredded
  mozzarella cheese

¾–1 pound salad shrimp (ready
  to eat)
3–4 spring onions, tops included,
  finely chopped
1 small tomato, seeds removed,
  finely chopped

In small mixing bowl, beat cream cheese, sour cream, and mayonnaise until smooth. Spread cream cheese mixture on a round serving platter. Cover cream cheese with cocktail sauce and sprinkle with mozzarella cheese, shrimp, onions, and tomato, in that order. Cover and chill. Serve with crackers or small pieces of assorted toasted bread.

Country Home Favorites (Virginia)

Shrimp Mold

Big hit on a cocktail table!

1 package unflavored gelatin
¼ cup water
1 cup mayonnaise
1 (8-ounce) package cream
  cheese, softened
Juice of ½ lemon
Dash of Worcestershire
1 pound cooked shrimp, cut in
  small pieces

1 cup finely chopped celery
1 small onion, minced
1 very small bottle olives,
  chopped
½ cup chopped green bell
  pepper

Dissolve gelatin in water. Whip mayonnaise, cream cheese, lemon juice, and Worcestershire until creamy. Add dissolved gelatin and rest of ingredients, mixing well. Pour into lightly greased mold. If using a fish-shaped mold, save 1 olive slice to make an eye.

The Smithfield Cookbook (Virginia)

Coconut Shrimp

This is a great "do-ahead" hors d'oeuvre.

1 pound medium shrimp	**2 tablespoons cream**
¼ cup flour	**¾ cup flaked coconut**
½ teaspoon salt	**⅓ cup dry bread crumbs**
½ teaspoon dry mustard	**3 cups vegetable oil**
1 egg	**Chinese Mustard Sauce**

Shell and devein shrimp, but leave tails intact. Combine flour, salt, and dry mustard in a small bowl. Beat egg and cream in another small bowl. Combine coconut and bread crumbs in shallow dish. Dip shrimp in flour mixture, then in egg-cream and finally in coconut-crumb mixture (coat well). At this point shrimp can be arranged in single layer and refrigerated.

When ready to cook, pour oil in medium saucepan (or wok) to 2-inch depth. Heat oil to 350°. Fry shrimp (6 or less at a time) for about 2 minutes. Turn once, cooking until golden brown. Remove with slotted spoon and drain on paper towels or paper bag. Keep warm in slow oven until all shrimp are cooked. Serve with Chinese Mustard Sauce and duck sauce.

Note: Can freeze and reheat in 350–370° oven for about 10 minutes. Serve on doilies to absorb any remaining grease.

CHINESE MUSTARD SAUCE:

⅓ cup dry mustard	**1 tablespoon honey**
2 teaspoons vinegar	**¼ cup cold water (maybe less)**

Mix all ingredients until well blended. Refrigerate.

Jaycee Cookin' (Maryland)

Marinated Shrimp in Avocado

This is one of my favorite appetizers. It also is good for a brown bag lunch if you wrap it all in Saran Wrap. Much more elegant than a sandwich.

½ cup salad oil
½ cup lime or lemon juice
2 tablespoons vinegar
1½ teaspoons salt
½ teaspoon each: dill seed
  and dry mustard

Dash of cayenne
2 teaspoons capers
1 pound shrimp, shelled,
  deveined
3 or 4 avocados, halved, peeled
Boston lettuce

Combine oil, lime juice, vinegar, seasonings, and capers for marinade. Toss with shrimp and chill several hours, stirring occasionally. Brush avocado halves with some of the marinade. Arrange on lettuce and fill with shrimp. Serve with remaining marinade. Makes 6–8 servings.

Could I Have Your Recipe? (Virginia)

Oysters Virginia Beach

½ pound mushrooms, thinly
  sliced
6 tablespoons butter, divided
3 tablespoons flour
1–2 dozen fresh oysters
⅓ cup dry sherry
3 tablespoons sliced green
  onions

3 tablespoons chopped parsley
¼ teaspoon salt
⅛ teaspoon cayenne pepper
⅛ teaspoon garlic powder
½ cup bread crumbs
Bacon, cooked, crumbled (optional)
Parmesan cheese (optional)

Preheat oven to 350°. Sauté mushrooms in 2 tablespoons butter; set aside. Melt remaining butter. Stir in flour; cook slightly. Add remaining ingredients except bread crumbs. Place in buttered 1½-quart casserole. Top with crumbs. Bake at 350° for 15 minutes. Ladle into individual shells for serving, and add optional toppings, if desired. Serves 6.

Tidewater on the Half Shell (Virginia)

Oyster Filling for Patty Shells

1 bunch spring onions, minced
¾ stick butter
3 tablespoons minced parsley
2 cloves garlic, pressed
5 tablespoons flour
1 pint oysters, drained, halved
Salt and pepper to taste

Sauté onions in butter; add parsley and garlic, and stir in flour till smooth. Add oysters (will get thinner as they cook, but a little water may be added if too thick). Season with salt and pepper. Yields enough filling for 3 dozen small patty shells.

High Hampton Hospitality (North Carolina)

Florentine Cheddar Squares

This is a great appetizer, especially served warm from the oven for an open house, tea, or pre-dinner hors d'oeuvre.

1 cup all-purpose flour
1 teaspoon baking powder
1 cup milk
1 stick margarine, melted
2 eggs, beaten
1 cup minced onion
10 ounces Cheddar cheese, shredded
1 (10-ounce) package frozen chopped spinach, cooked, squeezed dry

Mix all ingredients together in order given. Bake at 350° in a greased 9-inch square pan for 30 minutes. Cut into squares to serve. Makes about 36 squares. Freezes well.

Taste of Goodness (Virginia)

Parmesan Toast Strips

4 slices bread, toasted
¼ cup margarine, melted
½ teaspoon onion salt (optional)
1 cup finely crushed corn chips
¼ cup grated Parmesan cheese

Remove crust from bread, then cut each slice into 5 strips. Roll in mixture of margarine and salt. Combine corn chips and cheese; dip sticks in this and bake at 400° for 5–8 minutes until crisp. Makes 20.

Mushrooms, Turnip Greens & Pickled Eggs (North Carolina)

Olive Cheese Nuggets

¼ pound Cheddar cheese,
  grated
¼ cup butter or margarine,
  softened

¾ cup sifted all-purpose flour
⅛ teaspoon salt
½ teaspoon paprika
36–40 medium stuffed olives

Blend cheese and butter; add flour, salt, and paprika. Mix well to form dough. Using about 1 teaspoon dough, flatten out in palm and wrap around olive. Place on ungreased cookie sheet and bake at 400° for 12–15 minutes until light brown. These may be made in advance and refrigerated, or frozen baked or unbaked. Yields 36–40.

The Stuffed Cougar (Virginia)

Fred's Cocktail Wieners

1 (16-ounce) jar chili sauce
1 (8-ounce) jar grape jelly

2–3 packages Little Smokies
  sausages

Heat chili sauce and grape jelly in a saucepan over medium heat. Add Smokies and let simmer until Smokies are heated thoroughly. Flavor is better if entire mixture is allowed to simmer 30–40 minutes. Dish can also be prepared in a crockpot.

Kids in the Kitchen (Virginia)

Asparagus Ham Rolls

16 asparagus stalks, cooked
4 thin slices boiled ham
½ cup grated sharp Cheddar
  cheese

1 cup medium white sauce (2
  tablespoons butter, 2 tablespoons
  flour, 1 cup milk, salt and
  pepper)

Put asparagus stalks on each ham slice. Roll up and fasted with a toothpick. Broil 5 minutes on each side. Add cheese to heated sauce. Stir till melted and pour over ham rolls. Broil to golden brown. Garnish with toast points.

Dan River Family Cookbook (Virginia)

Virginia Ham Fantastics

2–3 (12-count) packages
  Parkerhouse rolls (or 20 count
  party rolls)
¾ pound Virginia ham, sliced
  paper thin
½ pound Swiss cheese slices

1 stick butter or margarine,
  softened
1–2 tablespoons mustard
2 tablespoons Worcestershire
1 tablespoon dried minced onion
1 tablespoon poppy seeds

Line 11x13-inch baking sheet with foil that has been lightly greased. Place rolls that have been filled with ample slices (cut quarter size) of ham and cheese on the foil-lined pan. Place rolls very close together. Spoon a mixture of butter, mustard, Worcestershire, onion, and poppy seeds over top of rolls. Cover with foil and refrigerate for several hours, or they may be baked right away. When ready to bake, preheat oven to 350°. Leave foil on to prevent scorching, and bake approximately 30 minutes. Serves 8.

Virginia Traditions (Virginia)

Sesame Chicken with Honey Dip

Served by popular request each year at an annual tailgate party.

CHICKEN:
½ cup mayonnaise
1½ teaspoons dry mustard
2 teaspoons instant minced onion

1 cup fine dry bread crumbs
½ cup sesame seeds
2 cups uncooked cubed chicken

Preheat oven to 400°. Mix mayonnaise, mustard, and minced onion in a shallow dish or pie pan; set aside. Mix crumbs and sesame seeds. Toss chicken in mayonnaise mixture, then roll in crumb mixture. Place on baking sheet. Bake at 400° for 12–15 minutes, or until lightly browned. Serve hot or at room temperature with dip. Yields 2 dozen.

HONEY DIP:
2 tablespoons honey

1 cup mayonnaise

Combine honey with mayonnaise.

A Matter of Taste (New Jersey)

Brandied Meatballs

I've had raves for this recipe each time I've served it.

BRANDIED PEACH SAUCE:

1 (18-ounce) jar peach preserves	½ cup brandy
¾ cup light brown sugar, firmly packed	½ cup peach brandy
	¼ teaspoon nutmeg

Combine ingredients in a bowl, blending well. Makes about 3 cups.

MEATBALLS:

2 pounds ground beef	¼ teaspoon pepper
¾ cup milk	2 drops hot sauce
½ cup bread crumbs	2 tablespoons hot cooking oil
1 tablespoon Worcestershire	1 tablespoon cornstarch, mixed
1½ teaspoons salt	with 1 tablespoon cold water
1 teaspoon garlic powder	(optional)
¼ teaspoon nutmeg	1 (20-ounce) can sliced peaches,
¼ teaspoon ginger	drained

Blend first 10 ingredients in a bowl. Shape mixture into 1- to 1½-inch balls. In a large heavy skillet, brown meatballs in hot oil. Remove with slotted spoon, set aside; keep warm. Reduce heat, blend Brandied Peach Sauce into meat drippings, and simmer 10 minutes. Add meatballs to sauce and coat thoroughly. Cover and simmer 45 minutes to 1 hour. If necessary, add cornstarch mixture to sauce, stirring constantly, and cook on low heat until thickened. Transfer to a chafing dish for buffet service. Garnish with canned sliced peaches. Makes about 40 meatballs.

Apron Strings (Virginia)

Although the first feast of thanksgiving took place at Plymouth Rock in 1622, a collective prayer of thanksgiving was held in the Virginia Colony on December 4, 1619, near the current site of Berkeley Plantation, marking the first Thanksgiving in North America. Thanksgiving Day is now an annual one-day holiday to give thanks, traditionally to God, for the things one has at the end of the harvest season. In 1939, President Roosevelt set the date for Thanksgiving to the fourth Thursday of November (approved by Congress in 1941).

Party Pork Tenderloin

1½ cups oil
¾ cup soy sauce
1 tablespoon dry mustard
1 tablespoon black pepper
⅓ cup lemon juice

⅓ cup white wine vinegar
1 clove garlic, crushed
1 (1- to 2-pound) package
  pork tenderloin
Rolls or party bread slices

Combine first 7 ingredients for marinade. Marinate pork overnight in refrigerator. Cook at 350° uncovered for 45 minutes. Slice thin and serve with rolls or party bread slices. Yields 48 appetizers or a main dish for 4.

Let Us Keep the Feast in Historic Beaufort (North Carolina)

Tailgate Tortillas

Take plenty along since tortilla roll-ups are awfully easy to eat.

2 (8-ounce) packages
  Neufchâtel cheese (or
  cream cheese), softened
1 cup chopped almonds,
  toasted
½ cup sliced green onions
2 tablespoons Dijon mustard

2 cloves garlic, minced
1 teaspoon dill weed
1 teaspoon dried sweet basil
2 large cracker bread rounds,
  or 6 large flour tortillas
1 pound thinly sliced ham
8 leaves red leaf lettuce

Blend cheese with almonds, green onions, mustard, garlic, dill weed, and basil. Soften cracker bread according to package directions, or lightly steam the tortillas. Spread cheese mixture on one side of each cracker bread or flour tortilla. Top with ham slices and lettuce, dividing equally. Roll tightly, sealing edges. Roll in aluminum foil and chill until ready to serve. To serve, cut in long diagonal slices, placing cut side down on serving plate. Yields 6–8 servings.

You're Invited (North Carolina)

Vegetable Pizza

2 (8-ounce) cans crescent rolls
2 (8-ounce) packages cream
  cheese, softened
1 cup sour cream
2 teaspoons dill weed
¼ teaspoon garlic powder

Variety of grated vegetables such
  as cauliflower, carrots, broccoli
  florets, bell pepper, celery,
  tomato, radish, etc.
Grated cheese

Press and seal seams of rolls on a cookie sheet. Prick so it won't
puff up. Bake according to directions. Cool. Mix cream cheese, sour
cream, dill weed, and garlic powder; spread over cooled crust. Top
with veggies and cheese last of all. Slice to serve. Serves 12.

Think Healthy (Virginia)

Kennett Square Mushrooms

20–25 fresh medium-sized
  mushrooms (approximately
  ½ pound)
2 tablespoons butter
1 small onion, minced
1 tablespoon Worcestershire

⅓ cup soft, fine bread crumbs
½ cup shredded sharp Cheddar
  cheese
Salt and pepper to taste
Parsley
2 tablespoons water

Select mushrooms with closed caps. Pull stems from mushrooms
and chop finely. Melt butter in skillet and add stems and onion.
Sauté until tender and translucent. Stir in remaining ingredients
except water. If preferred, parsley may be sprinkled on top instead of
mixed in with other ingredients. Fill mushroom caps with mixture,
mounding over top. Arrange mushrooms in ovenproof serving dish.
At this point mushrooms can be refrigerated up to 24 hours. Before
serving, add 2 tablespoons of water to dish. Bake at 350° for 20 minutes. Serve hot. Yields 20–25 mushrooms.

Winterthur's Culinary Collection (Delaware)

Onion Ring Loaf

This is better than Blooming Onions!

**4–6 mild white onions or sweet
  onions**
1 cup milk
3 eggs, beaten

Salt to taste
**Approximately 2 cups pancake
  mix, like Bisquick Baking Mix**
Oil for deep frying

Slice onions crosswise and separate into rings. Soak rings in mixture of milk, eggs, and salt to taste in bowl for 30 minutes. Dip each onion ring in pancake mix and fry in oil heated to 375° until golden brown. Pack fried onion rings solidly but without pressing, into an 8x4-inch loaf pan. Bake at 400° for 10–15 minutes. Turn onto serving plate. Makes 4 servings.

Country Chic's Home Cookin (Maryland)

Bambinos

PASTRY ROUNDS:
2 cups all-purpose flour
1 teaspoon salt

⅔ cup shortening
¼ cup water

Heat oven to 475°. Mix flour and salt; cut in shortening. Sprinkle with water and mix with fork. Divide in half and roll each to ⅛-inch thickness. Cut into 1½- to 2-inch circles. Place on foil-covered baking sheet and prick with fork. Bake 8–10 minutes or until lightly browned.

1 (6-ounce) can tomato paste
1 teaspoon garlic salt
¼ teaspoon oregano
**¼ pound American or mozzarella
  cheese, cubed**

**⅛ pound salami or pepperoni, cut
  into rounds**
Additional oregano

Before serving, heat oven to 400°. Combine tomato paste, garlic salt, and oregano. Spoon a small amount onto a pastry round. Top with small cube of cheese and a piece of meat. Sprinkle with oregano. Bake 3–5 minutes. Serve hot. Makes about 4 dozen.

Jarrett House Potpourri (North Carolina)

Hugs and Kisses

¼ cup butter or margarine,
  melted
1 tablespoon Worcestershire
1 teaspoon seasoned salt
1 cup pretzel sticks (bite-size
  lengths)
8 cups rice, corn, or wheat
  square cereal

Candy-coated chocolate candies,
  raisins, butterscotch morsels,
  miniature marshmallows,
  chocolate chips, or peanut butter
  morsels (optional)

Combine butter or margarine, Worcestershire, and seasoned salt, mixing well. Combine pretzels and cereal in large bowl. Drizzle seasoned butter over cereal mixture and mix gently until evenly coated. Spread mixture in 10x14x3-inch baking pan. Bake at 300° for 1 hour, stirring at 15-minute intervals. Spread mixture on paper towels and cool. Add 1 cup of one or several optional ingredients. Makes 10–12 cups.

Children's Party Book (Virginia)

Bread and Breakfast

Once the 175-room country estate of Henry Francis du Pont, Winterthur, located in Delaware's Brandywine Valley, is now world renowned for its vast woodland gardens and unrivaled collection of American decorative arts.

Butter Dips

⅓ cup butter
2¼ cups sifted all-purpose
   flour
1 tablespoon sugar

3½ teaspoons baking powder
1½ teaspoons salt
1 cup milk

Heat oven to 450°. Melt butter in oven in 9x13-inch pan. Remove pan when butter is melted. Sift together flour, sugar, baking powder, and salt. Add milk. Stir slowly with fork until dough just clings together. Turn onto well-floured board. Roll over to coat with flour. Knead lightly about 10 times. Roll out ½ inch thick into rectangle, 8x12 inches. With floured knife, cut dough in half lengthwise, then cut crosswise into 16 strips. Pick up strips in both hands and dip each strip on both sides in melted butter. Lay them close together in 2 rows in same pan in which butter is melted. Bake 15–20 minutes until golden brown. Serve hot. Makes 32 sticks.

Variations: (1) Add ½ cup grated Cheddar cheese to dry ingredients. (2) Add ½ clove finely minced garlic to butter before melting. (3) Sprinkle paprika, celery seed, or garlic salt over dips before baking.

High Hampton Hospitality (North Carolina)

Sour Cream Dinner Rolls

1 (8-ounce) carton sour cream
½ cup butter or margarine
½ cup plus 1 teaspoon sugar,
   divided
1¼ teaspoons salt
2 packages yeast

½ cup warm water
1 teaspoon sugar
2 large eggs
4 cups all-purpose flour
2 tablespoons melted butter

Heat sour cream, butter, ½ cup sugar, and salt till butter melts, then cool to 105°–115°. Proof yeast in warm water with a teaspoon of sugar, then add to cooled sour cream mixture. Stir in eggs and gradually add flour. Cover and chill 8 hours.

   Roll out dough to ¼-inch thickness and cut with a 2- to 3-inch biscuit cutter. Brush tops with melted butter, crease center of each roll with a knife, and fold over; press edges to seal. Place in greased pan and let rise 45 minutes or till doubled in size. Bake at 375° for 10–15 minutes or till golden brown. Makes about 4 dozen.

A Taste of Heaven (Virginia)

Skillet-Popover

Delight your family with this fancy giant-size popover for breakfast. I serve it with a light sprinkling of cinnamon sugar. You may choose syrup or warmed fruit preserves or lemon juice and powdered sugar. At any rate, it is sure to please. Be careful to follow the directions carefully and be certain to heat the frying pan.

½ cup butter
½ cup milk

½ cup all-purpose flour
2 eggs

Place butter in a heavy iron 9-inch skillet. Place pan in a preheated oven set at 475°. Mix milk, flour, and eggs lightly to make a batter. After butter has melted, tilt pan so that the entire surface will be coated with butter. Add batter and bake 12 minutes. Remove from oven and invert onto a large plate. Drizzle butter in the pan over popover. Sprinkle with cinnamon sugar. Roll it over in loose jellyroll fashion. Slice and serve. Serves 2–4.

Taste Buds (North Carolina)

Popovers Fontaine

If you have never had the thrill of seeing a "runny" batter bloom into a large golden cloud, try this recipe. Popovers are definitely a Sunday morning breakfast treat. Serve with fried ham and scrambled eggs. Butter generously and top with honey or syrup.

3 eggs
1 cup milk
3 tablespoons oil or melted
butter

1 cup all-purpose flour
½ teaspoon salt

Preheat oven to 400°. Lightly grease 8 (5-ounce) custard cups or an old-fashioned popover pan. In a medium bowl, with a rotary beater, beat until well combined the eggs, milk, and oil. Sift flour and salt into egg mixture. Beat just until smooth. Pour batter into greased custard cups, filling each half full. Place cups on a baking sheet and bake 45–50 minutes, until golden brown. Serve at once. Makes 8.

The Ham Book (Virginia)

Virginia Ground-Ham Biscuits

2 cups all-purpose flour
3 teaspoons baking powder
½ cup ground cooked Virginia
  or country ham

3 tablespoons shortening
¾ cup milk

Preheat oven to 450°. Sift dry ingredients together. Combine with ground ham. Cut shortening in with knife till it is like meal. Add milk. Roll out ¼ inch thick on floured board. Cut out with a biscuit cutter. Place on ungreased baking sheet. Bake 12–15 minutes or until brown. Makes about 20.

The Ham Book (Virginia)

Capital Landmarks Cheese Biscuits

½ pound sharp Cheddar cheese,
  grated
½ stick butter or margarine
2 cups Bisquick
6 drops Tabasco

¼ teaspoon pepper
½ teaspoon salt
1 teaspoon mustard powder
¼ teaspoon dill weed
½ cup water

Mix cheese and butter until soft. Coat with Bisquick. Add seasonings. Moisten to pie crust consistency with ½ cup water. Roll into small balls (approximately 7 dozen). Bake on ungreased cookie sheet in preheated oven for 20 minutes at 375°, or until lightly brown.

These will be slightly puffed and have a flaky texture. They freeze and reheat well. Serve at room temperature. Serves 30.

A Taste of History (North Carolina)

Seventy square miles make up the District of Columbia. Designed by Major Pierre Charles L'Enfant around 1791, it was the first American city planned for a specific purpose and became the nation's capital in 1891. The country had been governed from Philadelphia, Pennsylvania, previously. Both Virginia and Maryland donated part of their land for the capital district. The Virginia portion of DC was later ceded back to Virginia.

Ranch Biscuits

2 cups biscuit mix
4 teaspoons dry ranch salad
 dressing mix
⅔ cup milk

2 tablespoons butter or
 margarine, melted
1 teaspoon dried parsley
⅛ teaspoon garlic powder

In a bowl, stir biscuit mix, salad dressing mix, and milk until combined. Drop by large spoonfuls 2 inches apart onto a greased baking sheet. Bake at 425° for 10–15 minutes or until golden brown. In a small bowl, combine butter, parsley, and garlic powder; brush over warm biscuits. Yields 9 biscuits.

Mary B's Recipes (North Carolina)

Farmer's Spoon Bread

A fluffy and moist bread that is spooned from the dish from which it is baked. My favorite spoon bread.

1½ cups boiling water
1 cup cornmeal
1 tablespoon butter, softened
3 eggs, separated
1 cup buttermilk

1 teaspoon salt
1 teaspoon sugar
1 teaspoon baking powder
¼ teaspoon baking soda

In large bowl, stir boiling water into cornmeal. Blend in butter and egg yolks. Stir in buttermilk, salt, sugar, baking powder, and soda. Beat egg whites until soft peaks form; fold into batter. Pour into a greased 2-quart casserole. Bake at 375° for 45–50 minutes. Serve piping hot with butter.

Granny's Kitchen (Virginia)

Clara's Smithfield Inn Cornbread Cakes

Clara Ford Williams has presided over the Smithfield Inn's kitchen for more than 26 years. Her cornbread cakes are a specialty of the house.

1½ cups cornmeal
1 tablespoon flour
1 teaspoon sugar (or more)
1½ teaspoons baking powder

½ teaspoon salt
2 eggs, beaten
1½ cups buttermilk

Mix all ingredients together. Drop by large spoonfuls in shallow hot fat. Fry until brown on both sides.

The Smithfield Cookbook (Virginia)

Eastern North Carolina Cornbread

1 cup cornmeal
½ cup all-purpose flour
2 teaspoons baking powder
1 teaspoon salt

1 cup milk
2 eggs
½ cup vegetable oil

Preheat oven to 400°. Mix together cornmeal, flour, baking powder, and salt. Add in milk, eggs, and oil. Beat well and pour into a greased 8x8-inch baking dish. Bake for 20–25 minutes. This can be halved and cooked in a 5x9-inch baking dish.

From Our Home to Yours (North Carolina)

Cracklin' Cornbread

1 tablespoon lard (or
   shortening)
1 cup self-rising cornmeal
1 cup self-rising flour
1 tablespoon sugar

2 eggs
1½ cups milk (sweet or
   buttermilk)
½ cup cracklins

Put lard in a 6x12-inch pan and let it melt. Mix all other ingredients together well. Pour batter into pan and bake in 425° oven for 20–25 minutes.

Dan River Family Cookbook (Virginia)

Jalapeño Hush Puppies

1½ cups cornmeal
½ cup all-purpose flour
1½ teaspoons baking powder
1½ teaspoons salt
½ teaspoon black pepper

¾ cup milk
1 egg, beaten
3 tablespoons vegetable oil
¼ cup chopped jalapeños

Combine dry ingredients. Add remaining ingredients and stir until well blended. Drop by teaspoonfuls into hot oil until golden brown. Drain on paper towels.

From Chaney Creek to the Chesapeake (Virginia)

Sweet Potato Love Buns

½ cup scalded milk
1 cup sugar
½ cup butter
½ teaspoon salt
1 cup mashed sweet potatoes
3 packages yeast, softened in
　½ cup warm water

2 eggs, beaten
1 tablespoon grated orange rind
1 teaspoon orange juice
1 teaspoon lemon juice
¼ teaspoon nutmeg
5–6 cups all-purpose flour

Scald milk; combine sugar, butter, and salt. Into sugar mixture, add lukewarm milk, potatoes, yeast, eggs, rind, juices, and nutmeg. Stir in 2½ cups flour; beat until smooth. Add more flour to make a soft dough. Knead. Let rise to double; punch down; let rest 10 minutes. Shape into buns about 2 inches in diameter. Place 1 inch apart on greased baking pan. Let rise to double. Bake at 350° for 15–20 minutes. Freezes well. Yields 4–5 dozen buns.

A Taste of History (North Carolina)

Founded in Chapel Hill in 1789, the nation's oldest state college is the University of North Carolina.

Cheese Bread

1 loaf French or Italian bread	Oregano
Soft margarine	6 slices provolone cheese
Garlic powder	1 large onion, thinly sliced
Parmesan cheese	2 cups shredded sharp cheese

Split bread loaf in half, longways. Spread margarine on both sides of bread. On one side of bread, sprinkle garlic powder, Parmesan cheese, and oregano. Arrange slices of provolone cheese, sliced onion, and sharp cheese. Put top of loaf together, wrap in foil, and bake in oven at 350° for 15 minutes, or until warmed.

A Second Helping (New Jersey)

Strawberries and Cream Bread

1¾ cups all-purpose flour	2 eggs
½ teaspoon baking powder	½ cup sour cream
¼ teaspoon baking soda	1 teaspoon vanilla
½ teaspoon salt	1 teaspoon almond extract
¼ teaspoon cinnamon	1 cup coarsely chopped
½ cup butter	strawberries
¾ cup sugar	¾ cup chopped walnuts

Combine flour, baking powder, baking soda, salt, and cinnamon. In small bowl, cream butter. Gradually add sugar and beat until light. Beat in eggs, one at a time. Beat in sour cream, vanilla, and almond extract. Stir into flour mixture only until dry ingredients are moistened. Fold in strawberries and nuts. Grease 4x8-inch loaf pan. Turn mixture into pan. Bake at 350° for 60–65 minutes, or until wooden pick inserted in center comes out clean. Let stand in pan 10 minutes. Turn out onto a rack to cool. Makes 1 loaf.

Pungo Strawberry Festival Cookbook (Virginia)

Banana Nut Bread

½ cup granulated sugar
2 tablespoons brown sugar
5 tablespoons margarine,
  softened
1⅓ cups mashed ripe bananas
  (3 or 4 bananas)

1 egg
2 egg whites
2½ cups all-purpose flour
1 teaspoon baking soda
½ teaspoon salt
⅓ cup chopped walnuts

Preheat oven to 375°. Spray large loaf pan with nonstick cooking spray; set aside. Beat sugars and margarine in large bowl with electric mixer until light and fluffy. Add bananas, egg, and egg whites. Sift together flour, baking soda, and salt in medium bowl; add to banana mixture. Stir in walnuts. Pour into prepared loaf pan. Bake 1 hour or until wooden pick inserted in center comes out clean. Remove from pan. Cool on wire rack 10 minutes. Serve warm or cool completely. Makes 1 loaf (16 servings).

Sharing Our Best (Virginia)

Easy Banana Bread

2 cups all-purpose flour
2 teaspoons cinnamon
¾ cup vegetable oil
¼ teaspoon baking powder
3 medium-size ripe bananas
1 teaspoon salt
2 teaspoons baking soda

3 eggs (or equivalent egg
  substitute), beaten
1 cup sugar
2 teaspoons vanilla extract
½ cup chopped walnuts (optional)
½ cup raisins (optional)

Preheat oven to 350°. Mix all ingredients (if using electric mixer, 5–7 minutes on medium speed). Pour into greased loaf pan. Bake for 40 minutes (or until you get a clean fork on testing). Cool and serve. Serves 10–12.

Cooking Through the Years (New Jersey)

Cranberry Nut Bread

2 cups flour
1 cup sugar
1½ teaspoons baking powder
½ teaspoon baking soda
1 teaspoon salt
¼ cup shortening

¾ cup orange juice
1 tablespoon grated orange rind
1 egg
½ cup chopped nuts
1 cup coarsely chopped fresh
   cranberries

Sift together flour, sugar, baking powder, baking soda, and salt. Cut in shortening until like oatmeal. Add orange juice and rind with well-beaten egg. Pour all at once into dry ingredients, mixing just enough to dampen. Carefully fold in nuts and cranberries. Spoon into greased loaf pan. Bake at 350° about 1 hour. Cool and remove from pan.

The Glen Afton Cookbook (New Jersey)

Apricot Nut Bread

2½ cups flour*
1 cup sugar
3½ teaspoons baking powder
1 tablespoon plus 1 teaspoon
   grated orange peel
3 tablespoons oil

½ cup milk
¾ cup orange juice
1 egg
1 cup finely chopped nuts
1 cup finely chopped apricots

Heat oven to 350°. Grease and flour 1 (9x5-inch) loaf pan, or 2 (8½x4½-inch) loaf pans. Measure all ingredients into large mixer bowl; beat on medium speed ½ minute. Pour into pan(s). Bake 55–65 minutes or until wooden pick inserted in center comes out clean. Remove from pan(s); cool thoroughly before slicing.

*If using self-rising flour, omit baking powder and salt.

WYVE's Cookbook/Photo Album (Virginia)

About half of all the people in the United States live within a 500-mile radius of Richmond, Virginia.

Gingerbread with Peach Sauce

1 package gingerbread mix	½ cup mincemeat

Cook gingerbread mix with mincemeat as directed on package.

SAUCE:

1 (13-ounce) can sliced peaches, drained, reserve syrup	1 tablespoon lemon juice
¼ cup sugar	½ teaspoon lemon rind
1½ tablespoons cornstarch	2 tablespoons butter, melted
¼ teaspoon salt	½ cup mincemeat

To peach syrup (add water if necessary to make one cup), add sugar, cornstarch, and salt, and cook until clear and thick. Add lemon juice, rind, and butter, then fold in peaches and mincemeat. Serve warm over gingerbread. Makes 7–8 servings.

Knollwood's Cooking (North Carolina)

Buttermilk Muffins

1 cup buttermilk	1 cup self-rising flour
¼ teaspoon baking soda	1 egg, beaten

Combine buttermilk and soda. Add flour, stirring until smooth. Stir in egg. Spoon into greased muffin tins. Bake at 425° for 30–40 minutes.

The What in the World Are We Going to Have for Dinner? Cookbook (Virginia)

Pineapple Muffins

A small, tasty muffin attractively baked in a tiny muffin tin is a nice change. Serve with lots of whipped butter.

2 cups all-purpose flour	2 tablespoons sugar
1½ teaspoons baking powder	1 large egg
⅛ teaspoon salt	1 (8-ounce) can crushed pineapple in heavy syrup, undrained
¼ cup butter, softened	

Stir together flour, baking powder, and salt. Cream butter and sugar. Beat in egg until blended. Add flour mixture and pineapple. Stir only until moistened. Turn into paper-lined muffin tins. Bake at 350° for 30 minutes. Yields 12 large or 24–36 tiny muffins.

Taste Buds (North Carolina)

Banana Chocolate Chip Muffins

1½ cups sifted all-purpose
  flour
¼ teaspoon nutmeg
¼ teaspoon salt
¾ cup semisweet chocolate
  pieces
¾ cup chopped English
  walnuts or pecans

½ cup butter or margarine,
  softened
½ cup sugar
1 tablespoon hot water
1 teaspoon baking soda
1 egg, lightly beaten
1 cup mashed, peeled ripe bananas
  (about 2–3 medium)

In small bowl, sift together first 3 ingredients; add chocolate pieces and nuts, coating each well with flour mixture. In a medium bowl, cream butter until smooth. Gradually add sugar, beating well. In a 1-cup measure, blend hot water and baking soda together. In a small bowl, combine egg, mashed bananas, and soda-water, mixing well; stir into butter mixture. Add flour mixture, mixing just until dry ingredients are thoroughly moistened. Fill greased muffin pans ⅔ full. Bake in moderate (375°) oven for 20 minutes or until done. Yields 12 muffins.

More Richmond Receipts (Virginia)

Pumpkin Chocolate Chip Muffins

Chocolate Chips make these irresistible.

1⅔ cups flour
1 cup sugar
1 teaspoon pumpkin pie spice
1 teaspoon cinnamon
1 teaspoon baking soda
¼ teaspoon baking powder

¼ teaspoon salt
2 large eggs
1 cup canned pumpkin
½ cup butter, melted
1 cup chocolate chips

Thoroughly mix flour, sugar, pie spice, cinnamon, baking soda, baking powder, and salt in a large bowl. Beat together eggs, pumpkin, and butter. Pour over dry ingredients and mix until just moistened. Add chocolate chips. Spoon batter evenly into greased muffin tins. Bake at 350° for 20–25 minutes. Yields 1 dozen muffins.

Capital Classics (Washington, DC)

Miniature Glazed Orange Muffins

1 egg
¾ cup buttermilk
1 orange rind, grated
¼ cup orange juice
4 tablespoons butter, melted
1¾ cups unbleached all-purpose
   flour

⅓ cup sugar
1 teaspoon baking powder
½ teaspoon salt
½ teaspoon baking soda

Preheat oven to 400°. Beat egg lightly. Stir in buttermilk, orange rind, orange juice, and melted butter. Sift dry ingredients together, add to liquid ingredients, and stir until just mixed. The batter should be lumpy; do not overmix.

Fill greased muffin cups (or use muffin liners) ⅔ full. Bake 20–25 minutes at 400°. Prepare glaze while muffins are baking. Remove muffins from oven. Run knife around edges of muffin cups. While muffins are still warm, prick tops lightly and pour glaze over. Remove from pan when cool. Yields 3 dozen muffins.

ORANGE GLAZE:
¾ cup sugar
¾ cup orange juice

1 teaspoon lemon juice
1 orange rind, grated

Combine all ingredients in saucepan; cook and stir until sugar is dissolved. Bring mixture to a soft simmer to make a light syrup.

The Fearington House Cookbook (North Carolina)

Orange Breakfast Treat

1 tablespoon butter
6 ounces orange marmalade
¼ cup chopped nuts
1 cup brown sugar, firmly
   packed

½ teaspoon cinnamon
2 (10-ounce) cans Hungry Jack
   Buttermilk Biscuits
1 stick butter, melted

Grease a tube pan with butter. Drop marmalade in by teaspoons evenly around bottom. Sprinkle with nuts.

Mix sugar and cinnamon together in a small bowl. Dip biscuits in melted butter and then in sugar mixture one at a time. Stand them up close together around pan in 2 rows. Sprinkle any left over sugar or butter over top. Bake at 350° for 30–40 minutes or until golden brown. Cool 5 minutes. Invert onto plate.

Jarrett House Potpourri (North Carolina)

Butterscotch Breakfast Ring

This is a good recipe to have for holidays.

1 cup butterscotch morsels	**½ cup chopped pecans**
2 tablespoons butter	**1 (10-ounce) package refrigerated**
2 tablespoons flour	**crescent rolls**
⅛ teaspoon salt	**7 teaspoons corn syrup**

Preheat oven to 375°. Melt half of butterscotch morsels and the butter in the top of a double boiler over hot, not boiling water. Remove from heat. Stir in flour, salt, and nuts, mixing gently with a fork. Set aside.

Separate rolls into triangles. Arrange on a greased cookie sheet so the triangles form a circle. The edges should overlap slightly and the long ends point outward.

Spread 2 teaspoonfuls of butterscotch mixture on each triangle. Roll, jellyroll fashion, toward the center. Slash inside half of each roll. Bake 15 minutes, or until golden brown.

Meanwhile, combine remaining ½ cup butterscotch with corn syrup. Melt over hot water, stirring to blend. Let cool slightly, then drizzle over the breakfast ring. Serve hot or cold. Makes 1 ring.

Love Yourself Cookbook (North Carolina)

A destination attaraction for millions of tourists each year, the Smithsonian is composed of sixteen museums and galleries and the National Zoo, and numerous research facilities in the United States and abroad. The Smithsonian Institution in Washington DC was established in 1846 with funds bequeathed to the United States by James Smithson.

Sour Cream Blueberry
Coffee Cake

STREUSEL TOPPING:

4 tablespoons butter, melted

1 cup dark brown sugar

2 teaspoons cinnamon

½ cup chopped nuts

Mix ingredients. Set aside.

¾ cup butter, softened

1 cup sugar

2 extra large eggs

1 teaspoon vanilla

2 cups all-purpose flour

1 teaspoon baking powder

1 teaspoon baking soda

½ teaspoon salt

1½ cups sour cream

2½ cups blueberries

Grease and flour a 10-inch tube pan. Cream butter and sugar. Add eggs one at a time, beating well after each addition. Add vanilla. Combine flour, baking powder, baking soda, and salt. Stir dry mixture into butter mixture alternately with sour cream, ending with dry ingredients. Beat until smooth. Fold in blueberries.

Pour half of the batter into prepared pan. Sprinkle with half of the Streusel Topping, which is prepared by mixing ingredients until crumbly. Pour remaining half of batter into pan and sprinkle again with Streusel Topping. Bake at 350° for 50–55 minutes. Allow to cool 10 minutes and turn out onto wire rack.

Frantic Elegance (North Carolina)

Cape May French Toast Casserole

1 cup brown sugar
1 stick butter (½ cup)
2 tablespoons corn syrup
2 tart apples, peeled and sliced
1 loaf French bread, cut into
   ¾-inch slices

5 eggs, beaten
1½ cups milk
1 teaspoon vanilla

Cook sugar, butter, and corn syrup until syrupy. Pour into 9x13-inch dish. Spread apple slices on syrup. Place bread on apples. Whisk together eggs, milk, and vanilla. Pour over bread. Cover and refrigerate overnight.

Heat oven to 350°. Bake, uncovered, for 30–40 minutes. Serve with your choice of syrup. Makes 8 servings.

Cooking with the Allenhurst Garden Club (New Jersey)

Frugally Delicious French Toast

2 large eggs
½–1 cup milk (just enough
   for good dipping consistency)
6–8 slices bread
1 teaspoon ground cinnamon

2 teaspoons sugar
Pinch of salt (optional)
Butter
Syrup
Powdered sugar (optional)

Heat iron skillet or griddle pan to medium-high heat. Coat pan, if needed, with cooking spray or a dab of butter. In a wide-open bowl (cereal or soup bowl), lightly beat eggs and add milk, blending well. (You don't want it too thin or too thick.) Stir in cinnamon and sugar; add salt if desired.

When skillet is heated through, dip 1 slice of bread in egg mixture, coating both sides. Place coated bread on hot skillet and repeat with as many as will fit. If you can only cook 2 at a time in a pan or skillet, just re-stir egg mixture before each dipping. Cook each piece until lightly browned on both sides and egg coating looks fully cooked.

Place French toast on plates and serve warm with butter and syrup. If desired, you can dust with a little powdered sugar for a frugally elegant touch!

*Day old, white, whole wheat, honey wheat, or diagonally sliced French bread can be used.

Frugal Family Recipes (North Carolina)

Dollar Pancakes
with Blueberry Sauce

1 cup all-purpose flour
1 teaspoon sugar
1 tablespoon baking powder
½ teaspoon salt

1 large egg
¾ cup evaporated milk
½ cup water
2 tablespoons soft butter

Mix dry ingredients together. Beat egg, milk, and water together and add to dry ingredients. Beat well and add soft butter. (It mixes better if you melt the butter.) Spoon silver-dollar-sized pancakes on hot griddle and fry on both sides till done. Keep warm. Serve with lots of crispy fried bacon and pass the Blueberry Sauce.

BLUEBERRY SAUCE:
¾ cup water
¼ cup sugar
1 tablespoon lemon juice
1 teaspoon cornstarch
    mixed with 1 tablespoon
    water

1 (16-ounce) can blueberries,
    drained or 2 cups fresh
    blueberries

Boil water and sugar; add lemon juice. Mix in cornstarch mixture; cook 1 minute, stirring constantly. Add blueberries and cook about ½ minute.

Turnip Greens, Ham Hocks & Granny's Buns (North Carolina)

Potato Scramble

¼ cup butter
½ (26-ounce) package frozen
    grated potatoes
1 small onion, grated
8 eggs, beaten

3 tablespoons cream
1 cup chopped cooked bacon or
    ham
Salt and pepper to taste
1 cup grated Cheddar cheese

Melt butter in sauté pan and add potatoes and onion. Cook over medium heat until lightly browned. Combine next 4 ingredients. Pour over potatoes and cook as for scrambled eggs. Add cheese. Heat until melted. To serve, cut in pie wedges.

Bravo (North Carolina)

Brunch Casserole

4 cups cubed day-old white or
  French bread
2 cups shredded Cheddar cheese
10 eggs, lightly beaten
1 quart milk
1 teaspoon dry mustard
1 teaspoon salt
¼ teaspoon onion powder
Freshly ground pepper to taste
8–10 slices bacon, cooked,
  crumbled
½ cup sliced mushrooms
½ cup chopped, peeled tomatoes

Generously butter a 9x13-inch baking dish. Arrange bread cubes in baking dish and sprinkle with cheese. In a bowl, add the next 6 ingredients and mix. Pour evenly over bread. Sprinkle mixture with bacon, mushrooms, and tomatoes. Cover and chill up to 24 hours. To bake, preheat oven to 325° and bake, uncovered, for 1 hour or until set. Tent with foil if top begins to over brown. Makes 12 servings.

Stirring Performances (North Carolina)

Frances' Fancy Breakfast

3 English muffins, split in half
¼ cup butter
2 green onions (or 1 small onion),
  chopped
1 small green pepper, chopped
6–8 large fresh (or canned)
  mushrooms, sliced
4 eggs, beaten with a small amount
  of milk
Salt and pepper to taste
6 slices Canadian bacon
1 (10¾-ounce) can cream of
  mushroom soup, undiluted
1 cup grated Cheddar cheese

Lightly butter and toast English muffin halves. Sauté in butter the onions, green pepper, and mushrooms until softened. Add beaten eggs, season, and scramble. Top each muffin half with a slice of Canadian bacon. Mound some of the egg mixture on the bacon and then place a tablespoon of mushroom soup on top. Add grated cheese on top of the soup and heat under the broiler until the cheese is melted and browned. This makes a delightful breakfast or brunch when served with spiced apple rings or fresh fruit. Yields 6 servings.

Pass the Plate (North Carolina)

Sausage and Onion Squares

1 pound mild bulk sausage
1 large onion, chopped
2 cups Bisquick Baking Mix
⅔ cup milk
2 eggs, divided

2 teaspoons caraway seeds
1½ cups sour cream
¼ teaspoon salt
¼ teaspoon paprika

Cook sausage and onion until brown and onion is tender. Drain well. Combine Bisquick, milk, and 1 egg; mix well. Spread mixture in a greased 9x13x2-inch baking dish. Sprinkle with caraway seeds. Top with sausage and onion mixture. Combine sour cream, salt, and remaining egg and blend well. Pour over sausage mixture and sprinkle with paprika. Bake at 350° for 25–30 minutes. Cut into squares. Makes 4 servings.

Atlantic Highlands (New Jersey)

Baked Eggs with Three Cheeses

7 eggs, beaten
1 cup milk
2 teaspoons sugar
1 pound small curd cottage
  cheese
4 ounces cream cheese, cubed

1 pound shredded Monterey Jack
  or muenster cheese
⅔ cup butter or margarine, melted
½ cup flour
1 teaspoon baking powder

Beat together eggs, milk, and sugar. Add cheeses and melted butter and mix well. Mix in flour and baking powder, then pour into a 3-quart baking dish sprayed with non-stick pan coating. Bake 45–50 minutes at 350°, or until knife inserted in center comes out clean. May be prepared in advance and refrigerated, covered. If put in oven directly from refrigerator, uncover, and bake up to 60 minutes. Cut into rectangles to serve. Serves 12.

The Queen Victoria® Cookbook (New Jersey)

Krispy Kreme Doughnuts was founded by Vernon Rudolph in Winston-Salem, North Carolina, in 1937, and now operates more than 380 retail outlets selling premium quality doughnuts throughout the United States.

Frittata with Pasta, Vegetables, and Crab

½ pound capellini
⅓ cup finely chopped zucchini
⅓ cup finely chopped red or
 yellow pepper
⅓ cup finely chopped sweet
 onion

3 tablespoons butter
6 large eggs, whisked
½ cup grated provolone cheese
¼ cup Parmesan cheese
⅔ cup flaked crabmeat

Cook capellini al dente in boiling salted water. Drain and rinse with cold water. Sauté vegetables in melted butter. Do not overcook. Mix pasta with beaten eggs. Add vegetables, cheeses, and crab. Pour mixture into greased 9x13-inch pan. Cover with foil and bake in pre-heated 350° oven for ½ hour, or until frittata is golden. Serves 8.

Cooking with the Allenhurst Garden Club (New Jersey)

Sausage Cheese Loaves

Delicious for breakfast.

2 pounds bulk hot pork
 sausage, cooked,
 crumbled, drained
1 egg, beaten
1 (2-loaf) package frozen
 bread loaves, thawed

2 cups shredded mozzarella
 cheese
Egg wash (1 beaten egg with
 ⅛ cup water)

Mix sausage with egg and divide in half. Roll each bread loaf into a large rectangle and cover with 1 cup shredded cheese and ½ sausage and egg mixture. Carefully roll up each loaf like a jellyroll, sealing edges, and place in 2 lightly greased loaf pans. Brush top of loaves with egg wash and bake at 350° for 30–40 minutes or until brown. Yields 2 loaves. May be cooked ahead and reheated.

Note: May use 1 hot and 1 mild package sausage.

A Taste of the Outer Banks III (North Carolina)

Green Chile Cheese Grits

We love grits and this is a tasty way to serve them. This is great for breakfast served with bacon or sausage.

¾ cup uncooked quick-
   cooking grits
2¼ cups water
½ medium onion, chopped
1 (4-ounce) can green chiles
½ green bell pepper, chopped

1 teaspoon minced garlic
1 stick butter
5 eggs, beaten
2 cups shredded Monterey
   Jack or Cheddar cheese
¼ teaspoon salt

Cook grits and water in microwave 8–10 minutes or until done. In a skillet, sauté onion, chiles, peppers, and garlic in butter until tender. In a large bowl, beat eggs. Add cheese and salt. Add grits and onion mixture to egg mixture. Stir well and pour into a greased 8x8-inch baking dish. Bake at 350° for 45 minutes or until set.

Gritslickers (North Carolina)

Grits Casserole

This is good served with fruit and muffins.

4¼ cups water
1 cup yellow grits
1 teaspoon garlic salt
1 pound Cheddar cheese,
   grated

1 stick butter or margarine
4 eggs, beaten
½ cup milk
4 slices bacon, cooked and
   crumbled

Preheat oven to 400°. Put water in pot and bring to a boil. Stir in grits and cook 4–5 minutes until thick, stirring frequently. Add garlic salt, cheese, and butter, and mix well. In a small bowl, beat eggs together with milk and add slowly to grits. Pour mixture into a greased baking dish and bake 30 minutes. Remove from oven and sprinkle bacon over top. Serve hot. Serves 8.

Mama Dip's Family Cookbook (North Carolina)

Pan-Fried Grits
with Virginia Country Ham

The South is known for its love of grits. This corn is a naturally wonderful starchy side dish for other meals. Chef Kimmel added the intricate flavors of country ham and Cheddar cheese with just a hint of garlic and chives. Shaped in muffin tins, they are finished by pan frying.

1 quart water	**1 tablespoon dried chives**
1¼ cups grits	**¼ cup finely chopped Virginia**
2 teaspoons white pepper	**country ham**
1 teaspoon garlic powder	**1 cup grated Cheddar cheese**
2 teaspoons salt	**2 tablespoons vegetable oil**

In a large saucepan, bring water to a boil. Stir in all ingredients except cheese and oil. Stir until smooth. Cook over medium heat, whipping occasionally, for 15 minutes or until thick. Remove from heat. Mix in cheese. Grease muffin tins with nonstick spray. Fill each to the top with mixture. Let cool. Remove from pans. Split lengthwise. Pan-fry in skillet in hot oil until golden on each side. Yields 9 servings.

Recipe by Mark Kimmel, The Tobacco Company Restaurant, Richmond
Culinary Secrets of Great Virginia Chefs (Virginia)

Dame Witty's Welsh Rarebit

¼ cup butter	**¾ teaspoon prepared mustard**
½ cup all-purpose flour	**½ tablespoon Worcestershire**
3 cups milk	**1 teaspoon Tabasco**
1 pound very sharp Cheddar	**½ teaspoon salt**
cheese, broken into pieces	**½ bottle beer (optional)**

Melt butter, then add flour and stir until smooth. Pour in milk, continue stirring for 5 minutes in double boiler. Add cheese and seasonings and continue cooking until smooth. Finally add beer, if desired, and serve over crackers or toast triangles with a strip of bacon. Serves 6.

Delectable Cookery of Alexandria (Virginia)

Tom's Own Sausage Gravy

1 pound sausage, hot or regular
1 teaspoon minced garlic
3–4 tablespoons flour

1½ pints half-and-half
1 teaspoon beef bouillon
Frozen or homemade biscuits

Crumble sausage in large skillet and brown thoroughly; add garlic. Drain grease from sausage and stir in 3 or 4 tablespoons flour. Pour in half-and-half and beef bouillon. Heat and stir until it thickens. Cover and let simmer for 1–2 hours, stirring occasionally. Let cool; place in refrigerator overnight. Reheat gravy and serve over hot, baked biscuits.

Cookin' for the Cure (Virginia)

Edinburg Mill Restaurant's Sausage Gravy

1 pound mild sausage
4 tablespoons finely chopped
  onion
2 tablespoons sugar
1 teaspoon salt
½ teaspoon pepper

2 tablespoons Worcestershire
¼ cup all-purpose flour
½ cup water
½ cup milk
Dash of Kitchen Bouquet

Brown sausage in skillet, adding 1 tablespoon at a time to prevent sticking. When sausage is browned, add onions, sugar, salt, pepper, and Worcestershire; simmer 2 minutes. Add flour, sprinkling evenly on top of sausage. Add water and milk gradually until right consistency is achieved. Add a dash of Kitchen Bouquet for color. Simmer 10–15 minutes. Serves 6–8.

Editor's Extra: Great served over grits or split biscuits.

Virginia's Historic Restaurants and Their Recipes (Virginia)

Monte Cristo Club

6 slices whole-wheat bread
4 tablespoons strawberry
  preserves
4 slices boiled ham
4 slices cooked turkey

4 slices Swiss cheese
1 egg
¼ cup milk
Salt to taste
Butter for grilling

Spread each of 4 slices of bread with 1 tablespoon preserves. Top each of 2 of these slices with a slice of ham, turkey, and cheese, and a plain slice of bread. Place another slice of ham, turkey, and cheese on the plain slice.

Place remaining preserve-coated bread, preserve side down, on top. Beat together egg, milk, and salt. Dip sandwiches in egg mixture, then grill in a buttered skillet until golden brown and hot enough. Serve at once. Makes 2 servings.

Love Yourself Cookbook (North Carolina)

Soups, Chowders, and Stews

The defining characteristic of the North Carolina Coast is the Outer Banks, a chain of fragile barrier islands—home to 130 miles of unspoiled coastline. The Outer Banks has some of the most beautiful beaches in the country.

Creamy Broccoli Soup

1 small onion, minced
4 tablespoons butter or
  margarine
5 tablespoons all-purpose flour
1 teaspoon salt
3 cups light cream

1–2 cups chicken broth
2 (10-ounce) packages frozen
  chopped broccoli, slightly
  thawed
½ teaspoon nutmeg

Sauté onion in butter until tender; stir in flour and salt. Gradually add cream, stirring constantly. Add broth according to desired thickness of soup. Add broccoli and nutmeg. Cook over low heat 25 minutes. Stir occasionally. Yields 6–8 servings.

Variation: ⅛ teaspoon mace may be substituted for nutmeg. Cauliflower can be used in lieu of broccoli.

Market to Market (North Carolina)

Broccoli Cream Cheese Soup

½ cup chopped green
  onions
2 tablespoons butter
2 (8-ounce) packages cream
  cheese, cubed
2 cups half-and-half
2 cups chicken broth
3 (10-ounce) packages
  frozen chopped broccoli

1 teaspoon lemon juice
1 teaspoon salt
½ teaspoon black pepper
4 chicken breasts, cooked,
  boned, and cubed (optional)
Toasted almonds for garnish
Parsley for garnish

Sauté onion in butter in large saucepan. Add cream cheese, half-and-half, and broth. In separate saucepan, cook broccoli according to package directions, then drain. Add broccoli, lemon juice, salt, and pepper to broth mixture. You may add chicken at this time, if desired, and heat thoroughly. Garnish with almonds and parsley. Serves 10.

A River's Course (North Carolina)

Martha Washington's Porridge of Green Peas

This soup is from Mrs. Washington's collection of recipes—the flavor is very light and I have found that it is most pleasing when a wine is not served, as one does not want to diminish the delicacy of the flavor.

2 cups young green peas
2 cups boiling water
1 teaspoon sugar
1 teaspoon salt
Sprig of mint

2 cups milk
1 tablespoon flour
2 tablespoons butter
Black pepper

Drop peas into boiling water. Add sugar, salt, and mint. Cook slowly until peas are tender. Rub through a sieve. Add milk and bring to a boil. Mix flour and butter, and thicken soup with this. Add more salt, if necessary, and freshly ground black to taste.

The Virginia Presidential Homes Cookbook (Virginia)

Basil Tomato Soup

2 (28-ounce) cans crushed
   tomatoes
1 (14-ounce) can chicken broth
18–20 fresh basil leaves,
   minced

1 teaspoon sugar
1 cup whipping cream
½ cup margarine

In large saucepan, bring tomatoes and broth to a boil. Reduce heat; cover and simmer 10 minutes. Add basil and sugar. Reduce heat to low; stir in cream and butter. Cook until butter is melted. Yields 9 servings.

Mary B's Recipes (North Carolina)

Onion Soup

Chop up twelve large onions, boil them in three quarts of milk and water equally mixed, put in a bit of veal or fowl, and a piece of bacon, with pepper and salt. When the onions are boiled to pulp, thicken it with a large spoonful of butter mixed with one of flour. Take out the meat, and serve it up with toasted bread cut in small pieces in the soup.

The Virginia House-wife (Virginia)

Zesty Gazpacho

4 large ripe tomatoes, peeled,
    chopped
⅓ green bell pepper
⅓ cucumber, peeled
¼ onion, chopped
2 garlic gloves
3 tablespoons red wine vinegar

2 tablespoons olive oil
1 tablespoon salt
3 cups cubed French bread (crust
    removed), soaked in water
Garnish: onion, bell pepper,
    cucumber, sour cream, black
    olives

In processor or blender, purée tomatoes, bell pepper, cucumber, onion, and garlic. Blend in vinegar, oil, salt, and bread crumbs in batches. Transfer to a bowl, thin it to desired consistency with ice eater. Chill covered.

Garnish with minced onion, bell pepper, cucumber, and a dollop of sour cream with black olive curls. Makes 6 cups and serves 4–6. Yum!

Ship to Shore II (North Carolina)

Soup à la Julienne

Take carrots, turnips and potatoes and cut them in strips about ¾ of an inch long and 1½ of an inch wide. There should be ¾ cupful of each. Melt 2 tablespoonfuls of butter, add the vegetables and fry gently, stirring carefully, until they begin to shrivel. Then put them in the soup. When it boils, add ¼ cup of sorrel, and ½ cup of spinach, which should first have been scalded with boiling water to take the sharpness out, then drain and chop fine. Add to your Julienne also 3 stalks of celery and 2 beets cut up like turnips and carrots. Also ½ cup green peas, when they are in season.

This soup should be made with beef broth, about 2½ quarts, or if water is used 3 spoonfuls of dried beans that have been soaked should be put in. It should cook for two hours. Before serving cut 3 slices of bread in small cubes and brown in butter. Add to soup.

Thomas Jefferson's Cook Book (Virginia)

No one knew more about the geography of North America in his own day than Thomas Jefferson. A skilled surveyor and cartographer, he amassed a remarkable collection of explorers' accounts, geographic works, and maps for his personal library. Although Jefferson himself never traveled any further west than Warm Springs, Virginia, he was promoter of four attempts to reach the Pacific, and as president, he personally planned the successful expedition led by Meriwether Lewis and William Clark from 1804–1806.

Corn Soup with Shrimp

¼ cup oil
4 tablespoons flour
1 large onion, chopped
2 tablespoons chopped bell
  pepper
1 pound whole tomatoes,
  chopped (or use Ro-Tel
  tomatoes for spicier taste)

1 cup cubed ham
1½ cups freshly cut or canned corn
2 quarts water
Salt and pepper to taste
1 pound shrimp, cleaned, deveined
2 tablespoons chopped parsley

Make a golden brown roux with oil and flour, cooking slowly over low to medium heat and stirring constantly. Add onion and bell pepper; cook a few minutes, stirring often until wilted. Add ham, corn, and tomatoes; simmer about 30 minutes, stirring occasionally to keep from sticking. Add water, salt and pepper; simmer about 1 hour. Add shrimp and parsley and cook another 15 minutes. Serves 4–6.

Feeding the Flock (North Carolina)

Oyster and Artichoke Soup

¼ cup butter
1½ cups chopped green onions
2 garlic cloves, minced
3 tablespoons flour
2 (14-ounce) cans artichokes
3 cups chicken stock or broth

3 cups milk
1 teaspoon crushed red pepper
1 teaspoon salt
½ teaspoon anise seeds
1 quart oysters with liquor

Melt butter in a large heavy pot. Add onions and garlic; sauté 5 minutes. Add flour and cook 5 minutes, stirring constantly. Drain and rinse artichokes. Cut into quarters and add to pot. Add chicken broth, milk, and seasonings. Cook 20 minutes. Add oysters and their liquor. Simmer 10 minutes. Top with a lemon slice to serve. Serves 12.

Seafood Sorcery (North Carolina)

Crab and Asparagus Soup

½ cup margarine
½ cup flour
8 cups skim milk
2 tablespoons finely chopped
  onion
2 teaspoons instant chicken
  bouillon

½ teaspoon pepper
1 teaspoon salt
2 teaspoons parsley flakes
10 ounces frozen asparagus,
  cut in thirds
1 pound Maryland crabmeat,
  cartilage removed

Melt margarine in large saucepan over medium heat. Gradually blend in flour. Stir in milk. Add onion, bouillon, seasonings, and parsley. Continue stirring until mixture thickens slightly. Add asparagus and cook over medium-low heat for 20–30 minutes, stirring often. Add crabmeat and cook over medium heat for approximately 5 minutes. Serve hot. Yields 6 servings.

Gardeners in the Kitchen (Maryland)

Peanut Soup

A light soup that is quick to prepare.

1 packet dry onion soup mix
2 ribs celery, chopped or 4
  teaspoons parsley flakes
2 tablespoons butter

1 quart chicken stock
½ tablespoon flour
½ cup peanut butter
1 cup milk

Mix first 4 ingredients and heat to boiling, then add flour which has been mixed with cooled stock to the mixture. Pour this all through a strainer and then add peanut butter and milk. Cook at low heat—do not boil—until warmed and blended. Serve garnished with crushed peanuts.

Note: I usually use lowfat milk and some powdered milk to thicken to my own liking. Regular milk will do fine or cream for a very full-bodied soup.

The Smithfield Cookbook (Virginia)

Virginia Peanut Soup

¼ cup olive oil
½ pound carrots, chopped
  rough
½ pound yellow onions,
  chopped rough
½ pound celery stalks, cut
  rough
¼ cup concentrated chicken
  base
12 cups water

1 pound fresh chicken carcass
¼ cup fresh tarragon leaves
1½ cups clarified butter
½–¾ cup flour
¾ pound creamy peanut butter
¾ tablespoon Kitchen Bouquet
2 cups heavy cream
Salt and pepper to taste
Crushed peanuts for garnish

Preheat oven to 350°. Glaze a medium baking sheet with olive oil. Spread vegetables evenly over pan. Bake 1 hour, turning vegetables occasionally. Combine chicken base with water. Add vegetables, chicken carcass, and tarragon. Simmer 2 hours. Strain mixture thoroughly and refrigerate. After simmering, you should have about 8 cups usable stock. When stock has completely cooled, skim off fat. Melt butter in a medium saucepan. Whisk in ½ cup flour to make a roux, using a little more if necessary. Simmer on very low heat 30 minutes until roux becomes a dusty brown.

Transfer stock to a heavy-bottomed stockpot and begin heating. When stock is just below a boil, add peanut butter, stirring to blend. Add roux, stirring constantly so it doesn't settle on bottom of pan and burn. Stir in Kitchen Bouquet, then cream. Season with salt and pepper. Simmer on low heat another 10 minutes. Remove from stove and run through strainer again. May be stored in refrigerator for later use or served immediately. Garnish with crushed peanuts. Serves 8.

Recipe from Occoquan Inn Restaurant and Tavern, Occoquan
A Taste of Virginia History (Virginia)

Peanuts were first grown commercially in the United States in Sussex County, Virginia, in the mid 1840s. Because of their size and flavor, Virginia peanuts are known as the "cadillac of peanuts." Virginias have the largest kernels and account for most of the peanuts roasted and processed in-the-shell. When shelled, the larger kernels are sold as snack peanuts. Virginias are grown mainly in southeastern Virginia and northeastern North Carolina.

Martha Washington's
To Make a Frykecy

Original receipt by Martha Washington.

Take 2 Chicken, or hare, kill & flaw [skin] them hot. take out thery intrills & wipe them within, cut them in pieces & break theyr bones with a pestle. Y(n) put halfe a pound of butter into y(e) fry pan, & fry it till it be browne, y(n) put in y(e) Chiken & give it a walme [boil] or two. Y(n) put in halfe a pinte of faire water well seasoned with pepper, & salt, & a little after put in a handfull of parsley, & time, & an ounion sphred all smal. fry all these together till they be enough, & when it is ready to be dished up, put into y(e) pan y(e) youlks of 5 or 6 eggs, well beaten & mixed w(th) a little wine vinegar or juice of leamons. stir thes well together least it Curdle, y(n) dish it up without any more frying.

Though Martha Washington's receipt used here as an early example of chicken vricassee, the one given below has been adapted for nodern use from a combination of Colonial recipes. Serves 6–8.

½ cup unsalted butter
1–2 tablespoons lard
8 large chicken breast halves, or
   a combination of breasts and
   thighs
4–5 cups chicken stock, or as
   needed
1 large onion, chopped
1 teaspoon salt

¼ teaspoon pepper
1 teaspoon thyme
1 teaspoon marjoram
1 teaspoon rosemary
¼ teaspoon ground cloves
3 egg yolks, slightly beaten
¼ cup minced fresh parsley
1 tablespoon lemon juice

HEARTH:

In a large spider or Dutch oven over hot coals, melt butter and lard. Add chicken and sauté until golden brown. Barely cover with stock; add onion and seasoning.

Cover pan and bring stock to simmer. Maintain heat by replenishing coals until chicken is tender, about 45 minutes. Remove chicken to heated platter and place near edge of fire to keep warm.

Measure stock; there should be 3–3½ cups. Gradually add ½ cup hot stock to egg yolks, stirring constantly to prevent eggs from curdling. Return mixture to rest of stock and toss in parsley. Correct seasoning and allow sauce to simmer briefly, stirring all the while. Blend in lemon juice. Pour sauce over chicken and serve.

(continued)

(Martha Washington's To Make A Frykecy continued)

MODERN:

One tablespoon cooking oil may replace lard, if desired.

Brown chicken over medium-high heat and, after adding stock, bring to a boil.

Hearthside Cooking (Virginia)

PHOTO © VIRGINIA TOURISM CORPORATION

Built of wood in a neoclassical Georgian architectural style, the plantation home of George Washington—Mount Vernon—is set on 40 wooded acres located in Fairfax County, Virginia, overlooking the Potomac River. The house was built by the Washington family around 1735. Mount Vernon was named for Admiral Edward Vernon, Lawrence Washington's commander in the British Navy. Lawrence was George Washington's older half-brother who owned the family estate at the time. George inherited the property in 1761 and lived there until his death in 1799. Washington transformed the house's modest frame from one-and-a-half to two-and-a-half stories and extensively redecorated the interior. The north and south wings of the house were begun just before the start of the Revolutionary War. The very last room, the Large Dining Room, was completed after the war's end. The mansion has been restored, with much of the original furniture, family relics, and duplicate pieces of the period based upon Washington's detailed notes.

Corn and Cheese Chowder

2 cups water
2 cups diced potatoes
½ cup chopped onion
½ cup diced celery
2 tablespoons butter
½ teaspoon dried whole basil
1 large by leaf
1 (16-ounce) can cream corn or 1
   (10-ounce) package frozen

2 cups milk
1 cup chopped tomatoes
⅛ teaspoon pepper
½ cup grated Cheddar cheese
1 tablespoon minced fresh
   parsley

Combine water, potatoes, onion, celery, butter, basil, and bay leaf in large kettle and bring to a boil. Reduce heat and simmer 10 minutes or until potatoes are tender. Discard bay leaf. Stir in corn, milk, tomatoes, and pepper and heat thoroughly. Add cheese and cook over low heat, stirring constantly until cheese is melted. Sprinkle parsley over chowder in bowls and serve. Serves 8–10.

In Good Taste (North Carolina)

Golden Glow Corn Chowder

This is wonderful when you're out of everything else!

6 slices bacon, cut into 1-inch
   pieces
2 small onions, peeled, chopped
½ medium green bell pepper,
   seeded, cored, chopped
4 medium potatoes, peeled,
   cubed
2 cups water

1 (16-ounce) can whole-kernel
   corn, drained
1 cup evaporated milk or
   half-and-half
1 (2-ounce) jar chopped pimento,
   drained
Salt and pepper to taste

In a heavy skillet, pan-fry bacon over medium heat until crisp. Remove and drain on absorbent paper. Sauté onion and green pepper in bacon dripping over moderate heat until tender but not browned. Drain off excess drippings. In a heavy 2- to 3-quart saucepan, cook potatoes in water over moderate heat until tender. Add onion, green pepper, corn, milk, pimento, salt and pepper to taste. Heat through. Garnish each serving with crisp bacon pieces. Makes 4–6 servings.

Apron Strings (Virginia)

Flounder Chowder Fulgham

3 pounds whole flounder
2 cups water
2 medium onions
Bacon drippings as needed
½ pound fresh mushrooms
1½ sticks butter, divided

7 medium potatoes
2 teaspoons salt
½ teaspoons white pepper
1 pint heavy cream
⅛ cup sherry
1 tablespoon sugar

Clean and fillet flounder. Retain head, tail, and backbone and boil in 2 cups water for 30 minutes. Strain and retain broth. Dice onion and sauté slowly in bacon drippings. Dice mushrooms and sauté in 1 stick butter. Dice potatoes and put into broth along with fish and simmer together 1 hour. Add mushrooms, onions, salt, and pepper. Simmer ½ hour. Cool for 1 hour. Add cream, sherry, sugar, and remaining ½ stick butter. Heat slowly. Do not boil! Yields 8 servings.

The Great Taste of Virginia Seafood Cookbook (Virginia)

Captain Rasmussen's Clam Chowder

12 chowder clams
4 cups water
¼ cup butter
1 cup chopped onion
¾ diced celery
¾ cup diced carrots
½ cup diced green bell pepper
1 clove garlic, pressed

½ cup chopped plum tomatoes
¼ cup tomato purée
1 cup cubed potatoes
⅛ teaspoon rosemary
⅛ teaspoon thyme
½ teaspoon salt
⅛ teaspoon white pepper
¼ teaspoon pepper

Scrub clams well. Steam them in water. Remove clams from shells. Chop clams finely; reserve. Strain clam broth; reserve.

Melt butter in a large saucepan. Add onion, carrot, and green pepper and sauté over medium heat until vegetables are tender. Do not brown. Add garlic, tomatoes, tomato purée, potatoes, rosemary, thyme, salt, white and black peppers, and clam broth. Bring to a boil, reduce heat, simmer covered for 20 minutes. Taste for seasoning. Add chopped clams. Heat almost to the boiling point. Serves 8.

Note: If fresh clams are not available, 1 (8-ounce) bottle clam juice and 2 (6½-ounce) cans minced clams and their liquid may be substituted.

Favorite Meals from Williamsburg (Virginia)

Fish Chowder, Jersey Shore

1½–2 pounds Jersey Shore fish
   fillets
Cold salted water
2 ounces salted pork (or bacon)
1 large onion, chopped fine
8 medium potatoes, diced
2 cups boiling water

Salt and pepper to taste
1 quart milk, scalded
2 tablespoons butter
1 cup oyster or other crackers,
   crumbled
1 small can corn (optional)

Place fish in saucepan; cover with cold salty water. Bring to boil and boil for 5 minutes. Save stock. Remove any skin on the fish. Fry the salt pork (or bacon) until fat is rendered. Remove pork and drain on paper towels. Sauté onion in fat; add potatoes and boiling water. Boil for 5 minutes. Add fish and reserved stock. Simmer another 15 minutes. Check potatoes for doneness. Season with salt and pepper. Add milk, butter, and crackers. (In Belford, the cooks always added a small can of corn.) Makes 4 servings.

Atlantic Highlands (New Jersey)

Quahog "Chowdah"

½ pound butter
1 cup scallops
3 cups white corn
1 cup diced onion
1 cup diced celery
1 pound red potatoes, diced

1 teaspoon thyme
¼ cup parsley
1 quart clam juice
3 cups shucked top neck clams
3 ounces Worcestershire
1 cup heavy cream

Melt butter in large pan and lightly sauté scallops, corn, onion, celery, potatoes, thyme, and parsley. Add juice and bring to a boil. Lower heat and simmer 15 minutes. Add clams and Worcestershire and simmer for 5 minutes. Remove from heat and add cream. Serves 4.

Recipe from Chef/Owner David Twining, Nantuckets, Fenwick Isle, Delaware
Coastal Cuisine (New Jersey)

Shrimp Bisque

2 or 3 fresh mushrooms, sliced
1 tablespoon butter
1 (10¾-ounce) can condensed
  cream of shrimp soup
¾ cup milk or light cream
¾ cup cooked shrimp, peeled,
  deveined

Dash of pepper
2–4 tablespoons sherry
  (optional)
Paprika

Sauté mushrooms in butter until tender, 3–4 minutes. Combine soup and milk in a large saucepan, blending until smooth. Set aside 2 whole shrimp, and chop the rest and add to soup. Stir in mushrooms and pepper.

Cook over low heat until just below the boiling point; it must not boil. Remove from heat and stir in sherry, if desired. Ladle into hot bowls and garnish with a dusting of paprika and reserved shrimp. Makes 2 servings.

Love Yourself Cookbook (North Carolina)

Fresh Mushroom Bisque

2 tablespoons corn oil
¼ cup minced celery
¼ cup minced onion
2½ tablespoons flour
1 cup homemade or canned
  chicken stock, boiling
1½ cups low-fat or whole
  milk, warmed
½ teaspoon salt
⅛ teaspoon ground nutmeg

¼ teaspoon white pepper
½ teaspoon tarragon
4 teaspoons margarine
2 cups fresh thinly sliced
  mushrooms
2 tablespoons sherry (optional)
½ cup minced parsley for garnish
2 tablespoons toasted almond
  flakes for garnish

Heat oil in large saucepan. Add celery and onion. Cook until soft. Add flour and cook about 3 minutes. Do not brown. Add boiling chicken stock all at once and whisk. Cook until thick. Slowly add warm milk, salt, nutmeg, white pepper, and tarragon. Reduce heat and stir occasionally.

Melt margarine in heavy skillet and cook sliced mushrooms until tender. Add mushrooms to soup mixture. Before serving, add sherry, if desired. Garnish with parsley and almond flakes. Serves 8.

Dining by Fireflies (North Carolina)

Crab and Corn Bisque

½ cup chopped celery
½ cup chopped green onions
¼ cup chopped green pepper
  (optional)
½ cup butter or margarine
2 (10¾-ounce) cans cream of
  potato soup, undiluted
1 (17-ounce) can cream-style corn
1½ cups half-and-half
1½ cups milk

2 bay leaves
1 teaspoon dried whole thyme
1 teaspoon garlic powder
¼ teaspoon white pepper
Dash of hot sauce
¼ teaspoon white pepper
¼ teaspoon Old Bay Seasoning
1 pound crabmeat, or ½ pound
  shrimp and ½ pound crab
Chopped parsley

Sauté celery, green onions, and green pepper in butter in Dutch oven. Add soup, corn, half-and-half, milk, bay leaves, thyme, garlic powder, white pepper, hot sauce and seasoning; cook until thoroughly heated. Gently stir in crabmeat and heat thoroughly. Discard bay leaves and garnish with parsley.

Bountiful Blessings (Maryland)

Beaufort Grocery's Darn Fine Gumbo

4–6 pieces bacon, chopped
  and fried
½ cup clarified butter
1 cup chopped green bell
  peppers
1 cup chopped celery
1 cup chopped onion
2 tablespoons chopped garlic
1 tablespoon paprika
1 teaspoon oregano
1 teaspoon coriander
½ teaspoon cumin

½ teaspoon thyme
½ teaspoon cayenne
1 tablespoon gumbo filé
¾–1 cup flour
2–3 quarts chicken stock or water
1 cup chopped cooked chicken
1 cup chopped cooked sausage
1 (8-ounce) bag chopped okra
2 cups scallops or chopped fish
Salt and Tabasco to taste
Cooked rice
Parsley for garnish

Render fat from bacon in a large pot and mix in butter. Add green pepper, celery, and onion, and sauté until onion is translucent. Add garlic and spices and stir for 1 minute. Mix in flour and stir 5 minutes. Gradually add chicken stock and simmer 20 minutes. Add chicken, sausage, and okra and simmer 11–15 minutes. Add seafood and cook until just done. Add salt and Tabasco and adjust seasonings. Serve with cooked rice and garnish with parsley. Yields about 4 quarts.

North Carolina's Historic Restaurants and Their Recipes
(North Carolina)

White Chili

2 pounds boneless chicken breasts, cooked and diced into ½-inch cubes
1 tablespoon olive oil
2 medium onions, chopped
4 garlic cloves, minced
2 (4-ounce) cans chopped mild chiles
2 teaspoons cumin
¼ teaspoon cayenne
3 pounds cooked Great Northern beans (canned)
4 cups chicken stock or canned broth
20 ounces Monterey Jack cheese, divided
Sour cream (optional)
Chopped jalapeños (optional)

Cook and cube chicken; save stock. In same pan, when chicken is done, add oil and sauté onions. Stir in garlic, chiles, and spices. Add chicken, beans, stock, and 12 ounces of the cheese. Simmer for 15 minutes. Ladle into big bowls and top with remaining cheese. Serve with sour cream and chopped jalapeños, if desired.

A Taste of GBMC (Maryland)

Sinfully Rich Oyster Stew

4–6 tablespoons butter
1 cup milk
2 cups heavy cream
1½ pints oysters and liquor
Salt and fresh ground pepper to taste
Cayenne pepper to taste
Chopped parsley or paprika for garnish

Heat bowls and add 1 tablespoon butter to each. Keep bowls hot. Heat milk, cream, and oyster liquor to the boiling point. Add oysters and again bring to boiling point. Season with salt, pepper, and cayenne. Ladle into hot bowls and garnish with a little chopped parsley or paprika. Serves 4–6.

The Rappahannock Seafood Cookbook (Virginia)

5-Hour Beef Stew

1 envelope dry onion soup mix
1 (10¾-ounce) can cream of
    mushroom soup
1 (10¾-ounce) can cream of
    celery soup
3 pounds stew beef (or boneless
    chuck steak, cut up)

3 (15-ounce) cans potatoes,
    drained, or 3 potatoes, peeled,
    diced
4 stalks celery, cut up
2 large carrots, cut up
2 large onions, quartered

Mix together all soups. In large ovenproof casserole dish, place raw meat and remaining ingredients. Pour soups over all and mix well. Cover and bake in 250° oven for 5 hours. Go shopping, come home with a loaf of good bread, pour yourself a glass of wine, and enjoy supper.

A Laugh & A Glass of Wine (Virginia)

Blues Brothers World Famous Brunswick Stew

Tell your friends it took you all day to prepare. They'll believe you—it's that good!

4 pounds boneless chicken
    breasts, cut in bite-size pieces
1 pound onions, chopped
2 teaspoons margarine
3 pounds potatoes, cubed
2 (15-ounce) cans corn, drained
1 (15-ounce) can green beans,
    drained

1 (15-ounce) can baby lima
    beans, drained
2 (10¾-ounce) cans tomato soup
1 pound minced pork barbecue
2 teaspoons black pepper
2 teaspoons Tabasco
¼–½ teaspoon red pepper

Sauté chicken and onions in margarine. In a big pot, boil potatoes until semi-soft in just enough water to cover. Put vegetables, soup, barbecue, chicken and onions into pot with potatoes that have been drained. Add spices, stir, and simmer until hot.

A Taste of the Outer Banks II (North Carolina)

Brunswick Stew Family Size

1 (2½- to 3-pound) chicken
2 stalks celery
1 small onion
Water
2 quarts tomatoes, fresh or
　canned
1 cup chopped onion
3 medium white potatoes, peeled
　but still whole

1 quart butter beans, drain if
　canned
1 quart whole-kernel corn, drain if
　canned
5 tablespoons sugar
Salt to taste
Red and black pepper to taste

Place chicken, celery, and small onion in a large kettle. Add about a quart of water. Simmer until meat is tender or begins to loosen from bones. Lift chicken from broth and discard celery and onion. Remove meat from bones and cut into small pieces. Add tomatoes, chopped onion, and whole potatoes to broth. Continue cooking over medium heat. Remove potatoes when tender, mash, and return to stew. (Some cooks omit this step and dice potatoes before adding to stew. It has been noted, however, that stew freezes better when potatoes have been mashed; otherwise, they're soggy.) Add cut-up chicken, butter beans, corn, and sugar. Add salt and peppers to taste. Bring to a boil while stirring. Cover; lower heat and simmer slowly 3–5 hours, stirring occasionally to prevent sticking, or until tomatoes have cooked to pieces. Makes about 6 quarts.

Recipe from Brunswick County/Lake Gasten Tourism Association, Inc.

Taste & See (Virginia)

 The origin of Brunswick stew is uncertain, and there are two competing claims as to the place from which it hails. According to Brunswick County, Virginia, legend, the camp chef of a Virginia state legislator invented the recipe in 1828 on a hunting expedition and everyone was immediately hooked. Recipes for Brunswick stew vary greatly, but it is usually a tomato-based stew containing various types of lima beans/butter beans, corn, and other vegetables, and one or more types of meat.

Chicken Tortilla Stew

If you are having trouble making homemade chicken and dumplings, this is a good substitute.

1 (3½- to 4-pound) broiler chicken	¾ stick butter
2 (14½-ounce) cans chicken broth	1 tablespoon dried parsley (optional)
	7 (10-inch) flour tortillas

Wash chicken in salt water, then put it breast side down in a large pot, and cover with water. Bring water to a boil and reduce heat to medium. Let cook (but not boil) until chicken is tender, turning chicken over after about 40 minutes to cook evenly. Let chicken begin to cool down in the pot, then remove to a bowl to finish cooling. When cool, pull meat from bone. Cut or pull meat into strips. Skim fat from stock and strain. Add enough canned broth to stock to make 6 cups total; pour liquid into a pot. Add butter and parsley. Cut tortillas in 1½-inch squares. When pot begins to boil, alternately add chicken and tortillas, stirring after each addition. Simmer 10 minutes. Serves 6–8.

Mama Dip's Family Cookbook (North Carolina)

Summer Corn and Tomato Stew

2 large onions, chopped	2 tablespoons sugar
1 stick margarine	2 teaspoons curry powder
1 gallon fresh tomatoes, peeled, cored, quartered	12 ears fresh corn kernels, cut off cob
2 tablespoons salt	4 cups (16 ounces) grated
¼ teaspoon black pepper	Longhorn Cheddar cheese

In a stockpot, sauté onions in margarine until tender. Add tomatoes and next 4 ingredients. Cover and simmer 4 hours over low heat, stirring occasionally. Add corn and simmer 1 hour. Before serving, turn off heat and add grated cheese. Let cheese melt, stir once or twice, and serve immediately. Yields 8–10 servings.

Very Virginia (Virginia)

Salads

Monticello, near Charlottesville, Virginia, was the estate of Thomas Jefferson, principal author of the Declaration of Independence, third President of the United States, and founder of the University of Virginia. The house is of Jefferson's own design and the only home in the United States that has been designated a World Heritage Site.

Wilted Lettuce and Onion Salad

8 slices bacon
½ cup vinegar
½ cup water
2 teaspoons sugar

2 quarts torn leaf lettuce
8 green onions, cut into small
   pieces

Fry, cool, and crumble bacon in to pieces. In skillet with bacon drippings, add vinegar, water and sugar. Bring to a boil. In large salad bowl mix lettuce and onions; pour hot liquid over and toss. Top with crumbled bacon bits. Serve immediately.

I Remember (North Carolina)

Orange-Avocado Toss

1 medium head lettuce, torn in
   bite-size pieces
1 small cucumber, thinly sliced
2 tablespoons sliced green
   onions

1 avocado, peeled, seeded, sliced
1 (11-ounce) can Mandarin
   oranges, drained

DRESSING:
¼ cup orange juice
½ cup salad oil
2 tablespoons sugar

2 tablespoons red wine vinegar
1 tablespoon lemon juice
¼ teaspoon salt

In large salad bowl, combine lettuce, cucumber, avocado, Mandarin oranges, and green onions. In a screw-top jar combine Dressing ingredients. Cover tightly and shake well. Just before serving, pour over salad. Toss lightly. Serves 8.

Out of Our League (North Carolina)

PHOTO BY M. APRILL

With more than 30 acres of beautiful flowers, ferns, lawns, and ponds, Leaming's Run in rural Swainton, New Jersey, is the largest annual garden in the United States. It is divided into 25 distinctive gardens, each with a different theme, such as the bamboo garden, shade garden, and colonial farm garden. The garden is named after whaler Thomas Leaming, who built his home—which still stands today—there in 1706.

Salad with Warm Brie Dressing

The dressing tastes best when made with a young Brie, not quite ripe, with the rind snowy white.

CROUTONS:

5 slices whole wheat or
   multi-grain bread

3 tablespoons butter
1 clove garlic

Remove crusts from bread and cut into cubes. Melt butter in a heavy skillet. Put garlic through a garlic press and add to butter. Stir. Fry bread cubes in garlic butter until golden. Remove from skillet and drain on paper towels.

SALAD:

1 head romaine lettuce

1 bunch watercress

Wash and dry romaine. Slice vertically through the center spine of each leaf. Then slice each piece horizontally into 1½-inch strips. Wash, dry, and remove tough stems from watercress. Toss with romaine and arrange on individual plates.

WARM BRIE DRESSING:

½ cup vegetable oil
4 tablespoons chopped onion
1 tablespoon chopped garlic
⅓ cup tarragon vinegar

1 tablespoon lemon juice
3 teaspoons Dijon mustard
7 ounces Brie cheese

Heat oil in a heavy skillet and fry onion and garlic until limp and slightly golden. Turn heat to warm. Add vinegar, lemon juice, and mustard. Combine well. Remove the thin layer of rind from the Brie. Discard the rind. Cut cheese into chunks. Turn up the heat under the skillet. Add the Brie and stir with a wooden spoon until melted. Pour dressing over greens and top with croutons. Serve immediately while still warm. Yields 6 servings.

A Matter of Taste (New Jersey)

Romaine, Grapefruit and Avocado Salad

2 heads romaine lettuce,
   torn into bite-size pieces
2 avocados, sliced
¼ cup sliced ripe olives

2 cups fresh grapefruit
   sections
Red Wine Vinaigrette

Combine romaine, avocados, grapefruit, and olives in a large bowl. Add Red Wine Vinaigrette, tossing to coat.   Serve immediately. Serves 8–10.

RED WINE VINAIGRETTE:

½ cup olive oil
¼ cup red wine vinegar
¼ cup sugar
½ teaspoon salt

½ teaspoon celery seeds
½ teaspoon dry mustard
½ red onion, grated

Whisk together all ingredients.

Blackened Mountain Seasonings (North Carolina)

Corn Salad

1 (15-ounce) can whole-kernel
   corn
1 (11-ounce) can shoepeg corn
1 (2-ounce) jar chopped pimento
1 large onion, chopped finely
½ cup finely chopped celery

½ cup finely chopped green bell
   pepper
½ cup sugar
½ cup vinegar
1 teaspoon garlic salt

Drain corn and pimento. Combine corn, onions, celery, green pepper, and pimento, and set aside. Combine sugar, vinegar, and garlic salt; stir until sugar dissolves. Pour over vegetables and toss lightly. Cover and chill 8 hours.

WYVE's Bicentennial Cookbook (Virginia)

Fresh Broccoli Salad

1 bunch fresh broccoli, chopped
½ cup raisins
½ cup Spanish peanuts
2 stalks celery, chopped
1 carrot, grated
1 tablespoon Parmesan cheese

½ jar real bacon bits
1 cup mayonnaise-type salad
  dressing
2 tablespoons sugar
1 tablespoon vinegar

Combine broccoli, raisins, peanuts, celery, carrot, Parmesan cheese, and bacon bits in bowl; toss to mix. Combine salad dressing, sugar, and vinegar in small bowl; mix until sugar dissolves. Pour over broccoli mixture. Marinate 12 hours or longer before serving. Yields 6 servings.

Goodness Grows in North Carolina (North Carolina)

Broccoli Salad

1 large head broccoli
10 slices bacon, cooked,
  crumbled
5 green onions, sliced (optional)
½ cup raisins

½ cup chopped English walnuts
1 cup mayonnaise
2 tablespoons vinegar
¼ cup sugar

Trim off large leaves of broccoli, remove the tough ends of lower stalks and wash broccoli thoroughly. Cut florets and stems into bite-size pieces. Place in a large bowl. Add bacon, green onions, raisins, and nuts. Combine remaining ingredients, stirring well. Add dressing to broccoli mixture and toss gently. Cover and refrigerate 2–3 hours. Yields 6 servings.

Cooking with Class, Volume II (Virginia)

Artichoke Salad

Must prepare ahead.

1 (8-ounce) package
  chicken-flavored rice
1 tablespoon finely chopped
  onion
3 rings green pepper, finely
  chopped

15 stuffed green olives, sliced
2 (6-ounce) jars marinated
  artichokes, drained (reserve
  liquid), cut in pieces
¾ teaspoon curry powder
⅓ cup mayonnaise

Cook rice according to package directions, leaving out butter. Cool completely. Add onion, pepper, and olives to cooled rice. Mix ½ of artichoke liquid with curry powder and mayonnaise. Add artichokes to rice mixture; pour marinade mixture over all and refrigerate overnight. Yields 8–10 servings.

Note: This is attractive served in a glass bowl or platter on a bed of lettuce leaves.

Market to Market (North Carolina)

Cool Carrots

2 bunches carrots, peeled, thinly
  sliced (or baby carrots)
½ teaspoon salt
1 (10¾-ounce) can tomato
  soup, undiluted
¾ cup vinegar
¾ cup sugar

½ cup vegetable oil
1 teaspoon dry mustard
1 bell pepper, chopped (green or
  red)
1 jar small sour pickled onions
1 teaspoon herb seasonings
  (optional)

Boil carrots 10 minutes in water with salt. Drain. Boil next 6 ingredients 5 minutes. Remove from stove and add drained sour pickled onions and herb seasonings. Pour over carrots. Marinate 6–8 hours. Serve hot or cold.

Christmas Favorites (North Carolina)

New Potato Salad

Make a day ahead of serving.

8–10 new potatoes
1 bunch green onions, sliced

3 stalks celery, chopped
3 hard-boiled eggs, chopped

Boil new potatoes and mix in large bowl with onions, celery, and eggs.

DRESSING:
1 teaspoon salt
1 teaspoon basil
½ teaspoon pepper
1 tablespoon Dijon mustard

2 cloves garlic, minced
3 tablespoons red wine vinegar
½ cup mayonnaise
⅓ cup olive oil

Combine salt, pepper, basil, Dijon mustard, garlic, and vinegar in small bowl, stirring in mayonnaise and whisk in oil. Pour over potatoes and let sit overnight.

Knollwood's Cooking (North Carolina)

Creamy Potato Salad

CREAMY DRESSING:
¾ cup mayonnaise
½ cup plain yogurt
1 tablespoon Dijon mustard
1 tablespoon cider vinegar
1½ teaspoons salt

½ teaspoon dry mustard
1¼ teaspoons celery seed
¼ teaspoon paprika
⅛ teaspoon garlic powder

Combine and chill until ready to toss with Potato Salad.

POTATO SALAD:
2 pounds potatoes, peeled
  and cubed
4 slices bacon, cooked and
  crumbled
3 eggs, hard-boiled and
  chopped
1 (2-ounce) jar pimientos,
  diced and drained

½ cup sliced green onions
½ cup chopped green bell
  pepper
½ cup chopped celery
3 tablespoons chopped fresh
  cilantro or parsley
Creamy Dressing

Cook potatoes in enough salted boiling water to cover for at least 10 minutes, or until tender; drain and cool. In large bowl, combine with remaining ingredients, toss gently, and chill. Serves 8.

A Pinch of Gold (North Carolina)

Spring Salad

1 cup mayonnaise
½ cup sour cream
3 boiled potatoes, peeled, cubed
3 hard-cooked eggs, chopped
½ cucumber, diced
3 pickles, chopped
¼ pound lean ham, chopped

4–5 green onions, chopped
½ (10-ounce) package peas, cooked
Salt
¼ head lettuce, cut in ⅛-inch strips

Mix mayonnaise and sour cream together. Combine potatoes, eggs, cucumber, pickles, ham, onions, peas, and salt to taste. Add about ¾ of mayonnaise mixture. Chill. When ready to serve, fold in lettuce and mound onto a large serving plate. Ice with remaining mayonnaise mixture and garnish with cherry tomatoes and green onions.

Culinary Contentment (Virginia)

Mixed Pasta Salad

Mixed Pasta Salad is indeed a treat for a hot summer evening meal. This dish has the added attraction of needing to be prepared early in the day in order for the flavors to mingle. Serve on a bed of lettuce with crusty rolls and butter.

2 cups fresh broccoli florets, blanched
1 cup sliced pitted ripe olives
1½ cups cherry tomatoes, sliced in half
½ cup canned mushrooms
2 thinly sliced green onions
1 (8-ounce) bottle of oil and vinegar salad dressing

4 ounces fettuccine noodles, cooked, drained, chilled
4 ounces spinach fettuccine noodles, cooked, drained, chilled
4 ounces boiled ham, sliced in strips
½ cup grated Parmesan cheese
½ cup crumbled, fried bacon

Marinate broccoli, olives, tomatoes, mushrooms, and onions in salad dressing at least 5 hours.

Drain, reserving the dressing. Combine vegetables with noodles, ham, cheese, and bacon. Toss with reserved dressing. Serve on lettuce leaves. Sprinkle with additional cheese, bacon, and parsley flakes, if desired. Serves 6.

Taste Buds (North Carolina)

Craisin Chicken Salad

4 cups cubed cooked
   chicken breasts
1½ cups mayonnaise
1 teaspoon salt
½ teaspoon black pepper

1½ cups craisins (dried
   cranberries)
½ cup chopped celery
⅓ cup chopped scallions
1 cup toasted pine nuts

Mix together in a large bowl the chicken, mayonnaise, salt, pepper, craisins, celery, and scallions. Refrigerate at least one hour before serving. Mix in toasted pine nuts just before serving.

Serving with Grace (North Carolina)

Curried Chicken Salad

3 cups cubed cooked chicken
1 (8-ounce) can sliced water
   chestnuts, drained

1¾ cups chopped seedless grapes
1 cup finely chopped celery

DRESSING:
¾ cup mayonnaise or salad
   dressing
1 teaspoon curry powder
2 teaspoons soy sauce

2 teaspoons lemon juice
Salt to taste
1 (11-ounce) can Mandarin orange
   sections, drained (optional)

In a large bowl combine chicken, water chestnuts, grapes, and celery. Prepare Dressing in small bowl. Stir together mayonnaise, curry powder, soy sauce, lemon juice, and salt. Mix well. Stir dressing into chicken mixture; add Mandarin oranges, then toss to coat. Cover and chill up to 5 hours. Makes 6–8 servings.

Best of Friends (Maryland)

Chicken Salad in a Cream Puff

CHICKEN SALAD:

2 cups cubed, cooked chicken
1 cup halved seedless green
  grapes
½ cup shredded Swiss cheese
½ cup sliced celery

3 tablespoons sliced green
  onions
½ cup dairy sour cream
¼ cup mayonnaise
¼ cup toasted sliced almonds

Combine chicken, grapes, cheese, celery, onions, sour cream, and mayonnaise. Chill until ready to serve.

CREAM PUFF:

½ cup margarine
1 cup boiling water
1 cup all-purpose flour

¼ teaspoon salt
4 eggs
Leaf lettuce for garnish

Preheat oven to 400°. Add margarine to boiling water and stir until melted; add flour and salt all at once. Stir until well blended and a ball forms. Set aside to cool for 10 minutes. Add eggs to flour mixture, one at a time. Stir after each addition until thoroughly blended. butter a 9-inch pie pan. Spread batter evenly in bottom and on sides. Bake 30–35 minutes, or until puffed and lightly browned.

When ready to serve, line pastry with lettuce leaves and fill with chicken salad. Sprinkle toasted almonds on top. To serve, cut into wedges. Yields 4–6 servings.

Hint: Cream puff may be made one day ahead and re-crisped in moderate (325°) oven for 5 minutes. chicken salad may be prepared 1 to 3 days ahead.

Even More Special (North Carolina)

Rice and Pea Salad

3 cups cooked rice, cooled
1 green bell pepper,
    chopped
1 cup chopped celery
1 cup chopped onion

1 (14-ounce) can green peas
2 carrots, grated
1 (8-ounce) bottle creamy
    Italian dressing

Mix all ingredients together. Refrigerate overnight.

Heavenly Dishes (North Carolina)

Elmer's Pasta Seafood Salad

Absolutely delicious!

SALAD:
1 pound medium shrimp,
    cooked, deveined
    (cut each into 3 pieces)
1½ cups coarsely sliced
    ripe olives
1½ cups coarsely chopped
    crisp kosher dill pickles

½ cup finely diced onion
¾ cup finely diced celery
4 hard-boiled eggs, chopped
1 pound large elbow
    macaroni, cooked al dente

Combine all Salad ingredients.

DRESSING:
3 tablespoons olive oil
    (good grade)
1 cup mayonnaise
2 tablespoons Worcestershire
1 tablespoon prepared
    mustard

2 tablespoons lemon juice
1 tablespoon Tabasco
1 tablespoon Old Bay Seafood
    Seasoning
1 teaspoon Ac'cent
Salt and pepper to taste

Whip together olive oil and mayonnaise. Add Worcestershire, mustard, lemon juice, and Tabasco, mixing after each addition. Add seasonings. Mix all ingredients thoroughly. Pour Dressing over Salad mixture and chill. Serve on a bed of lettuce.

A Taste of the Outer Banks (North Carolina)

Tidewater Shrimp Salad

1 (16-ounce) package small shell
pasta
2 pounds frozen salad shrimp,
thawed, drained
1 cup chopped celery
6 green onions, chopped
1 cup mayonnaise

½ cup Russian salad dressing
2 tablespoons capers
1 tablespoon lemon juice
1 tablespoon celery seeds
¼ teaspoon salt
¼ teaspoon pepper
¼ teaspoon Old Bay Seasoning

Cook pasta using package directions (without adding fat or salt) until al dente; drain. Combine shrimp, celery, and green onions in a bowl and mix well. Combine mayonnaise, salad dressing, capers, lemon juice, celery seeds, salt, pepper, and Old Bay Seasoning in a bowl and mix well. Add mayonnaise mixture to the shrimp mixture and toss to coat. Stir in pasta. Chill, covered, until serving time. Yields 20 servings.

Vintage Virginia (Virginia)

Diamond Shoals extends fourteen miles out into the Atlantic Ocean and is comprised of shifting sandbars lurking shallowly under the waters of Cape Hatteras. Strong currents and hidden shoals have sunk many a ship. Hence this area of North Carolina's coast is known as the "Graveyard of the Atlantic." The remains of more than 2,000 ships have settled to the ocean.

Shrimp and Crab Salad

1 (3- to 4-ounce) can black
  olives, divided
½ pound cooked and peeled
  shrimp
¾ cup mayonnaise

1 pound white crabmeat
1 cup diced celery
1 teaspoon lemon herb seasoning
Dash of garlic powder
Salt and pepper to taste

Reserve half the olives for garnish, and quarter those remaining. Mix ingredients in order given. Toss and serve on bed of lettuce. Garnish with whole black olives and tomato wedges if desired. Yields 4–6 servings.

The Great Taste of Virginia Seafood Cookbook (Virginia)

Crab Salad

This is for crab lovers. It has a mild flavor so as not to cover up the crab. Also great for a luncheon or light dinner.

1 pound lump crabmeat
4 cups shredded lettuce
½ cup minced celery
¼ cup minced scallions
2 hard-boiled eggs, chopped
¼ cup mayonnaise
¼ cup sour cream
½ teaspoon dry mustard

1 teaspoon Worcestershire
1 small jar pimento, diced
1 teaspoon chopped fresh parsley
1 teaspoon chopped fresh chives
½ teaspoon salt
2 teaspoons Old Bay Seasoning
2 tomatoes, cut into wedges

Pick through crabmeat and set aside. Soak shredded lettuce in ice water; set aside. Add celery, scallions, and eggs to crabmeat; set aside. In small bowl mix mayonnaise, sour cream, dry mustard, Worcestershire, pimento, parsley, chives, salt, and Old Bay until well combined. Drain lettuce well. Mix mayonnaise mixture and crab mixture together. Chill lettuce and crab salad (separately) for 1 hour. To serve place lettuce on plate and top with ¼ of crab salad. Arrange tomato wedges around. Serves 4.

A Taste of Tradition (Delaware)

Tutti-Fruitti Glazed Salad

An attractive, great-tasting salad—so easy. Serve this salad in a pretty glass bowl—makes a great buffet salad for autumn.

1 (29-ounce) can peach slices
1 (20-ounce) can pineapple
  chunks
1 (17-ounce) can pear chunks
1 cup seedless white grapes or
  1 (17-ounce) can fruit cocktail

3 bananas, sliced
2 unpared red apples, cut into
  chunks (optional)
½ cup orange juice (optional)
1 (3¾-ounce) package vanilla or
  lemon instant pudding

Drain canned fruits; reserve pineapple juice. Dip bananas and apples in orange or pineapple juice; drain and save juice. Mix pudding with 1 cup pineapple juice (or orange juice). Pour over fruits. Chill.

Variation: If you like the tang of orange, add 1 tablespoon Tang to pudding. May use any combination of fruits desired.

Granny's Kitchen (Virginia)

Magnificent Spring Salad

1 (16-ounce) can grapefruit
  segments, drained (reserve
  juice)
1 (10.5-ounce) can Mandarin
  oranges, drained (reserve juice)
1 medium cucumber, sliced thin
1 small onion, thinly sliced and
  separated into rings

Orange juice
⅔ cup wine vinegar
⅓ cup sugar
¼ teaspoon salt
Pepper to taste
2 avocados, seeded, peeled, and
  sliced
Lettuce

In a large bowl, combine grapefruit, oranges, cucumbers, and onions. Measure reserved juices and add enough orange juice to make 1 cup. Combine juice mixture, vinegar, sugar, salt and pepper; pour over fruit. Cover and marinate in refrigerator for 2–3 hours. At serving time, add avocado slices and toss to coat. Remove ingredients from marinade and arrange on lettuce-lined plates. Drizzle some marinade on top. Serves 8–10.

Where There's a Will... (Maryland)

Wedding Bell Pear Salads

12 canned Bartlett pear halves
1 (5-ounce) jar Old English
   cheese
1 (3-ounce) package cream
   cheese, softened
2 tablespoons finely chopped
   celery

1 tablespoon minced green onion
1 tablespoon minced parsley
⅛ teaspoon tarragon
Green onion for garnish
Salad greens

Drain pears and place cut-side down on absorbent paper. Cream together Old English and cream cheeses, celery, green onion, parsley, and tarragon. Spread on cut sides of pear halves; place halves together in pairs to form whole pears. Garnish with piece of green onion to resemble stem. Chill. To serve, place pears upright on greens on a platter. Makes 6 salads.

What's New in Wedding Food (North Carolina)

Emerald Salad

1 (6-ounce) package lime Jell-O
¾ cup boiling water
1½ cups grated cucumber and
   rind
2 tablespoons grated onion

1 (8-ounce) carton cottage
   cheese
1 cup mayonnaise
¾ cup slivered almonds

Mix Jell-O and water really well. Let cucumbers drain until they don't even drip. Mix cucumbers and onion with Jell-O mixture. Fold in cottage cheese and mayonnaise. Add almonds. Serves 12.

Recipes from Our Front Porch (North Carolina)

The Emerald Hollow Mine is the only emerald mine in the United States open for public prospecting. Nestled snugly in the foothills of the beautiful Brushy Mountains, this emerald mine is located in the small town of Hiddenite. This area is recognized as one of the most unique and interesting geological locations on the North American continent. The largest emerald found in North Carolina (1,438 carats) was found at Hiddenite. Hiddenite is also famous as the only place on earth where the very rare gemstone "Hiddenite" can be found.

Asheville Salad

1 (10¾-ounce) can tomato
  soup
1 (3-ounce) package cream
  cheese
1 (¼-ounce) package plain
  gelatin
⅓ cup cold water

1 cup sliced stuffed olives,
  cut fine
1 cup finely cut celery
1 cup finely cut onion
1 cup finely cut bell pepper
½ cup mayonnaise
Shrimp or avocado (optional)

Put soup and cheese together on stove to dissolve. Add gelatin that has been dissolved in cold water and mix well. Cool. Add olives, vegetables, and mayonnaise. Mix well. Pour into ring mold to congeal. Unmold on lettuce or endive and fill center of mold with shrimp or avocado, if desired.

God & Country Cookbook (North Carolina)

Margarita Berry Slaw

Turn on a Jimmy Buffet recording and pass out the margarita glasses filled with slaw. Your guests will be amused and pleasantly surprised as they savor this unusual salad. Unexpected and enticing flavors for your backyard picnic.

MARGARITA DRESSING:
¾ cup frozen margarita
  mix, thawed
¼ cup apple cider vinegar

¼ cup vegetable oil
¾ teaspoon celery salt

Combine dressing ingredients.

1½ pounds green cabbage,
  shredded
½ pound red cabbage,
  shredded
3 carrots, shredded

1 cup dried cranberries
2 medium Granny Smith
  apples, peeled, cored, cut
  into small cubes

Toss together cabbages, carrots, cranberries, and apple cubes in a large mixing bowl. Pour Margarita Dressing over cabbage mixture and toss well. Cover and refrigerate a minimum of 6 hours or overnight. Yields 12 servings.

You're Invited (North Carolina)

Vegetables

PHOTO COURTESY OF NEW JERSEY DEPARTMENT OF AGRICULTURE.

New Jersey is known as the "Garden State" for a good reason—over 150 types of fruits and vegetables are grown there, such as tomatoes, blueberries, cranberries, peaches, spinach, bell peppers, asparagus, eggplant, and lettuce.

Blender Carrot Ring "Quickie"

2½ cups diced, cooked carrots
3 eggs
1 slice of onion
4 sprigs parsley
1 tablespoon butter, melted

1 teaspoon salt
¼ teaspoon pepper
1 tablespoon brown sugar
1 slice bread, crumbled

Place all but crumbled bread in blender container; blend until carrots are finely cut. Fold in bread crumbs and turn into a buttered 8-inch ring mold. Set in shallow pan of water and bake in moderately hot (375°) oven for 30 minutes or until firm. Unmold and fill with creamed peas, if desired. Serves 6.

High Hampton Hospitality (North Carolina)

Carrot Soufflé

A sweet carrot dish.

2 cups diced carrots, cooked and
    drained
⅓ cup sugar
¼ cup butter

1 teaspoon vanilla extract
2 eggs
½ cup milk

Blend ingredients in a blender until thick and smooth. Pour into a buttered soufflé dish. Bake in a preheated 450° oven for 30 minutes. Serve immediately. Yields 4 servings.

Capital Celebrations (Washington, DC)

C1888. KURZ & ALLISON

More major Civil War battles were fought in Virginia from 1861 through 1865 than in any other state. One-third of the nation's most important Civil War battlefields are in Virginia, and most are open to the public. Shown here is a depction of the Battle of Fredericksburg fought in 1862.

Scalloped Corn

2 eggs
1 cup milk
⅔ cup cracker or bread
  crumbs
2 cups cooked or canned corn

1 teaspoon minced onion
½ teaspoon salt
⅛ teaspoon pepper
1 tablespoon sugar
3 tablespoons butter, melted

Beat eggs and add milk and crumbs. Add corn, onion, seasoning, and butter. Mix together well and pour in a greased casserole dish. Bake at 350° for 40 minutes. Serves 6.

Mennonite Community Cookbook (Virginia)

Fresh Corn Casserole

8 slices bacon
8 ears fresh corn, cut from cob
1 cup chopped green
  bell pepper
½ cup chopped onion

1 teaspoon salt
½ teaspoon pepper
½ teaspoon dry mustard
3 fresh tomatoes, peeled and
  sliced

Preheat oven to 350°. Fry bacon in large skillet until crisp. Drain on paper towels. In same skillet, pour off all but 2 tablespoons bacon drippings. Add corn, bell pepper, and onion. Sauté 5 minutes.

Combine crumbled bacon, salt, pepper, and mustard in small bowl. In greased 2-quart baking dish, layer ½ corn mixture, ½ bacon mixture, and ½ tomatoes. Repeat layers. Bake uncovered 35 minutes. Serves 8.

Dining by Fireflies (North Carolina)

Scalloped Tomatoes

2 cups thinly sliced onions
2 tablespoons margarine
1 (20-ounce) can tomatoes
3 slices toasted bread, cubed

¼ teaspoon pepper
½ teaspoon celery salt
2 tablespoons brown sugar
1 cup shredded Cheddar cheese

Sauté onions in margarine until transparent; remove from pan and drain. Combine tomatoes with bread cubes and add seasonings, sugar, and onions. Pour into buttered casserole. Top with cheese and bake uncovered at 350° for 1 hour. Yields 6 servings.

Heart of the Mountains (North Carolina)

Tomato Pie

1 (9-inch) deep-dish pie shell
5 large tomatoes, peeled
  and thickly sliced
½ teaspoon salt
½ teaspoon pepper
3 teaspoons dried basil

Garlic powder to taste
¾ cup mayonnaise
1¼ cups grated mozzarella
  or Swiss cheese
Thinly sliced onions
  (optional)

Bake pie shell 10 minutes at 375°. Layer tomatoes in shell, sprinkling each layer with salt, pepper, basil, and garlic powder. Combine mayonnaise and cheese. Spread over tomatoes (and onions, if used). Bake at 350° for 35 minutes or until brown. Allow to stand at least 5 minutes before serving.

Making Time (North Carolina)

Candied Tomatoes

1 onion, chopped
1 tablespoon butter
1 quart tomatoes, quartered
½ cup chopped green bell
  pepper

½ teaspoon salt
1 cup sugar

Brown onion in butter in iron skillet. Add tomatoes, green pepper, salt, and sugar. Simmer over low heat 1½ hours; stir occasionally. Serves 4.

The Hunt Country Cookbook (Virginia)

Smithfield Inn Stewed Tomatoes

One of the renowned dishes of the Smithfield Inn.

1 pint tomatoes, slightly mashed
2 (day-old) biscuits
¼ cup or less sugar
½ teaspoon vanilla

½ teaspoon lemon extract
1 teaspoon flour
1 tablespoon butter

Combine ingredients. Pour into greased casserole dish and bake at 350° for 30–40 minutes.

The Smithfield Cookbook (Virginia)

Broccoli-Stuffed Tomatoes

6 medium tomatoes
Salt and pepper to taste
1 bunch fresh broccoli
1 cup grated Swiss cheese
1 cup fresh bread crumbs
½ cup mayonnaise

2 tablespoons minced onion
2 tablespoons freshly grated
   Parmesan cheese
Green onion fans for garnish
   (optional)

Wash tomatoes, cut off tops and scoop out pulp, leaving shells intact. Sprinkle cavities of tomatoes with salt and pepper, and invert on wire rack to drain 30 minutes.

Preheat oven to 350°. Remove tough stems from broccoli. Blanch florets in boiling water until crisp-tender (3–4 minutes). Drain and chop coarsely. Combine broccoli, Swiss cheese, bread crumbs, mayonnaise, and minced onion; mix well.

Stuff tomato shells with broccoli mixture; sprinkle with Parmesan cheese. (May be prepared ahead to this point and refrigerated.) Place tomatoes in oven-proof dish and bake 30 minutes. Serve with green onion fans, if desired. Yields 6 servings.

Note: Substitute Monterey Jack or Dilled Havarti for Swiss cheese if desired.

Even More Special (North Carolina)

Eggplant Parmigiana Barbara

This recipe may be altered for a meatless meal by eliminating ground beef and doubling or tripling amount of mozzarella.

½ cup chopped onion
1 clove garlic, minced
1 pound ground beef
2 tablespoons butter or
　margarine
1 (16-ounce) can tomatoes
1 (6-ounce) can tomato paste
2 teaspoons dried oregano
1 teaspoon basil
1½ teaspoons salt

¼ teaspoon pepper
½ cup water
1 tablespoon brown sugar
1 large eggplant
2 eggs, beaten slightly
½ cup dry bread crumbs
¼ cup salad oil
1¼ cups Parmesan cheese
6–8 ounces mozzarella, shredded

In large skillet sauté onion, garlic, and ground beef in butter until meat is no longer red. Add tomatoes, tomato paste, oregano, basil, salt, and pepper. Stir well. Add water and brown sugar. Bring all ingredients in skillet to a boil. Simmer uncovered 20 minutes.

Heat oven to 350°. Spray baking dish with nonstick product. Peel eggplant and cut into ½-inch slices. Combine eggs and 1 tablespoon water; mix well. Dip eggplant in egg mixture; coat well. Dip in crumbs and coat well. Sauté eggplant in oil until brown and arrange in bottom of baking dish; sprinkle with half Parmesan; top with half mozzarella cheese and cover with half of tomato sauce. Repeat. Bake uncovered 20 minutes. Arrange remaining mozzarella cheese over top and bake 20 minutes longer or until mozzarella is melted and slightly brown. Yields 6 servings.

Pass the Plate (North Carolina)

Putt-Putt Golf was invented by Don Clayton in 1954 in Fayetteville, North Carolina, where the headquarters are still located today.

Ratatouille

½ pound eggplant, unpeeled
½ pound zucchini, unpeeled
1 teaspoon salt
3 cloves garlic, chopped fine
2 large onions, sliced thin
⅓ cup olive oil
2 green bell peppers, seeded, sliced

6–8 ripe tomatoes, or 1 (28-ounce) can tomatoes, drained
3 tablespoons minced fresh parsley
1 teaspoon dry basil, or more
Salt and pepper to taste
Grated Parmesan cheese and minced parsley for garnish

Cube eggplant and slice zucchini. Toss in a porcelain or stainless steel bowl with salt and let stand 30 minutes; drain. Meanwhile, sauté garlic and onions in oil until soft; add peppers and cook 5 minutes, stirring and tossing. Stir in eggplant and zucchini and cook 5 minutes. Peel tomatoes, cut in wedges, and remove seeds; add to eggplant mixture with herbs. Correct seasoning with salt and pepper. Simmer, covered, 30 minutes, stirring gently every now and then. Serve garnished with Parmesan cheese and more minced parsley. Serves 6–8.

Note: An electric skillet is ideal for this dish. An enameled or stainless steel skillet may be used, but avoid cast-iron here. Ratatouille may be served cold as well as hot.

The Belle Grove Plantation Cookbook (Virginia)

Snow-Capped Broccoli Spears

2 (10-ounce) packages frozen broccoli spears
1 tablespoon butter or margarine, melted
2 egg whites

¼ teaspoon salt
½ cup mayonnaise or salad dressing
Parmesan cheese, grated

Preheat oven to 350°. Cook broccoli according to package directions and drain well. Arrange stem ends toward center of an oven-proof platter or 9-inch pie plate. Brush with butter. In a small bowl, beat egg whites and salt until stiff peaks form. Gently fold in mayonnaise. Spoon mixture in center of broccoli and sprinkle with Parmesan cheese. Bake at 350° for 12–15 minutes. Yields 6 serving.

Market to Market (North Carolina)

Broccoli Casserole

1 (10-ounce) package frozen
   chopped broccoli
½ (10¾-ounce) can cream of
   mushroom soup
Dash of red pepper
½ cup grated sharp Cheddar
   cheese

1 egg, beaten
1 tablespoon grated onion
½ cup mayonnaise
½ cup crumbled cheese
   crackers
1 tablespoon butter, melted

Cook broccoli for 10 minutes; drain. Mix with over ingredients, except cheese crackers and butter. Pour into casserole and top with crumbled crackers mixed with butter. Bake at 300° until bubbly.

Have Fun Cooking with Me (North Carolina)

Broccoli Rice Bake

2 (10-ounce) packages chopped
   broccoli
1 onion, chopped
1 pat butter
1 cup Minute Rice

1 can cream of mushroom soup
1 (8-ounce) jar Cheez Whiz
1 (6.5-ounce) jar mushrooms
1 (2.8-ounce) can French's French
   Fried Onions

Cook and drain broccoli. Sauté chopped onion in butter. Add Minute Rice; cover, turn off heat and let set 5 minutes. Mix all ingredients, except French fried onions, and put in casserole dish. Bake at 350° for 30 minutes. Top casserole with French fried onions for last 8 minutes of baking.

Our Favorite Recipes–Book Three (New Jersey)

 At twenty-eight miles long, Virginia Beach is the world's longest resort beach. In terms of population, Virginia Beach is the largest city in Virginia.

Zesty Cheezy Cauliflower

1 medium head cauliflower	¼ cup mayonnaise
2 tablespoons water	2 teaspoons spicy mustard
¼ cup sour cream	1 cup shredded Cheddar cheese

Break cauliflower up into florets. Put in 2-quart round casserole dish. Add 2 tablespoons water. Cover. Microwave on HIGH 6–8 minutes or until almost tender. Let stand. Drain.

Mix sour cream, mayonnaise, and mustard. Toss gently with cauliflower. Sprinkle with cheese. Microwave on MEDIUM (50%) 2–4 minutes. Serve. Serves 4–6.

Note: Cauliflower can be cooked whole. Add 1 or 2 tablespoons water and microwave, covered, on HIGH 8–10 minutes. Let stand. The above mixture can be spread over the whole cauliflower.

The Microwave Touch (North Carolina)

Asparagus Casserole

7 tablespoons margarine, divided	1 (8-ounce) can sliced water chestnuts
4 tablespoons flour	1 (4-ounce) jar chopped pimento
2 cups milk	1 (4-ounce) can mushrooms
Salt and pepper to taste	4 hard-cooked eggs
1 (8-ounce) can asparagus, drained	Bread crumbs

Mix a thick white sauce of 4 tablespoons margarine, flour, milk, and salt and pepper. Alternate vegetables and eggs in a casserole dish with the white sauce. Sprinkle top with bread crumbs and dot remaining 3 tablespoons margarine. Bake at 325° for 30–40 minutes.

Jarrett House Potpourri (North Carolina)

Cabbage Casserole

1 stick margarine
2 cups crumbled cornflakes
6–7 cups shredded cabbage
2 cups chopped onions

1 (8-ounce) can sliced water
  chestnuts, drained
  (optional)
2 cups grated Cheddar cheese

Mix margarine and cornflakes. Place ½ of mixture in bottom of 9x13-inch dish. Spread cabbage over cornflakes and sprinkle with onions and water chestnuts, if desired.

SAUCE:

1 (8-ounce) container sour
  cream, or ½ cup mayonnaise
1 cup milk

1 (10¾-ounce) can cream
  of celery soup
Salt and pepper to taste

Mix all ingredients and pour over cabbage. Top with remaining corn-flake mixture. Bake in 350° oven 30–40 minutes. Remove from oven. Top with grated cheese. Allow to melt before serving. Yields 8–10 servings.

The Best of Mayberry (North Carolina)

Zucchini Deluxe

6 large zucchini
1 cup fresh bread crumbs
¼ cup chopped onion
1 tomato, chopped
½ teaspoon salt

¼ teaspoon pepper
2 tablespoons margarine, melted
½ pound Cheddar cheese,
  grated
¼ cup milk

Wash and trim ends of zucchini. Cook, covered, in boiling salted water 5–8 minutes; drain. Cut in half lengthwise. Scoop out center of each. Chop up and combine with bread crumbs, onion, tomato, seasonings, and margarine. Toss lightly. Fill shells and place in baking dish. Heat cheese and milk in saucepan over low heat, stirring until sauce is smooth. Pour sauce over stuffed zucchini. Bake in 350° oven 25–30 minutes. Serves 6–12.

In Good Taste (North Carolina)

Mock Crab Cakes

2 cups grated zucchini
2 cups dry bread crumbs
2–3 teaspoons Old Bay
  Seasoning

3 green onions, chopped
2 eggs, beaten
1 teaspoon mayonnaise
Tartar sauce (optional)

Drain grated zucchini in 2 or more layers of paper towels; press firmly. Combine all ingredients and spoon into hot oil (about 1 inch of oil); brown on both sides. Serve with tartar sauce, if desired.

Have Fun Cooking with Me Again and Again (North Carolina)

Ranch Squash Casserole

The key to this creamy casserole is the ranch dressing.

2 pounds yellow squash, sliced
1 cup sliced onion
¾ cup mayonnaise
2 eggs, slightly beaten
½ cup crushed unsalted
  saltine crackers

1 envelope ranch buttermilk
  dressing
1 cup shredded Cheddar cheese
2 tablespoons butter, melted
½ cup fresh bread crumbs

Cook squash and onion together in water until tender; drain well. In a bowl, mix mayonnaise, eggs, saltines, ranch dressing, and shredded cheese together. Mash squash with a fork and combine with ranch mixture. Pour into a greased casserole dish. Mix melted butter with bread crumbs and put on top of casserole. Bake 20–25 minutes in a 350° oven.

Someone's in the Kitchen with Melanie (North Carolina)

Green Beans and Zucchini Bundles

1½ pounds green beans, stringed
2 zucchini squash, 2 inches in diameter
½ cup vegetable oil

¼ cup white wine vinegar
2 tablespoons Dijon mustard
2 tablespoons honey
2 cloves garlic, minced
2 teaspoons fresh basil

Cook beans in salted water until crisp tender, about 7 minutes. Cool beans in ice water; drain; set aside. Cut zucchini into 8 (1½-inch) slices. Carve out the centers so that you have rings with ¼-inch rims.

Steam zucchini rings 2–3 minutes until crisp tender. Immerse rings in ice water and drain well. Poke 8–12 beans through each zucchini ring. Arrange bundles in a 9x13-inch casserole dish.

Combine remaining ingredients in a blender and pour over beans. Cover and refrigerate for 24 hours. Makes 8 servings.

Stirring Performances (North Carolina)

Green Bean Casserole

2 (16-ounce) cans French-style green beans, drained
1 (8-ounce) can sliced water chestnuts, drained
1 (15-ounce) can bean sprouts, drained
1 (8-ounce) can sliced mushrooms, drained

1 medium onion, chopped
1½ (10¾-ounce) cans cream of mushroom soup
Salt and pepper to taste
1 cup grated sharp Cheddar cheese
1 (3½-ounce) can French fried onion rings

In a 2-quart casserole layer half beans, water chestnuts, bean sprouts, mushrooms, and onion. Cover with half of soup. Sprinkle with salt and pepper and half of cheese. Repeat layering. Top with French fried onions. Bake at 400° for 20 minutes, covered. Remove cover and bake additional 10 minutes.

Command Performances (Virginia)

Garlicky Green Beans

This dish is delicious enough to set before a king.

1 pound fresh green beans, tips
  removed
2 tablespoons butter
2 tablespoons olive oil
4 garlic cloves, minced
8 sun-dried tomatoes, finely
  chopped

3 tablespoons bread crumbs
3 tablespoons grated Parmesan
  cheese
Salt and pepper

Rinse beans and microwave for 3–5 minutes on full power. Heat butter and olive oil in skillet. Add garlic and tomatoes and sauté for 3 minutes. Add beans, bread crumbs, and cheese. Mix and remove from heat. Season with salt and pepper. Yields 6 servings.

Food Fabulous Food (New Jersey)

Boiled Butter Beans—Lima Beans

Butter beans and lima beans are cooked in the same manner. The lima bean is larger and more mealy. They may be seasoned with butter, ham, or salt meat.

2 cups fresh butter beans, or
  lima beans
4 cups water
1 teaspoon salt
1 teaspoon sugar

2 tablespoons butter, or piece of
  boiling meat about 2 inches
  square, 1-inch thick
½ cup milk or cream (optional)
Pepper to taste

Wash and pick over beans; cover with water in a saucepan with lid. Add salt and sugar. Boil about 10 minutes, then add butter; or if meat is to be used, add meat. Boil slowly until beans are tender, about 45 minutes to 1 hour. If pan becomes too dry, add a little warm water. There should be a little broth left with the beans. If desired, just before serving, add milk or cream and season to taste with pepper; reheat. Serve 4–6.

Marion Brown's Southern Cook Book (North Carolina)

North Carolina Baked Beans

3 (32-ounce) cans pork and
  beans, liquid drained
2 pounds country-style
  sausage, browned and
  crumbled
2 medium onions, thinly
  sliced

1 cup dark corn syrup
1 cup brown sugar
4 tablespoons prepared
  yellow mustard
3 teaspoons dry mustard
2 teaspoons Worcestershire

Preheat oven to 350°. Prepare a bean pot or deep casserole, about 10x14-inches, by spraying with vegetable spray. Pour drained pork and beans into bean pot. Add cooked sausage and onions. Pour in corn syrup, brown sugar, prepared and dry mustards, and Worcestershire. Blend thoroughly. Bake for 90 minutes. Cooking the day before and reheating for 30 minutes before serving greatly increases flavor. Serves 10–12.

The Curran Connection Cookbook (North Carolina)

Bootleg Beans

3 strips bacon, diced
1 small onion, chopped
1 (16-ounce) can pork and beans

1 tablespoon brown sugar
2 tablespoons vinegar
2 tablespoons ketchup

Fry bacon until half cooked; add onion. When onion is lightly browned, pour off excess fat. Add pork and beans, brown sugar, vinegar, and ketchup. Stir well and cover. Let simmer 30–45 minutes, or bake slowly at 300° for 2 hours. Yields 4 servings.

Note: Add sliced hot dogs last 10 minutes, if desired. Great for picnics or barbecues.

Heart of the Mountains (North Carolina)

 Virginia actually extends 95 miles farther west than West Virginia.

Delaware Succotash

2 thin slices salt pork
1 pint shelled lima beans or
  1 package frozen, thawed
Water
8 ears of fresh corn or frozen,
  thawed

1 large ripe tomato, cubed
1 teaspoon salt
¼ teaspoon pepper
Dash of nutmeg

Lay salt pork in bottom of a saucepan and cover with lima beans. Add enough water to cover and cook over low heat until beans are tender. Cut kernels from fresh corn and combine with beans, cubed tomato, and seasonings. Cover and continue cooking over low heat for 10–15 minutes. Stir frequently. Yields 6 servings.

South Coastal Cuisine (Delaware)

Spinach Madeline

2 (10-ounce) packages frozen
  chopped spinach
4 tablespoons butter
2 tablespoons flour
2 tablespoons chopped onion
½ cup evaporated milk
½ cup spinach liquor
½ teaspoon black pepper

¾ teaspoon celery salt
¾ teaspoon garlic salt
½ teaspoon salt
1 (6-ounce) ball jalapeño cheese,
  or any pepper-hot cheese
1 teaspoon Worcestershire
Pinch of red pepper (optional)

Cook spinach according to directions. Drain and reserve liquid. Melt butter and add flour, stirring well. Add onion and cook until soft, not brown. Add evaporated milk, liquor, seasonings, and cheese, and stir until cheese is melted. Fold in spinach. Cover top with buttered bread crumbs. Bake in moderate (350°) oven until bubbling. Serves 5–6.

    This freezes well. If you do not freeze, make at least 24 hours ahead since it improves flavor.

Taste of the Town (North Carolina)

Spinach-Artichoke Casserole

½ cup chopped onion
½ cup butter or margarine
2 (10-ounce) packages frozen
  chopped spinach, thawed,
  drained
1 (14-ounce) can artichoke hearts
  (in water), cut-up coarsely
½ cup grated Parmesan cheese
1 cup sour cream
1 (4-ounce) can chopped
  mushrooms
¼ teaspoon red pepper

Sauté onion in butter. Combine all other ingredients and add to onions. Bake in a deep (2½- or 3-quart) casserole dish covered at 350° for 25 minutes. (Can be baked in microwave at 50% power for 25 minutes). Serves 4 when used as a main dish or 6 when used as a vegetable.

Historic Lexington Cooks (Virginia)

Spinach Soufflé

2 packages chopped frozen
  spinach
1 package dry onion soup mix
1 pint sour cream
1 cup Pepperidge Farm crumbs
3 tablespoons butter, melted

Boil spinach, drain well. Reserve juice and use as needed to keep dish from becoming too dry. Mix sour cream and onion soup together and let stand ½ hour. Then add to spinach with ¾ of the bread crumbs, mixed with melted butter. Bake in a greased dish at 275° for 30 minutes or until hot. Add rest of soaked crumbs sprinkled on top. Makes 6 servings.

Centenary Cookbook (North Carolina)

Baked Potato Sauce

A great alternative to sour cream.

1 cup Hellmann's mayonnaise
½ cup grated Parmesan cheese
¼ cup grated onion
¼ cup butter, softened
½ teaspoon hot pepper

Combine all ingredients. This mixture will keep indefinitely under refrigeration. Yields 2 cups.

A Dash of Down East (North Carolina)

Gourmet Potatoes

2 cups shredded Cheddar cheese
½ cup plus 2 tablespoons
   butter, divided
1½ cups sour cream (at room
   temperature)
½ cup chopped green onions
1 teaspoon salt
½ teaspoon pepper
8 medium potatoes, peeled,
   coarsely shredded

Heat cheese and ½ cup butter in saucepan over low heat until partially melted, stirring occasionally; remove from heat. Stir in sour cream, green onions, salt, and pepper. Fold in potatoes. Spoon into greased 8-inch glass baking dish. Dot with 2 tablespoons butter. Bake at 350° for 25 minutes or microwave, covered, on HIGH for 12 minutes. Yields 8 servings.

Goodness Grows in North Carolina (North Carolina)

Clawson's Emporium's
Original Dirigible

1 (1-pound) potato
1 tablespoon butter
1 tablespoon chopped onion
1 tablespoon chopped green bell
   pepper
⅛ cup diced ham
⅛ cup diced turkey
⅛ cup shredded provolone
   cheese
⅛ cup shredded Cheddar cheese
¼ cup sour cream
Pinch of chives
2 slices cooked bacon, crumbled

Bake potato at 400° for 1 hour or until done. Split open and rake with fork. Work in butter, onion, and pepper; work in diced ham, turkey, and cheeses. Close potato and heat until cheese melts. Remove, open, and top halves with sour cream, chives, and bacon.

   For a seafood dirigible, substitute cooked, minced crab and shrimp for ham and turkey. Serves 1.

North Carolina's Historic Restaurants (North Carolina)

Ranch Potato Casserole

5 cups cooked, cubed potatoes, drained
1 cup sour cream
½ cup ranch dressing
1¼ cups shredded Swiss cheese, divided

¼ cup chopped onion
2 tablespoons minced parsley
½ teaspoon dill
1 teaspoon chives
Paprika

In a bowl, combine potatoes, sour cream, dressing, 1 cup cheese, onion, parsley, dill, and chives; transfer to a greased baking dish. Sprinkle with remaining cheese and paprika. Bake, uncovered, at 350° until bubbly. Makes 8 servings.

Cabbage to Caviar (North Carolina)

Washington Red Skins

4 pounds red potatoes
1 stick butter, more or less, depending on size of baking dish

4 cloves garlic, or to taste, minced
1½ teaspoons salt, or to taste
½ teaspoon ground white pepper, or to taste

Scrub the potatoes and cut into halves, if large. Steam the potatoes in their skins for 25 minutes or until done (this will depend on size) using a vegetable steamer or just a colander set over water in a big pot. Cool and refrigerate them.

When ready to cook again, roughly chop the potatoes, leaving the skins on. Rub baking dish with about one tablespoon of the butter. Toss potatoes with garlic, salt and pepper, and press into the pan. Melt remaining butter and pour over top. Bake on the top rack of a 350° oven for about an hour, until the potatoes are crisp and golden. Serves 8.

Best of Friends (Maryland)

WWW.WIKIPEDIA.COM

On December 25, 1776, George Washington made his famous overnight crossing of the Delaware River from Pennsylvania to surprise the British in Trenton, New Jersey.

Sweet Potato Cups

4–6 medium-size sweet potatoes
1 stick butter
1 (15-ounce) can crushed
   pineapple, undrained
3 eggs, beaten

½ cup dark rum
½ cup chopped walnuts
1 cup miniature marshmallows
Orange shells

Boil unpeeled potatoes until soft; drain, peel, and mash. To hot potatoes, add butter, undrained pineapple, eggs, rum, nuts, and marshmallows. Blend well. Mound into 6–8 orange shells. This can be done ahead of time. Heat in a 325° oven for 30 minutes, or until heated through. Makes 6–8 servings.

Korner's Folly Cookbook (North Carolina)

Candied Yams

3–4 medium sweet potatoes
¾ cup sugar
Pinch of nutmeg
Pinch of salt

Pinch of cinnamon
1–2 tablespoons water
1 teaspoon vanilla
1 tablespoon butter

Boil sweet potatoes until done. Peel, slice, and place in buttered glass baking dish. In saucepan, combine sugar, nutmeg, salt, and cinnamon. Add sufficient water to moisten. Simmer 3 minutes. Add vanilla. Dot potatoes with butter and pour sauce over potatoes. Bake at 350° for 20 minutes.

Secret Recipes (North Carolina)

State Fair Onion Rings

2 large Bermuda or sweet onions
Cooking oil
½ cup all-purpose flour

½ teaspoon salt
⅔ cup milk
Additional salt to sprinkle

Cut onions into ¼-inch slices. Separate into rings. Heat about 2 inches of oil in frying pan. Mix flour and ½ teaspoon salt. Soak rings in milk and dip into flour mixture. Fry a few at a time and drain on paper towels. Sprinkle with additional salt.

From Our Home to Yours (North Carolina)

Gourmet Smothered Onions Amandine

⅓ cup butter
1 cup whole or slivered almonds
1 tablespoon brown sugar
1 teaspoon salt

Dash each of cayenne pepper,
  nutmeg, and ground cloves
3 dozen very small onions (frozen
  ones do well)

Melt butter in a casserole on top of stove and add everything except the onions. Stir until well blended. Add onions and stir until they are well coated. Cover and bake in a moderate oven (350°) about an hour, stirring 3 or 4 times. Makes 5 servings.

Cooking Along the Susquehanna (Maryland)

Sweet Onion Pudding

6 large eggs
2 cups whipping cream
1 (3-ounce) package shredded
  Parmesan cheese
3 tablespoons all-purpose
  flour

2 tablespoons sugar
2 teaspoons baking powder
1 teaspoon salt
½ cup butter or margarine
6 medium-size sweet onions,
  thinly sliced

Stir together first 3 ingredients in large bowl, blending well. Combine flour, sugar, baking powder, and salt; gradually stir into egg mixture. Set aside.

Melt butter in large skillet over medium heat. Add onions. Cook, stirring often, 30–40 minutes or until caramel colored. Remove from heat. Stir onions into egg mixture, then spoon into a lightly greased 9x13-inch baking dish. Bake 30 minutes at 350° or until pudding is set. Makes 8 servings.

Cooking with the Sandhills Woman's Exchange (North Carolina)

Middleburg Medley

1 medium onion, sliced
1 red bell pepper, sliced
2 tablespoons vegetable oil
3 garlic cloves, minced
2 small to medium zucchini, sliced
2 small to medium yellow squash, sliced
1 cup frozen whole-kernel corn
1 large tomato, peeled, chopped
2 jalapeño peppers, seeded, chopped
2–3 teaspoons chopped fresh basil
½ teaspoon dried Italian seasoning
½ teaspoon salt
½ cup grated Parmesan cheese

Sauté onion and bell pepper in hot oil in a large skillet over medium heat, stirring often, 4 minutes. Add garlic and cook 1–2 minutes or until vegetables are tender. Add zucchini and yellow squash, and cook, stirring often, 7 minutes.

Add corn and next 5 ingredients; reduce heat and simmer, stirring often, 7–10 minutes. Sprinkle vegetable medley with Parmesan cheese. Serve immediately with cooked pasta or as a side dish. Serves 2–4.

What Can I Bring? (Virginia)

Cranberry-Apple Bake

3 cups red apples, unpeeled and sliced
2 cups raw cranberries
1 cup sugar
1 cup quick oats, uncooked
½ cup chopped pecans
⅓ cup flour
½ cup brown sugar
1 stick margarine, melted

Combine apples and cranberries in 2-quart casserole dish. Mix remaining ingredients, except margarine, and spread over apples and cranberries. Spoon melted margarine over top. Bake at 325° for 45–60 minutes. Can be used with a meal or as a dessert with whipped topping. Freezes well. Yields 6–8 servings.

Making Time (North Carolina)

Fried Apples

4 medium Yellow Delicious apples
⅓ cup butter, softened
¾ cup packed brown sugar

1 tablespoon plus 1 teaspoon cornstarch
½ teaspoon cinnamon
1½ cups water

Slice, but do not peel apples; place in heavy 10-inch skillet. Combine butter, brown sugar, cornstarch, and cinnamon together, mixing well. Toss with apples, stirring to coat all pieces. Add water to skillet. Put lid on skillet and cook over medium heat 12–15 minutes till apples are fork-tender and sauce is thick, stirring occasionally. To serve, either spoon all in a medium-size serving bowl or divide into 4 individual serving bowls, ladling ½ cup sauce into each bowl.

Note: After the apples are tender, you can remove skillet from heat and add 2 tablespoons apple liqueur (Applejack).

Turnip Greens, Ham Hocks & Granny's Buns (North Carolina)

Curried Fruit

1 (29-ounce) can peach slices
1 (29-ounce) can pear slices
1 (20-ounce) can pineapple chunks

1 (20-ounce) can apricot halves
⅓ cup butter
¾ cup brown sugar
4 teaspoons curry powder

Drain fruit. Arrange in a 3-quart ovenproof dish. Melt butter and add brown sugar and curry powder. Stir to blend. Pour over fruit and stir to cover fruit evenly. May be made ahead to this point and refrigerated overnight. In fact, it benefits from being made in advance and letting the flavors marry. Bake one hour at 325°. Serves 12.

Note: This recipe is very flexible. Use fruits you like best: if you like pineapple, for example, use two cans instead of one. Canned cherries (not pie filling) are very pleasant, or you can use maraschino cherries if you like them, though they "bleed" their color onto the other fruit if it is allowed to sit overnight. You can use fresh fruit in this recipe, but it is not necessary, and in fact quite a bit more work, and the fresh advantage is lost in the baking process.

The Queen Victoria® Cookbook (New Jersey)

Pasta, Rice, Etc.

PHOTO COURTESY OF NC DIVISION OF TOURISM, FILM AND SPORTS DEVELOPMENT. BILL RUSS, PHOTOGRAPHER.

Linn Cove Viaduct on the Blue Ridge Parkway in Watauga County, North Carolina, is the most complicated concrete bridge ever built. The viaduct's construction had to overcome an elevation of 4,100 feet without damaging one of the world's oldest mountains, Grandfather Mountain. The viaduct's 7-mile portion of the Parkway's 469 miles was finally completed in 1987, twenty years after the rest of the parkway.

Crockpot Macaroni and Cheese

1 (8-ounce) package dry elbow
  macaroni
1 (12-ounce) can evaporated
  milk
1½ cups whole milk
2 eggs
¼ cup butter, melted
1 teaspoon salt
½ teaspoon pepper
3 cups shredded sharp Cheddar
  cheese, divided

Cook macaroni in boiling, salted water 5 minutes. Drain; pour into crockpot. Mix all other ingredients, except 1 cup cheese. Add to macaroni; stir well. Put remaining cup of cheese on top of macaroni. Do not stir. Cook in covered crockpot on HIGH 2 hours.

Favorite Recipes: Barbara's Best Volume II (Virginia)

Creamy Macaroni and Cheese

1 (8-ounce) box elbow macaroni
¼ cup butter or margarine
¼ cup flour
½ teaspoon salt
¼ teaspoon pepper
¼ teaspoon dry mustard
¼ teaspoon Worcestershire
2 cups milk
3 cups shredded Cheddar cheese,
  divided
1 cup buttered bread crumbs

Cook macaroni as directed on the box. Drain and reserve. Preheat oven to 350°. Heat butter in a 3-quart saucepan over low heat until melted. Using a whisk, stir in flour, salt, pepper, mustard, and Worcestershire. Cook over low heat, stirring constantly, until mixture is smooth and bubbly. Remove from heat. Stir in milk. Heat to boiling, stirring constantly. Boil and stir for 1 minute. Add 2½ cups cheese; cook on low, stirring constantly, until melted. Stir in macaroni gently. Pour into an ungreased 2-quart casserole dish. Top with buttered crumbs, mixed with remaining ½ cup cheese. Bake uncovered 20–30 minutes or until bubbly.

Country Chic's Home Cookin (Maryland)

Crabmeat-Sauced Pasta

This sauce is delightful over any pasta, but especially favored in my home over linguine.

1 (5½-ounce) package frozen
   crabmeat, thawed
2 tablespoons butter
1 green onion, including tops,
   sliced
2 or 3 mushrooms, sliced
2 tablespoons flour
Salt to taste

¼ tablespoon dry mustard
Pepper to taste
1 cup milk
1 tablespoon lemon juice
2 tablespoons dry white wine
   (optional)
1 tablespoon ketchup
2 cups hot cooked pasta

Drain crab and cut into small pieces. Combine butter, onion, and mushrooms in a skillet. Sauté until onion is opaque but not browned, about 3 minutes.

Stir flour into butter in the pan. Blend in salt, mustard, and pepper. Slowly add milk, whisking until smooth. Cook, stirring, until mixture thickens slightly. Stir in crab, lemon juice, wine, and ketchup. Stirring often, continue to cook over medium heat until crab is done and mixture is about to boil. Serve steaming hot over pasta. Makes 2 servings.

Love Yourself Cookbook (North Carolina)

Pasta Primavera

¼ cup butter
1 small onion, chopped
1 clove garlic, minced
3 ounces cauliflower, in pieces
½ carrot, sliced
½ zucchini, sliced
½ pound fresh asparagus, cut in
   ¼-inch pieces
¼ pound fresh mushrooms,
   sliced

½ cup heavy cream
¼ cup chicken stock
1 teaspoon dried basil
Salt and pepper to taste
½ cup frozen peas, thawed
2 scallions, thinly sliced
12 ounces vermicelli or linguine,
   cooked al dente
Freshly grated Parmesan cheese

In large skillet, melt butter and sauté onion and garlic. Add cauliflower and carrot; cook 3 minutes. Add zucchini, asparagus, and mushrooms to skillet and cook 2 minutes more. Add cream, stock, and seasonings, and cook until liquid is slightly reduced. Add peas and scallions and cook briefly. Serve sauce over cooked and drained noodles. Sprinkle with lots of fresh Parmesan cheese. Yields 4 servings.

Even More Special (North Carolina)

Baked Spaghetti

1 medium onion, chopped
1 pound ground beef
2–3 teaspoons oil
¾ cup tomato juice
3 (8-ounce) cans tomato sauce
¼ teaspoon marjoram
¼ teaspoon oregano
¼ teaspoon basil
¼ teaspoon rosemary
Dash of garlic salt
Salt and pepper to taste
1 teaspoon sugar
½ pound thin spaghetti
  (2 inches long)
¼ pound grated Cheddar cheese

Cook onion and beef in oil until lightly brown; drain. Add tomato juice, sauce, spices and sugar. Simmer until thickened. Cook spaghetti by package directions. Mix spaghetti with sauce mixture and ½ the cheese. Spread in baking dish coated with cooking spray. Top with remaining cheese. Bake at 350° for 20–25 minutes. Cut into squares. Serves 6.

Seasoned Seniors' Specials (North Carolina)

Mark's Baked Pepperoni Spaghetti

1 (6-ounce) package spaghetti
2 tablespoons butter
⅓ cup Parmesan cheese
2 eggs, well beaten
1 pound lean ground beef
1 (26-ounce) jar spaghetti sauce
  with mushrooms
1 cup ricotta cheese
1 package pepperoni slices
½ cup grated mozzarella
  cheese

Cook spaghetti according to package directions; drain. Stir butter, Parmesan cheese, and eggs into cooked spaghetti. Spray a 9x13-inch baking pan with vegetable spray. Put spaghetti in bottom of pan. Spread Parmesan mixture on top. Brown ground beef; drain well. Add spaghetti sauce and simmer 10 minutes. Spread ricotta cheese over noodles and Parmesan mixture. Spread meat mixture on top of ricotta cheese mixture. Top with pepperoni and mozzarella cheese. Cover and bake at 350° for 30–40 minutes. Uncover and continue baking until cheese begins to brown.

The Westwood Clubhouse Cookbook (Virginia)

Seafood Lasagna

8 lasagna noodles
1 cup chopped onion
2 tablespoons butter or margarine
1 (8-ounce) package cream
    cheese, softened
1½ cups cream-style cottage
    cheese
1 beaten egg
2 teaspoons dried basil, crushed
½ teaspoon salt
⅛ teaspoon pepper

2 cans condensed cream of
    mushroom soup
⅓ cup milk
⅓ cup dry white wine
1 pound shelled shrimp, cooked
    and halved
1 (7½-ounce) can crabmeat,
    drained
¼ cup grated Parmesan cheese
½ cup shredded sharp American
    cheese

Cook noodles according to directions; drain. Arrange 4 noodles in bottom of greased 9x13x2-inch baking dish. Cook onion in butter or margarine until tender. Blend in cream cheese. Stir in cottage cheese, egg, basil, salt, and pepper; spread half atop noodles. Combine soup, milk, and wine. Stir in shrimp and crab; spread half over cottage cheese layer. Repeat layers, beginning with remaining noodles. Sprinkle with Parmesan cheese. Bake, uncovered, in 350° oven for 45 minutes. Top with American cheese. Bake 2–3 minutes more. Let stand 15 minutes before serving. Makes 12 servings.

A Taste of GBMC (Maryland)

Spinach Lasagne

½ pound fresh spinach
½ onion, chopped
1 garlic clove, minced
1 tablespoon olive oil
1 cup low-fat cottage cheese
1 egg, beaten
Salt and pepper to taste

1 teaspoon basil
½ teaspoon oregano
2 tablespoons chopped parsley
½ pound lasagne noodles
½ pound mozzarella cheese
3 cups tomato sauce

Wash spinach carefully, tearing out stems, and chop coarsely. Sauté chopped onion and minced garlic in oil. Combine sautéed onion and garlic with spinach, cottage cheese, and beaten egg. Mix well. Season with salt, pepper, basil, oregano, and parsley.

Cook lasagne noodles until tender. Coarsely grate mozzarella cheese. In a buttered oblong baking dish, layer noodles, cottage cheese mixture, mozzarella cheese, and tomato sauce, in order listed. Repeat layering 3 times, making sure tomato sauce is on top. Cover with aluminum foil. Bake at 350° for 40 minutes. Remove foil and bake 10 minutes more. Serve with garlic bread and green salad. Serves 4.

In Good Taste (North Carolina)

Lasagna Pie

1 (13-ounce) container small curd
    cottage cheese or ricotta
½ cup grated Parmesan cheese
1 pound extra lean ground beef
1 medium onion, chopped
1 green bell pepper, chopped
1 teaspoon dried oregano
½ teaspoon dried basil

1 (6-ounce) can tomato paste
1½ cups shredded mozzarella
    cheese, divided
Salt and pepper to taste
1 cup milk
⅔ cup packaged biscuit mix
2 eggs

Preheat oven to 400°. Lightly grease 10-inch pie pan. Place cottage cheese in a layer on bottom, then top with Parmesan cheese. Brown beef over medium-low heat, and add onion and green pepper, cooking until onion is translucent. Add oregano, basil, tomato paste, ¾ cup mozzarella, salt and pepper to taste. Spoon over cheese layers in pie pan.

Beat milk, biscuit mix, and eggs 1 minute until smooth (1 minute or so with hand beater). Pour into pie pan. Bake about 30 minutes, or until golden brown. Knife inserted halfway between center and edge will come out clean. Sprinkle with remaining mozzarella. Let stand 5–10 minutes before serving.

The Other Side of the House (Virginia)

The wild ponies of Assateague and Chincoteague islands, Virginia, are actually small horses just larger than a Shetland pony. There are two theories of how the ponies came to live on the islands. One legend is that a Spanish galleon wrecked off of Assateague Island and the surviving ponies swam ashore. However, the more likely theory is that early 17th-century colonists let their animals loose on the island to avoid the tax on fenced livestock. Whichever theory is true, Virginia's wild ponies have been living on the islands for hundreds of years.

Vermicelli with Scallops

1 pound bay scallops
2 tablespoons fresh lemon juice
2 tablespoons chopped parsley
1 onion, chopped
1 clove garlic, minced
2 tablespoons olive oil
2 tablespoons butter, divided
1½ cups canned Italian
 tomatoes, undrained, cut up
2 tablespoons chopped fresh
 basil, or ½ teaspoon dried,
 crushed basil

½ teaspoon dried oregano
½ teaspoon dried, crushed thyme
 leaves
1 (12-ounce) package vermicelli,
 cooked
2 tablespoons heavy cream
Dash of ground nutmeg

Rinse scallops and place in glass dish; sprinkle with lemon juice and chopped parsley. Cover and marinate in refrigerator while preparing sauce.

Cook and stir onion and garlic in oil and 1 tablespoon butter in large skillet over medium-high heat until onion is tender. Add tomatoes with juice, basil, oregano, and thyme. Reduce heat to low. Cover; simmer 30 minutes, stirring occasionally. Meanwhile, cook vermicelli; drain. Keep sauce and vermicelli warm in their own utensils.

Drain scallops. In another large skillet, add remaining 1 tablespoon butter and scallops. Cook and stir over medium heat until scallops are cooked through and light golden brown on each side (about 10 minutes total), adding more butter if necessary. Add cream, nutmeg, and tomato sauce mixture. Place warm vermicelli in a large bowl and pour scallops and sauce over it. Toss gently to coat. Serves 4.

It's Delicious! (Virginia)

Deep in the mountains of Graham County, North Carolina, lies a 3800-acre tract of the most beautiful forest in America. On July 30, 1936, the area was dedicated to the poet Joyce Kilmer as a living memorial. It was his simple but beautiful words in the poem "Trees" that prompted forestry officials and friends of nature to set aside the acreage that is now Joyce Kilmer Memorial Forest.

Chicken Pecan Fettuccine

This is a mouth-watering combination of ingredients.

**1 pound chicken breasts, skinned
and boned**
¾ cup butter, divided
3 cups sliced fresh mushrooms
1 cup sliced green onions
¾ teaspoon salt, divided
**½ teaspoon freshly ground black
pepper, divided**
½ teaspoon garlic powder, divided

10 ounces fresh fettuccine
1 egg yolk
⅔ cup half-and-half
**2 tablespoons freshly chopped
parsley**
**½ cup freshly grated Parmesan
cheese**
1 cup chopped pecans, toasted

Cut chicken into ¾-inch pieces. Melt ¼ cup butter in a large skillet. Sauté chicken until lightly browned. Remove chicken from skillet and set aside. To drippings in skillet, add mushrooms, green onions, ½ teaspoon salt, ¼ teaspoon pepper, and ¼ teaspoon garlic powder. Sauté until mushrooms are tender. Return chicken to skillet and simmer for 20 minutes, or until chicken is done. Cook fettuccine in boiling salted water until al denté. Drain well.

Melt remaining ½ cup butter and combine with egg yolk, half-and-half, parsley, and remaining salt, pepper, and garlic powder. Stir butter sauce into fettuccine. Sprinkle with cheese, tossing until well mixed. Add chicken and mushroom mixture; toss until combined. To serve, arrange fettuccine on a warm platter and sprinkle with toasted pecans. Yields 6 servings.

A Matter of Taste (New Jersey)

"Trees" by Joyce Kilmer:

I think that I shall never see
A poem lovely as a tree.
A tree whose hungry mouth is prest
Against the earth's sweet flowing breast;
A tree that looks at God all day,
And lifts her leafy arms to pray;
A tree that may in summer wear
A nest of robins in her hair;
Upon whose bosom snow has lain;
Who intimately lives with rain.
Poems are made by fools like me,
But only God can make a tree.

Old World Manicotti

12 large manicotti shells
4 cups shredded mozzarella
   cheese, divided
2 cups ricotta cheese
6 tablespoons chopped fresh
   basil, or 2 tablespoons dried

1 (26-ounce) jar prepared spaghetti
   sauce, divided
½ cup grated Parmesan or Romano
   cheese

Cook pasta according to package directions. Drain; rinse with cool water. Let pasta dry on paper towels.

Preheat oven to 350°. Spray a 9x13-inch baking dish with nonstick cooking spray. In medium bowl, stir together 3 cups mozzarella with ricotta and basil. Using a teaspoon, carefully stuff pasta shells with prepared cheese mixture. Spoon 2 cups spaghetti sauce into prepared baking dish. Arrange stuffed pasta over sauce; pour remaining sauce over top of pasta and sprinkle with remaining mozzarella. Bake 15 minutes; sprinkle with grated cheese, and bake 10 minutes longer. Serve hot.

Cooking with Love & Memories (North Carolina)

Risotto with Tomato, Corn and Basil

2½ cups water
2 cups milk (whole or low fat)
2 tablespoons butter
1 cup minced onion
1 garlic clove, minced
¾ cup uncooked Arborio rice
3 tablespoons white wine

1½ cups corn kernels
1 ripe tomato, seeded, chopped fine
½ cup grated Parmesan cheese
½ cup thinly sliced basil,
   divided
½ teaspoon salt
Pepper to taste

Heat water and milk to a simmer. Keep heat low. Melt butter in a separate pan and sauté onion 3–4 minutes. Add garlic and rice. Stir constantly for 1 minute. Add wine. Stir until absorbed. Begin to add milk/water mixture ½ cup at a time. Wait until each addition is absorbed before adding the next amount. When rice has cooked 15 minutes and most of the liquid has absorbed, add corn, tomato, and remaining milk/water mixture. Cook, stirring frequently, until rice is tender, but still slightly chewy. Risotto should take 18–20 minutes to cook.

Stir in cheese, ½ the basil, salt, and pepper. Spoon onto plates and top with remaining basil. Serves 4.

Cooking with Grace (Virginia)

Rice Pilaf

PLAIN PILAF:

1 large onion, sliced
4 tablespoons butter

1 cup uncooked rice
2 cups bouillon (beef or chicken)

Brown sliced onion in butter. Add rice. Cook in butter and onion mixture over low heat 4–5 minutes, stirring often. Rice will be lightly colored. Heat liquid bouillon to boiling point and pour over rice. Cover dish or pan tightly and bake in 350° oven 25–30 minutes or until liquid is absorbed. Yields 8 servings

Variations: (1) Add 1 (4-ounce) can mushrooms, drained. (2) Add sliced green bell peppers. (3) Add chopped water chestnuts.

Editor's Extra: I sometimes like slivered almonds, too.

Nothing Could Be Finer (North Carolina)

Browned Rice with Peas

1 cup rice
2½ cups boiling water
½ cup butter
¼ cup chopped onion
¼ cup sliced mushrooms,
  drained

10 ounces frozen peas, thawed
1 (8-ounce) can water chestnuts,
  drained, diced
3 tablespoons soy sauce

Preheat oven to 350°. In dry skillet, brown rice, stirring often. Turn into a 1½-quart casserole dish; add water and stir with fork to separate grains. Cover and bake 30 minutes or until rice is tender.

Meanwhile in skillet, over low heat, melt butter; add onion and mushrooms and sauté. Remove from heat; add peas, chestnuts, and soy sauce. Add to rice and blend gently. Bake uncovered 15 minutes. Serves 8.

Hint: Add 1 tablespoon oil, butter, or margarine to rice before boiling to make grains separate, and rice will never stick to pan.

Virginia Hospitality (Virginia)

Shrimp and Sausage Jambalaya

1 pound smoked sausage,
  thinly sliced
3 tablespoons olive oil
⅔ cup chopped bell pepper
2 cloves garlic, minced
¾ cup chopped fresh parsley
1 cup chopped celery
2 (16-ounce) cans diced
  tomatoes, undrained
2 cups chicken broth
1 cup chopped green onions

1½ teaspoons thyme
2 bay leaves
2 teaspoons oregano
1 tablespoon Creole seasoning
½ teaspoon salt
½ teaspoon cayenne pepper
½ teaspoon black pepper
2 cups converted long-grain
  rice, washed
3 pounds raw shrimp, peeled

In a 4-quart heavy pot, sauté sausage; remove with slotted spoon. Add oil to pan drippings and sauté bell pepper, garlic, parsley, and celery 5 minutes. Add tomatoes and liquid, broth, and onions. Stir in thyme, bay leaves, oregano, Creole seasoning, salt, cayenne pepper, and black pepper. Add rice which has been washed and rinsed 3 times. Add sausage and cook 30 minutes, covered, over low heat, stirring occasionally. After most liquid has been absorbed by rice, add shrimp and cook until pink. Transfer mixture to an oblong baking dish. Bake approximately 25 minutes until heated through. Serves 12–14.

Note: Be sure rice is not crunchy after 30 minutes of cooking. If not done, add more chicken broth and continue cooking until done.

A River's Course (North Carolina)

Gwenzy's Crabmeat Quiche

A recipe tester declared this recipe to be "insanely delicious."

1 (10-inch) deep-dish pie shell, unbaked
2 cups drained, flaked backfin crabmeat
½ cup thinly sliced green onions with tops
½ cup evaporated milk
2 tablespoons flour
2–3 eggs, beaten
½ cup mayonnaise
1 teaspoon Worcestershire
¼ teaspoon dry mustard
1 (8-ounce) package shredded Swiss cheese

Prick bottom and side of pie shell with a fork. Bake at 450° for 8 minutes. Remove from oven. Reduce oven temperature to 350°.

Combine crabmeat and green onions in a large bowl. Mix evaporated milk and flour in a bowl until smooth. Beat in eggs. Add a mixture of mayonnaise, Worcestershire, and dry mustard, and beat a few seconds. Stir into crabmeat mixture. Add cheese and mix well. Pour into prebaked pie shell. Place on a baking sheet. Bake 45 minutes or until firm. Yields 6–8 servings.

Seaboard to Sideboard (North Carolina)

Crustless Crab Quiche

½ pound fresh mushrooms, thinly sliced
2 tablespoons butter
4 eggs
1 cup sour cream
1 cup small-curd cottage cheese
½ cup grated Parmesan cheese
4 tablespoons flour
1 teaspoon onion powder
¼ teaspoon salt
4 drops Tabasco
2 cups shredded Monterey Jack cheese
16 ounces fresh backfin crabmeat

Preheat oven to 350°. Sauté mushrooms in butter. Drain on paper towels. In blender, combine remaining ingredients except Monterey Jack cheese and crabmeat. Blend until thoroughly mixed. Pour mixture into large bowl. Stir in mushrooms, cheese, and crabmeat. Pour into a greased 9- or 10-inch quiche dish or 10-inch pie plate. Bake at 350° for 45 minutes or until knife comes out clean. Let stand 5 minutes before cutting. Serves 6–8.

Note: May be prepared ahead and brought to room temperature before baking. One-half pound slivered ham may be substituted for crab.

Tidewater on the Half Shell (Virginia)

Crab Quiche Surprise

Pie crust for a 9-inch quiche pan
½ cup grated Swiss cheese
½ cup grated Cheddar cheese
1 tiny zucchini, peeled, sliced
1 tiny yellow squash, peeled,
  sliced
1 small onion, diced

1 tablespoon olive oil
3 ounces crabmeat
2 eggs
½ cup sour cream
Salt and pepper to taste
1 teaspoon parsley

Preheat oven to 350°. Mix cheeses together and sprinkle ¾ cup in bottom of crust. Sauté zucchini, yellow squash, and onion in olive oil for 3 minutes (just to get them started). Spread crabmeat, zucchini, squash, and onion on top of cheese. Mix together eggs, sour cream, remaining cheese, salt, and pepper to taste and spread on top of quiche. Sprinkle parsley on top. Bake 35–40 minutes until set.

The Great Taste of Virginia Seafood Cookbook (Virginia)

Snow Hill Inn's Crab Quiche

1 sheet puff pastry
5 eggs, beaten
1 cup heavy cream
8 ounces sharp Cheddar cheese,
  grated

6 ounces Swiss cheese, grated
½ teaspoon seafood seasoning
1 teaspoon chopped cilantro
¾ pound crabmeat

Fit puff pastry into a large pie pan. Combine eggs, cream, and cheeses. Add seasonings and stir in crabmeat. Pour into pastry shell and bake at 375° for 45 minutes, or until a knife inserted in center comes out clean. Serves 8.

Recipe from Snow Hill Inn, Snow Hill, Maryland
Maryland's Historic Restaurants and their Recipes (Maryland)

Meats

One of the Seven Natural Wonders of the World, VIrginia's Natural Bridge is 215 feet high (17 stories) and 90 feet long. Thomas Jefferson bought the bridge and 157 surrounding acres from King George of England in 1774. The price of the purchase was 20 schillings. George Washington's initials are carved in it.

Beef Burgundy

2 pounds beef cubes
4 tablespoons A-1 Steak Sauce
1 package onion soup mix
1 cup red wine
1 can cream of celery soup

Preheat oven to 300°. Mix all ingredients in ovenproof dish. Cook 3 hours. Serves 4.

A Taste of GBMC (Maryland)

Elegant Filet Mignons

A superb butter sauce!

4 (1½- to 2-inch thick) filet mignons
2–3 teaspoons freshly cracked black pepper
2 teaspoons extra virgin olive oil
4–7 tablespoons butter, divided
3–6 shallots, sliced in half
½ cup beef bouillon
2–3 tablespoons red wine vinegar
1–2 tablespoons Worcestershire
Sliced green onions, for garnish

Dry filets and sprinkle each side generously with ½ teaspoon pepper; press pepper into beef. Place on plate and cover; refrigerate 2–3 hours. In a skillet, heat olive oil and add 1 tablespoon butter; cook fillets quickly on each side (approximately 4–6 per side). Place meat on a warm platter; keep warm.

Pour excess pan drippings from skillet; add 2–3 tablespoons butter to pan. Sauté shallots for one minute over medium heat; add beef bouillon. Increase heat and boil to reduce pan juices to 2 tablespoons. Be sure to scrape bottom of pan well while sauce is cooking; add red wine vinegar and Worcestershire; boil one minute. Add remaining 2 -3 tablespoons butter and mix with pan juices; pour over filets. Garnish with sliced green onions. Serve immediately. Serves 4.

Note: Do not overcook this elegant beef dish! Sliced mushrooms can be substituted for shallots. Use only extra virgin olive oil for this recipe.

Words Worth Eating (Virginia)

Medallions of Beef and Sautéed Shiitake Mushrooms with Red Wine Sauce

6 tablespoons butter or
  margarine, divided
4 small shallots, minced
1 garlic clove, minced
½ cup Worcestershire
½ cup red wine (Bordeaux)

¼ pound mushrooms (fresh, sliced
  Shiitake, if possible)
1½ pounds beef tenderloin
  medallions
Cognac as needed
1 teaspoon flour

In a sauté pan, melt 2 tablespoons butter. Sauté shallots; then add garlic. After 2 minutes, add Worcestershire and wine. Simmer until sauce is reduced by one third. Add mushrooms.

In a separate pan, melt remaining butter and, when hot, sauté the beef to desired degree of doneness. Flame beef with cognac. Remove beef. Add flour to pan and stir. Mix beef drippings into sauce. Set medallions on a bed of rice and pour sauce over. Serves 4.

The Great Chefs of Virginia Cookbook (Virginia)

Pot Roast 1950s Style

We've been enjoying this oldie-but-goodie for a long time. It makes its own gravy and is especially good with potatoes and carrots, which can be cooked in with the roast or added after the first hour. This dish is even better the second day.

1 (2- to 3-pound) boneless
  pot roast
Salt and pepper to taste
1 (10¾-ounce) can cream
  of mushroom soup

½ cup boiling water
1 package dry onion soup mix
1 clove garlic, crushed, or ½
  teaspoon garlic powder
  (optional)

Place roast on heavy-duty foil in roasting pan, Dutch oven, or casserole dish; salt and pepper to taste. Mix mushroom soup, water, dry onion soup mix, and garlic, if desired, and spread over top of roast. Bring foil up and fold over to seal. Bake covered 2–3 hours at 350° or until meat is tender.

Sing for Your Supper (North Carolina)

Coca-Cola Brisket

1 (3- to 4-pound) brisket of beef	2 large onions, chopped
1 (10- or 12-ounce) can or bottle	1 tablespoon paprika
Coca-Cola Classic	2 envelopes dry onion soup mix
Oil	Water

In a plastic or crockery bowl, place brisket and cover with Coca-Cola (use more, if needed). Refrigerate covered for 24 hours.

Remove meat from marinade. Discard marinade. In Dutch oven large enough for brisket to lie flat, pour a thin coating of vegetable oil. Over very high heat, sear meat on both sides on the stove top. Remove pan from heat and remove meat from pan. Add onions to pan. Sprinkle paprika and both envelopes of dry soup mix over onions and mix. Lay brisket on top. Add enough water to come up sides of brisket. Cover with lid. Bake at 325° for 2–2½ hours. Check occasionally to make sure liquid is not drying out too much. Slice and serve with onion mixture as gravy.

My Table at Brightwood (Virginia)

Fresh Brisket

1 (4- to 5-pound) brisket	Onion, celery, and garlic salt to
2 (5-ounce) bottles liquid smoke	taste

Place brisket in baking dish. Pour liquid smoke over meat. Sprinkle with salts; cover and refrigerate overnight. Discard marinade. Pour Worcestershire over meat, fat side up in baking pan. Cover tightly with foil and bake 5 hours at 275°.

BARBECUE SAUCE:

1 (46-ounce) can tomato juice	1 (20-ounce) bottle ketchup
1 medium onion, grated	2 tablespoons Worcestershire
1 (8-ounce) can tomato sauce	2 teaspoons lemon juice
2 tablespoons brown sugar	2 teaspoons chili powder
1 teaspoon dry mustard	

Combine ingredients and simmer slowly until desired thickness. Uncover meat and pour half the sauce over and bake uncovered for 1 hour longer. Baste occasionally. Freeze remaining sauce. Brisket also freezes well.

Knollwood's Cooking (North Carolina)

Cube Steak with Milk Gravy

Here in the South, we love to fry meat, and pretty much every time we do, we want gravy made with the "crumbles" left in the oil after the meat is cooked. This is an easy-to-follow recipe to help you make gravy. A truly southern dish. Serve with rice, biscuits, or rolls.

½ cup flour
4–6 cube steaks

½ cup vegetable oil
Salt and pepper to taste

Place flour in large zipper bag. Toss steaks in flour, one at a time, to coat. Heat oil in skillet. Brown steaks 5–7 minutes on each side. Salt and pepper while cooking.

GRAVY:

1 tablespoon drippings from skillet
2 tablespoons flour
1½ cups milk

2 teaspoons beef bouillon granules
⅛ teaspoon pepper
½ cup water, if needed

Remove meat from skillet. Drain all but about 1 tablespoon of drippings. Heat and add flour. Gradually add milk. Stir constantly. Bring to a boil for 2 minutes. Reduce heat and add bouillon and pepper. Simmer 4–5 minutes. Add water if gravy is too thick. Serve over steaks.

Gritslickers (North Carolina)

Sunday Dinner Steaks

6–8 beef cubed steaks
¾ cup all-purpose flour
¾ teaspoon black pepper
Oil
1 envelope onion mushroom soup mix

1 (8-ounce) can mushrooms, undrained
1 medium onion, sliced thin
2 (10-ounce) cans beef gravy
2 cans water

Dredge steaks in flour/pepper mixture. Brown lightly on both sides in hot oil. Put steaks in 9x13-inch pan. Sprinkle with onion soup mix. Cover with mushrooms. Layer onion slices on top. Mix gravy and water together and pour over steaks and onion. Do not stir. Cover tightly with foil. Bake at 250° for 3–4 hours.

Favorite Recipes: Bayside Baptist Church (Virginia)

Stuffed Round Steak

4 slices bacon, diced
1 onion, chopped
2 cups toasted bread crumbs
2½ tablespoons minced parsley
½ teaspoon celery salt
½ teaspoon sage

3–3½ pounds thin round steak,
   cut into 6 pieces
½ teaspoon salt
¼ teaspoon pepper
1 cup bouillon
1–2 (8-ounce) cans tomato sauce

To make stuffing sauté bacon with onion; mix in bread crumbs; add parsley, celery salt, and sage. Sprinkle steak with salt and pepper. Spread each portion of steak with dressing and roll up. Hold together with toothpicks. Place in a large skillet; pour bouillon over; cover and simmer 1 hour. Pour on tomato sauce; cover and simmer another 45 minutes or until done. If gravy is thin, uncover and cook until it thickens. Serves 6.

Mushrooms, Turnip Greens & Pickled Eggs (North Carolina)

Steak and Onion Pie

1 cup onion, sliced
¼ cup shortening
1 pound round steak, cut into
   small pieces
¼ cup flour
2 teaspoons salt
½ teaspoon paprika

Dash of ginger
Dash of allspice
2½ cups boiling water
2 cups raw potatoes, diced
⅛ teaspoon pepper
Dough for 1 pie crust

Cook onion slowly in shortening until yellow. Remove onion; set aside. Roll meat in mixture of flour, seasonings, and spices. Brown in hot shortening. Add boiling water; simmer, covered, until meat is tender, about one hour. Add potatoes and cook for 10 minutes longer.

Roll pie dough into circle, about ¼-inch thick. Make several openings for steam to escape. Pour meat and potatoes into greased 8-inch casserole. Cover with reserved onion. Fit pastry over top and seal edges. Bake in a 450° oven for 25–30 minutes. Serves 6.

Our Favorite Recipes (Maryland)

Betty's Beef Stroganoff

2 pounds round steak or sirloin,
  cut in ½-inch strips
⅓ cup flour
1 teaspoon salt
¾ teaspoon Ac'cent
⅓ cup plus 3 tablespoons
  butter, divided
½ cup finely chopped onion

1 small clove garlic, crushed
1 cup beef broth
1 tablespoon sherry
½ pound mushrooms, sliced
1 cup sour cream
1 teaspoon Worcestershire
Rice or noodles, cooked

Trim meat and coat evenly with a mixture of flour, salt, and Ac'cent. Heat ⅓ cup butter in a heavy 10-inch skillet over low heat. Add meat strips, onion, and garlic. Brown over medium heat, turning frequently.

When meat is browned, slowly add broth and sherry. Bring liquid rapidly to boiling, reduce heat, cover, and simmer until meat is tender. While meat is cooking, sauté mushrooms in remaining 3 tablespoons butter. Blend sour cream and Worcestershire and add to meat in small amounts along with mushrooms. Return to heat and continue cooking 3–5 minutes. Do not boil at this point. Serve immediately over rice or noodles.

Thought for Food (Virginia)

White-tailed deer live all over North Carolina, from Mount Mitchell (highest peak east of the Mississippi River) to the marshy sounds bordering the Atlantic Ocean. Most of the biggest bucks have come from the central section of the state, which features a lot of private land in mixed woods and pastures. North Carolina's population of white-tailed deer is estimated to be 1.1 million.

Grandmother's Meatloaf

2 slices bread, torn into cubes
⅓ cup milk
1 pound ground chuck
½ cup chopped onion
¼ cup chopped celery
⅛ cup chopped green bell
  pepper

1 teaspoon salt
Dash of black pepper
1½ teaspoons Worcestershire
1 egg, beaten
1 (8-ounce) can tomato sauce,
  divided

Soak bread in milk in large bowl. Add rest of ingredients, except ½ can tomato sauce, to soaked bread and mix together well. Bake in 350° oven 30–45 minutes. Make Meatloaf Sauce and spoon over meatloaf. Bake another 15 minutes. This recipe can easily be doubled. Serve with scalloped potatoes, a salad, and French bread. Serves 2–3.

MEATLOAF SAUCE:

Reserved ½ can tomato sauce
4 teaspoons brown sugar

½ teaspoon dry mustard
Dash of nutmeg

Combine ingredients and spoon over meatloaf.

Someone's in the Kitchen with Melanie (North Carolina)

Hurry-Up Meatloaf

¾ pound ground beef
1 (8-ounce) can tomato sauce,
  divided
½ cup soft bread crumbs
1 egg, slightly beaten
1 tablespoon dried onion flakes

½ teaspoon salt
⅛ teaspoon pepper
1 tablespoon brown sugar
2 tablespoons dried parsley flakes
1 tablespoon Worcestershire

Combine ground beef, ½ cup tomato sauce, bread crumbs, egg, onion flakes, salt, and pepper; mix well. Shape meat mixture into 4 individual loaves. Place on lightly greased (7x11-inch) baking pan. Bake at 450° for 30 minutes. Combine remaining tomato sauce, brown sugar, parsley flakes, and Worcestershire. Mix well and pour over loaves and bake an additional 5 minutes. Yields 2 servings.

WYVE's Bicentennial Cookbook (Virginia)

Sweet-Sour Meatballs on Rice

¾ pound ground chuck
3 tablespoons minced green
   onions
1 egg
¼ teaspoon salt
¼ teaspoon ground ginger
4 tablespoons soy sauce, divided
2 tablespoons vegetable oil
1 green bell pepper, cut in strips

1 (8¼-ounce) can sliced pineapple
1 cup frozen sliced carrots, cooked,
   drained, liquid reserved
¼ cup sliced water chestnuts
1½ tablespoons sugar
1½ tablespoons white vinegar
1 tablespoon cornstarch
2 servings hot cooked rice

Combine first 5 ingredients with 2 tablespoons soy sauce. Mix well and shape in balls, using 2 measuring tablespoons for each. (Balls hold shape best when chilled before cooking.) Sauté in oil in skillet until done; remove and keep warm.

Add green pepper to skillet and sauté 2 minutes. Drain pineapple, reserving syrup. Cut pineapple in chunks and add to skillet with carrots and water chestnuts. Sauté 3 minutes, then add meatballs. In small saucepan, mix remaining soy sauce, reserved liquids (add water to make 1 cup), sugar, vinegar, and cornstarch. Bring to a boil, stirring, until thickened and clear. Pour over contents of skillet and simmer 5 minutes. Serve on rice. Makes 2 servings.

Recipe submitted by Joy N. Starkey, Charles City, James City, New Kent
Country Treasures (Virginia)

The American Revolution refers to the period during the last half of the 18th century in which the thirteen colonies that became the United States of America gained independence from the British Empire. The thirteen colonies were British colonies in North America founded between 1607 and 1732. Although Britain held a dozen additional colonies in North America and the West Indies, the colonies referred to as the "thirteen" are those that rebelled against British rule in 1775 and proclaimed their independence as the United States of America on July 4, 1776. (The thirteen colonies are New Hampshire, Massachusetts, Rhode Island, Connecticut, New York, New Jersey, Pennsylvania, Delaware, Maryland, Virginia, North Carolina, South Carolina, and Georgia.) The majority of the fighting ended with the surrender of Britain's General Cornwallis in Yorktown, Virginia, on October 19, 1781. However, minor battles continued for another two years. The Treaty of Paris was finally signed on September 3, 1783, officially ending the American Revolution.

Popover Pizza

1 pound ground beef
1 (15-ounce) can tomato sauce
½ cup chopped green pepper
1 cup plus 2 tablespoons Bisquick
   Baking Mix, divided
1 tablespoon parsley

½ teaspoon pepper
2 cups Cheddar cheese, shredded
¾ cup water
¼ cup butter or margarine
4 eggs
¼ cup chopped green onions

Brown ground beef in a 10-inch skillet. Stir in tomato sauce, green pepper, 2 tablespoons Bisquick, parsley, and pepper. Heat to boiling. Boil and stir 1 minute. Pour into ungreased 9x13-inch pan. Sprinkle with cheese. Heat water and margarine to boiling in a 3-quart saucepan. Add 1 cup Bisquick all at once. Stir vigorously over low heat until mixture forms a ball, about 1½ minutes. Remove from heat. Beat in eggs, one at a time; continue beating until smooth. Spread over beef mixture. Sprinkle with onions. Bake in 400° oven for about 25–30 minutes, until puffy and golden brown. Serve immediately. Serves 6.

What's Cookin' (Maryland)

Hungry Jack Beef and Bean Round-Up

1½ pounds ground beef
¼ cup chopped onions
1 cup barbecue sauce
1 tablespoon brown sugar
1 (16-ounce) can baked beans
   with brown sugar

1 (10-ounce) can Hungry Jack
   biscuits
½ cup (2 ounces) shredded
   Cheddar cheese

Heat oven to 375°. Brown ground beef and onions in skillet. Drain. Stir in barbecue sauce, brown sugar, and beans. Heat until bubbly. Pour into 1½- to 2½-quart casserole. Separate biscuit dough into biscuits. Cut in half, crosswise. Place biscuits, cut-side-down, over hot meat mixture in spoke fashion around edge of casserole. Sprinkle cheese over biscuits. Bake 22–27 minutes, or until biscuits are golden brown. Serves 6.

A Cookbook of Treasures (Delaware)

Stuffed Green Peppers

6 medium green bell peppers
1 pound ground beef
⅓ cup chopped celery
⅓ cup chopped onions
1 teaspoon salt
1 teaspoon mustard
¼ cup ketchup

1 egg, beaten
1 teaspoon hot sauce
1 teaspoon A-1 sauce
1 teaspoon Worcestershire
1 teaspoon white pepper
½ cup bread crumbs
½ teaspoon garlic salt

Cut off tops of peppers and remove seeds. Parboil pepper cups in small amount of salted water for 5 minutes; drain. Mix remaining ingredients together; divide into 6 portions and stuff peppers. Prepare Sauce. Pour approximately ¼ cup of Sauce into a baking dish which has been sprayed with vegetable spray. Place stuffed peppers in dish. Pour 1–1½ cups Sauce on top. Bake in preheated 375° oven for 45–50 minutes. Spoon on additional Sauce, if needed.

SAUCE:

½ cup sugar
1 tablespoon hot sauce
1 tablespoon A-1 sauce
1 tablespoon Worcestershire
1 (42-ounce) can tomato juice

1 tablespoon salt
2 teaspoons white pepper
½ cup ketchup
2 tablespoons cornstarch
1 (4-ounce) can tomato juice

Mix first 8 ingredients together and heat. Mix cornstarch and tomato juice; add to mixture, stirring constantly. Simmer until thickened. Makes enough Sauce for 12 peppers.

Mrs. Rowe's Favorite Recipes (Virginia)

Hot Wheel Burgers

1½ pounds lean ground beef
1 (10¾-ounce) can tomato soup
1½ teaspoons dried minced
    onion
1 tablespoon prepared mustard
1 tablespoon Worcestershire

1 teaspoon horseradish
1 teaspoon salt
Hamburger buns
Sliced tomatoes
Cheese slices

Combine first 7 ingredients. Spread thinly on hamburger bun halves. Broil about 4 inches from heat for 12 minutes. Top with tomato slices and cheese. Broil until cheese melts. Makes 6.

Children's Party Book (Virginia)

Hamburger-Potato Bake

2 pounds ground chuck
2 eggs, beaten
2 cups bread crumbs
2 tablespoons ketchup
4 teaspoons salt
4 teaspoons pepper

Combine meat, eggs, bread crumbs, ketchup, salt, and pepper. Mix well, adding more crumbs if needed to make mixture firm. Put in ungreased oblong glass baking dish and bake at 350° for 20–30 minutes, or until brown.

TOPPING:

8 medium potatoes
1 carton sour cream
1 stick butter or margarine
3 ounces cream cheese, softened
Garlic salt to taste
Salt and pepper to taste
8 ounces grated sharp Cheddar
cheese

Cook potatoes until done. Peel and mash, adding sour cream, butter, cream cheese, garlic salt, salt, and pepper. Whip. Spread over meat mixture. Sprinkle with Cheddar cheese. Return to oven and bake until cheese melts and is slightly browned.

Jarrett House Potpourri (North Carolina)

Unsandwich Reuben Casserole

1 (12-ounce) can corned beef
1 (16-ounce) can sauerkraut,
drained
2 cups shredded Swiss cheese
½ cup Thousand Island
Dressing
1 large tomato, sliced
1 cup pumpernickel bread crumbs
2 tablespoons butter
Salt and pepper to taste
2 tablespoons caraway seeds

Layer each ingredient in a 2-quart casserole in order give. Bake at 350° for 30 minutes. Let set 5 minutes before serving.

A Cookbook of Pinehurst Courses (North Carolina)

Veal and Peppers

2 pounds veal cubes
1 tablespoon paprika
Vegetable cooking spray
1 cup chopped onions
2 medium tomatoes, chopped

1 cup crushed tomatoes
2 medium green peppers, chopped
2 medium red peppers, sliced
2 cups cooked noodles

Sprinkle veal with paprika, and brown in vegetable cooking spray. Add onions and sauté until golden. Add tomatoes and peppers. Cover and simmer one hour. Serve with noodles. Serves 4.

Sealed with a Knish (Maryland)

North Carolina Barbecue Sauce

In North Carolina the most traditional barbecue sauce is a straight-forward mix of vinegar and red pepper. To my taste, it is a classic, hardly interfering with the smoky roast and just setting it off. Ketchup and mustard sauces make a thick, sticky coating. The vinegar sauce gives the roast a crisp coat and cuts the fat.

1 cup apple cider vinegar
½–¾ cup water
⅔ cup minced onion
1 garlic clove, crushed
½ teaspoon salt
1 teaspoon ground black pepper
1–2 teaspoons red pepper flakes

1 teaspoon sugar
1 bay leaf
⅔ teaspoon thyme
3 tablespoons peanut oil
2–3 teaspoons dry mustard
4 -6 teaspoons cold water

Combine all ingredients except last 2 in a small stainless steel or enamel saucepan. Bring to a rapid boil, then simmer 5 minutes. Remove from heat. Dissolve mustard in cold water, then thin it out with some of the hot vinegar sauce. Stir mustard into sauce. Let cool, bottle, and store in refrigerator. Yields about 2 cups.

Bill Neal's Southern Cooking (North Carolina)

On a bun or as an entrée, served up with coleslaw, hushpuppies, or baked beans . . . in the Tar Heel State, you'll find BBQ any way you like it. BBQ is basic fare, and there is no question in North Carolina that it should be pit-cooked and always pork—chopped pork cooked slowly so the hickory flavor is just right. And the key ingredient is the sauce. The great debate in North Carolina is over what kind of sauce is best—Eastern Carolina BBQ features a vinegar-based sauce, while western North Carolinians use a tomato-based sauce. Which is better? Well that depends on which side of the state you happen to be in at the moment!

Oven Barbecued Spareribs

4 pounds spareribs
1 tablespoon lemon pepper
  seasoning
½ cup ketchup
½ cup barbecue sauce
1 (6-ounce) can frozen orange
  juice, thawed and diluted

½ cup butter
2 tablespoons brown sugar
1 tablespoon soy sauce
2 teaspoons mustard
Green onions or 1 large white
  onion, finely chopped

Cut ribs into serving sizes and sprinkle with lemon pepper seasoning. Place ribs in shallow baking dish. Cover and bake at 350° for 45 minutes. Combine remaining ingredients in a medium saucepan, stirring well; bring to a boil. Reduce heat and simmer sauce uncovered for 10 minutes. Remove ribs from oven and baste with sauce. Cover and return to oven and bake an additional 45 minutes, turning and basting occasionally with remaining sauce. Serves 4.

Feeding the Flock (First Baptist Church, Boiling Spring Lake)
(North Carolina)

Marinated Pork Roast with Apricot Sauce

Really delicious.

2 garlic cloves, peeled, minced
½ cup plus 2 tablespoons dry
  sherry, divided
½ cup plus 1 tablespoon
  soy sauce, divided
2 tablespoons dry mustard

2 teaspoons thyme
1 teaspoon ginger
1 (5- to 6-pound) boneless pork loin,
  rolled, tied
1 (10-ounce) jar apricot preserves

In a 2-cup measure, combine garlic, ½ cup sherry, ½ cup soy sauce, mustard, thyme, and ginger, blending well. Arrange pork loin in a deep bowl or dish; pour marinade over meat. Cover and refrigerate 2–3 days, turning meat frequently. Remove meat from marinade.

Insert meat thermometer into center of roast, away from fat. Arrange roast on a rack in a shallow roasting pan and bake in slow (325°) oven 2½–3 hours or until thermometer registers 170°. In a saucepan, combine preserves, remaining 2 tablespoons sherry and 1 tablespoon soy sauce; heat until bubbly hot; serve sauce with roast. Makes 8–10 servings.

Apron Strings (Virginia)

Pork Tenderloin
with Mustard Cream Sauce

1 (1-pound) pork tenderloin	4 green onions
⅓ cup flour	⅓ cup dry white wine
½ teaspoon each salt and pepper	1 cup heavy cream
3 tablespoons butter or margarine	¼ cup Dijon mustard
	Salt and pepper to taste

Cut pork tenderloin into ½-inch slices. Place between pieces of wax paper and pound to ¼-inch thickness with a meat mallet. Mix flour, salt, and pepper together and coat pork medallions with mixture, shaking off excess. Sauté pork medallions ⅓ at a time in butter in a skillet for 2 minutes on each side; remove to a warm platter, reserving the drippings.

Slice green onions, keeping white and green parts separate. Reserve green portions. Add white portions to drippings in skillet and sauté 1 minute or until tender. Stir in wine and cook 3 minutes or until reduced to 2 tablespoons. Add cream and simmer 5 minutes or until thickened to desired consistency. Whisk in Dijon mustard and season with additional salt and pepper to taste. Spoon over pork medallions and sprinkle with reserved green onion tops. Serve immediately. Serves 4.

Oh My Stars! Recipes that Shine (Virginia)

Baked Stuffed Pork Chops

DRESSING:

3 cups bread crumbs
1 small onion, minced
2 stalks celery, finely chopped
½ teaspoon salt

White pepper to taste
1 teaspoon sage
Broth, any kind

Mix together and add only enough broth to hold crumbs together. Do not make Dressing too wet.

4 (1½-inch-thick) pork chops
1 cup all-purpose flour
1 teaspoon salt
⅓ teaspoon white pepper
1 egg, well beaten

1 tablespoon prepared mustard
¾ cup milk
1 cup Dressing, divided
1 cup cooking oil

Prepare pork chops by cutting slit along fat side and into chop to form a pocket. Combine flour, salt, and pepper. Prepare egg wash by mixing egg, mustard, and milk. Using ¼ cup Dressing, stuff tightly into each pocket and press fatty edges together to close. Dip each chop into egg wash, then flour. In very hot oil, fry until golden brown. Remove; drain and place in large casserole dish. Cover with thin gravy. Cover with foil and bake uncovered an additional 30 minutes.

Mrs. Rowe's Favorite Recipes (Virginia)

Maryland Pork Chops

8 pork chops
2 tablespoons oil
½ teaspoon salt
½ teaspoon sage
4 tart apples, cored and sliced
  in rings

½ cup brown sugar
2 tablespoons flour
1 cup hot water
1 tablespoon cider vinegar
½ cup seedless raisins

Brown pork chops in oil in skillet. Sprinkle with salt and sage. Place in a baking dish. Top with apple rings; sprinkle with sugar. Blend flour into oil in skillet; stir until brown; add water and vinegar. Cook until thickened. Add raisins and pour over pork chops. Bake at 350° for 1 hour. Makes 6–8 servings.

Come, Dine with Us! (Maryland)

Baked Virginia Ham

Visitors to Williamsburg who plan to carry home a Virginia ham as a souvenir are advised to heed these preliminary directions or they may be sadly disappointed: Scrub the ham to remove coating of seasonings, cover it with water, and soak for 24 hours. Place ham, skin side down, in a pan with enough fresh water to cover; bring to a boil, reduce heat, and simmer, covered, 20–25 minutes per pound. When done, skin the ham and trim off excess fat.

1 (10- to 12-pound) Virginia ham	**1 teaspoon cloves**
2 tablespoons light brown sugar	**3 teaspoons honey, dry sherry, or**
1 tablespoon bread crumbs	**sweet pickle vinegar**

Preheat oven to 375°. Combine brown sugar, bread crumbs, and cloves. Press the mixture into the ham. Place ham in a roasting pan. Bake at 375° for 15 minutes or until sugar melts. Drizzle honey, sherry, or sweet pickle vinegar over ham. Bake at 375° for 15 minutes.

Note: These directions apply to a Virginia ham that has been cured for at least 12 months. If the ham has been cured less than 12 months, follow the instructions on the wrapper or hang the ham and allow it to age.

Favorite Meals from Williamsburg (Virginia)

Famous since the mid-1700s for its salt-cured hams, Smithfield recently (2002) celebrated the 100th birthday of its oldest ham, which was cured in 1902. This ham, which is on display still today at the Isle of Wight County Museum in Virginia, may very well be the world's oldest edible dried meat.

Best Baked Ham Ever

1 (10- to 15-pound) semi-
  boneless, fully cooked ham
2 cups sugar
1 cup cider vinegar
1 stick cinnamon
12 whole cloves

6 allspice berries
Additional cloves to stud ham
White pepper to taste
1½ cups brown sugar
1 cup sherry

Preheat oven to 350°. Wash ham and place in large roasting pan with lid. Add sugar, vinegar, cinnamon stick, cloves, and allspice berries. Fill pan with water, cover, and place in oven. Cook 15 minutes per pound, turning ham often. Remove from oven and cool.

Lower oven temperature to 250°. Remove top skin, but leave fat on ham. Place ham in washed and dried roasting pan and stud at intervals with cloves. Sprinkle liberally with white pepper and spread brown sugar all over. Pour sherry into pan and bake, uncovered, for 1 hour. After 30 minutes of cooking time, baste every 10 minutes with pan juices. Remove from oven and keep covered and warm until serving time. Makes 20 servings.

MUSTARD SAUCE:

2 teaspoons dry mustard
¼ teaspoon salt
1 teaspoon sugar
2 tablespoons flour

¾ cup water
2 tablespoons vinegar, warmed
2 egg yolks, beaten
2 tablespoons butter, melted

Combine mustard, salt, sugar, and flour. Place in top of double boiler. Add egg yolks and butter, stirring until thickened. Do not boil or eggs will curdle. Can be prepared one day ahead and reheated to serve.

Stirring Performances (North Carolina)

Poultry

Sailing is a popular sport along the East Coast, as well as a favorite recreational pastime. Situated on picturesque Chesapeake Bay, Annapolis, Maryland, is often referred to as the Sailing Capital of the United States.

Southern-Fried Chicken, Virginia Style

Many Richmonders use only bacon dripping for frying chicken. It gives a very special flavor.

1 cup all-purpose flour	3 (3-pound) frying chickens, cut
1 tablespoon salt	into serving pieces
1 tablespoon paprika	1½ cups shortening, cooking oil,
1½ teaspoons poultry seasoning	or bacon drippings (or a
¾ teaspoon pepper	combination)

Combine first 5 ingredients in a paper or plastic Ziploc bag. Place 3 or 4 chicken pieces in bag at a time, close, and shake to coat well with seasoned flour. In a large skillet, melt fat, add chicken pieces, and cook over moderate (350°) heat until browned and crisp on both sides (do not crowd chicken pieces in skillet). Transfer chicken to 2 (9x13-inch) baking pans and cover securely with aluminum foil. Bake in moderate (350°) oven for 40 minutes. Uncover and continue baking 15–20 minutes longer, or until chicken is tender and outside is crisp. Yields 12 servings.

Richmond Receipts (Virginia)

Barbecued Chicken

1 frying-size chicken, quartered	2 bay leaves
1 onion, sliced	½ cup water
¾ cup ketchup	1 tablespoon sugar
4 tablespoons Worcestershire	¼ teaspoon salt
2 teaspoons prepared mustard	Tabasco
¾ cup vinegar	

Place chicken in roasting pan with slice of onion on top of each piece. Combine remaining ingredients for sauce and pour over chicken and cook at 350° for 2 hours. Baste frequently.

Queen Anne's Table (North Carolina)

Roast Sticky Chicken

4 teaspoons salt
2 teaspoons paprika
1 teaspoon cayenne pepper
1 teaspoon onion powder
1 teaspoon thyme

1 teaspoon white pepper
½ teaspoon garlic powder
½ teaspoon black pepper
1 large roasting chicken
1 cup chopped onion

In a small bowl, thoroughly combine all the spices. Remove giblets from chicken, clean the cavity well, and pat dry with paper towels. Rub spice mixture into chicken, both inside and out, making sure it is evenly distributed and down deep into the skin. Place in a resealable plastic bag, seal, and refrigerate overnight.

When ready to roast chicken, stuff cavity with onion, and place in a shallow baking pan. Roast uncovered at 250° for 5 hours. After the first hour, baste chicken occasionally (every half hour or so) with pan juices. The pan juices will start to caramelize on bottom of pan and chicken will turn golden brown. If chicken contains a pop-up thermometer, ignore it. Let chicken rest about 10 minutes before carving.

Seasoned Seniors' Specials (North Carolina)

Herbed Chicken Casserole

½ cup margarine
1 (8-ounce) package Pepperidge
 Farm Herb Dressing
1 (10¾-ounce) can cream
 of mushroom soup
1 (10¾-ounce) can cream of
 chicken soup

1 (8-ounce) container sour cream
1 unsalted chicken boiled,
 meat removed (save broth)
1¾ cups reserved broth

Melt margarine and mix with dressing mix. Put ½ of dressing on bottom of 9x13-inch baking dish. Mix together soups and sour cream. Spread ½ of soup mixture over dressing and arrange chicken on top. Put ¼ of remaining dressing on top of chicken and spread remaining ½ of soup mixture over dressing. Put remainder of dressing over top of soup. Pour chicken broth over all. Bake at 350° for 30 minutes or until bubbly. Great served with cranberry sauce. Yields 6–8 servings.

Pass the Plate (North Carolina)

Chicken Pillows

1 whole chicken breast, halved, skinned, boned
1 clove garlic, halved
2 slices prosciutto or boiled ham
2 thin slices mozzarella cheese
2 tablespoons seasoned bread crumbs
2 tablespoons medium dry sherry
2 tablespoons clarified butter
Salt and freshly ground pepper
1 tablespoon chopped parsley

Pound chicken breast pieces to a thickness of ¼ inch. Rub each chicken breast piece with cut clove of garlic. Place prosciutto and cheese over chicken. Sprinkle with bread crumbs. Roll up, starting at broader end, and secure with wooden picks. Place in lightly greased shallow baking dish.

Combine sherry and butter and heat briefly. Pour over chicken. Season with salt and pepper. Bake at 350° for 20–25 minutes or until chicken is done. Sprinkle with parsley.

Command Performances (Virginia)

Chicken in a Package

1 large chicken breast, halved, skinned, boned
Salt and pepper to taste
Spicy mustard
2 small potatoes, thinly sliced
2 small onions, thinly sliced
2 carrots, cut into julienne strips
4–6 mushrooms, sliced
2 tablespoons butter
Paprika

Preheat oven to 350°. Sprinkle chicken with salt and pepper. Spread each breast half lightly with mustard; set aside.

On a large square of heavy-duty foil, alternate slices from one potato and one onion so that they overlap slightly. Repeat with remaining onion and potato on other square of foil. Sprinkle half of carrot strips over one, the rest over the other. Divide mushrooms between pieces of foil. Cut butter into bits and sprinkle over vegetables. Lay a chicken breast half on each pile of vegetables. Sprinkle both liberally with paprika.

Seal foil and lay packets on a cookie sheet. Bake 25–30 minutes, or until chicken is done and vegetables are tender. Serve at once. Makes 2 servings.

Love Yourself Cookbook (North Carolina)

Cream Cheese and Spinach Stuffed Chicken Rolls

6 boneless chicken breast halves
1 (8-ounce) package cream
   cheese, softened
½ cup chopped cooked spinach
1 clove garlic, minced
⅛ teaspoon nutmeg

Salt and pepper to taste
1 large egg, beaten with
   1 tablespoon water
½ cup unseasoned bread crumbs
3 tablespoons margarine, melted

Heat oven to 375°. Flatten chicken between sheets of plastic wrap to uniform ¼-inch thickness. In large bowl, beat cream cheese with spinach, garlic, nutmeg, salt and pepper. Spoon equal amount of mixture across narrow end of each breast. Roll jellyroll-style. Dip in egg, then in crumbs; shake off excess. In baking dish, arrange chicken in single layer, seam-side-down; drizzle with melted margarine. Bake 25–30 minutes or until golden brown. Makes 6 servings.

Atlantic Highlands (New Jersey)

Country Chicken

2 sweet or hot sausage links,
   sliced
2 red potatoes, diced
6 tablespoons extra virgin olive
   oil, divided
2 boneless, skinless chicken
   breasts

2 tablespoons flour for coating
2 shallots, chopped
2 cloves garlic, pressed
3 ounces white wine
1 (7-ounce) jar roasted red
   peppers, drained
3 teaspoons sweet basil

In a small skillet (or sauté pan) brown sausage and potatoes in 1 tablespoon olive oil, turning frequently to avoid burning. Remove potatoes and sausage from pan and allow to drain on paper towels. Heat remainder of olive oil in a large skillet. While oil is heating, slice each chicken breast lengthwise into 4 pieces; coat with flour. Sauté chicken in olive oil for 2 minutes. Add shallots and garlic and continue to sauté until chicken is lightly browned. Reduce heat. Add wine, sausage, potatoes, roasted red peppers, and basil, cooking for 5 minutes more.

Collected Recipes (New Jersey)

Peanut-Crusted Picnic Chicken

2 cups dry roasted peanuts,
  ground fine
⅔ cup yellow cornmeal
5 large cloves garlic, minced
2 tablespoons minced fresh
  ginger

1 teaspoon pepper
2 tablespoons salt
3 cups flour, divided
2 cups buttermilk
8 chicken breast halves

Preheat oven to 350°. Combine first 6 ingredients and ⅔ cup flour in medium bowl. Place remaining 2⅓ cups flour and buttermilk in separate bowls. Dredge chicken in flour, dip in buttermilk, and roll in peanut mixture.

Bake chicken, covered tightly with foil, 45 minutes in greased, shallow baking dish. Carefully remove foil and bake another 20–25 minutes or until chicken is golden brown. Remove chicken from baking dish and cool. Chicken will crisp as it cools. Serves 8.

Dining by Fireflies (North Carolina)

Lazy Day Chicken

2–3 pounds chicken breasts
⅓ cup all-purpose flour
1 package dry onion soup mix
2–3 carrots, sliced
2–3 stalks celery, sliced
1 (4-ounce) can mushrooms,
  drained (optional)

½ cup sherry
1 (10¾-ounce) can cream of
  chicken soup
Paprika

Oil large baking dish. Dredge chicken in flour and place in dish. Sprinkle onion soup over top. Place sliced vegetables on soup mix. Combine sherry and cream soup. Spread over chicken and vegetables. Dot with paprika. Cover with foil and bake at 350° for at least 1 hour 15 minutes.

A Southern Lady's Spirit (Virginia)

Chicken Suzanne

Our absolutely number one favorite dish at the restaurant. We have had more requests for this recipe than any other.

6 (8-ounce) boneless chicken breast halves
1 cup flour
1 egg, beaten with 1 cup milk

3 cups good quality fresh bread crumbs
½–1 cup light cooking oil

Dip chicken breasts in flour, dip in egg/milk mixture, then thoroughly coat in bread crumbs.

Sauté in hot oil until well browned on each side. Cook until done (do not overcook). Serve with a dollop of herb butter. Serves 6.

HERB BUTTER:

½ cup chopped green onions
½ cup chopped fresh parsley
2 cloves garlic
1 teaspoon basil (2 tablespoons fresh)
½ teaspoon oregano (½ tablespoon fresh)
1 teaspoon marjoram (1 tablespoon fresh)

1 teaspoon tarragon (1 tablespoon fresh)
1 teaspoon dill weed (1 teaspoon fresh)
1 teaspoon black pepper
Dash of Tabasco
1 pound unsalted butter

Mix all above thoroughly in food processor.

The herb butter is delicious on toasted French bread, or toast triangles. Can also be used on steaks, hamburgers, veal scaloppini or steamed vegetables.

Cooking with Heart in Hand (Virginia)

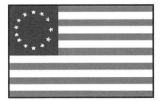

History students know that Betsy Ross sewed the first American flag, but did you know it was designed by a New Jersey congressman? Francis Hopkinson, a signer of the Declaration of Independence, designed the first American flag, which was adopted by the Continental Congress in 1777. Tradition holds the first time Betsy Ross's famous flag was flown was at the Battle of Cooch's Bridge in Delaware.

Crab Stuffed Chicken Breasts

6 boned chicken breasts
½ cup chopped onion
½ cup chopped celery
3 tablespoons butter
3 tablespoons white wine

1 (7-ounce) can crabmeat, or
   fresh
½ cup Pepperidge Farm stuffing
2 tablespoons flour
½ teaspoon paprika

Salt and pepper chicken breasts and pound. Cook onion and celery in butter. Remove from heat and add wine, crabmeat, and stuffing. Put inside chicken breasts and secure with toothpicks. Combine flour and paprika and coat chicken. Drizzle with butter and bake uncovered at 375° for 40 minutes. Pour Sauce over when serving. Serves 6.

SAUCE:

1 envelope Hollandaise Sauce
   Mix
¾ cup milk

2 tablespoons white wine
½ cup Swiss cheese

Heat ingredients and spoon over chicken.

A Taste of History (North Carolina)

Cranberry Chicken

6 chicken breasts
1 (15-ounce) can whole-
   berry cranberry sauce

1 (8-ounce) bottle fat-free
   Catalina salad dressing
1 package dry onion soup mix

Place chicken in baking pan. Mix together remaining ingredients; pour over chicken. Bake in preheated 400° oven for 1 hour and 30 minutes or until chicken is done. Serve over white rice. Serves 6.

Celebrations...Food, Family, and Fun! (North Carolina)

Chicken and Spinach Enchilada Casserole

This is a great entrée for a casual dinner party.

2 pounds boneless chicken
 breasts
4 tablespoons (½ stick) unsalted
 butter
1 large onion, chopped
1 (10-ounce) box frozen chopped
 spinach, thawed and drained
3 cups sour cream
1 teaspoon ground cumin

1 (4-ounce) can chopped green
 chiles (or more to taste)
¼ cup milk
Salt and freshly ground pepper to
 taste
12 flour tortillas
8 ounces shredded Monterey Jack
 cheese

Place chicken breasts in a skillet and add water to just cover. Poach on medium-low heat until cooked through, approximately 15–20 minutes. Remove from water and cool. Shred or cut into bite-sized pieces and place in a mixing bowl.

Preheat oven to 350°. Grease a 9x13-inch baking dish. In a small skillet, melt the butter and sauté the onion until tender, about 5 minutes. In a large bowl, combine cooked onion, spinach, sour cream, cumin, chiles, and milk. Season with salt and pepper. Add half the sauce to the shredded chicken and mix well. Layer 3 tortillas in bottom of casserole dish. Cover with ⅓ of the chicken mixture. Repeat process 3 times, ending with a layer of tortillas. Cover casserole with remaining sauce, spreading evenly with a spatula. Top with grated cheese. Bake casserole approximately 40 minutes, or until heated through and bubbly and cheese begins to brown. Serve hot. Serves 6–8.

In the Kitchen with Kendi, Volume 1 (Maryland)

CHOWAN COUNTY TOURISM
DEVELOPMENT AUTHORITY

In 1774, fifty-one of Edenton, North Carolina's leading ladies signed a pledge to cease use of East India Tea, thus showing that they were in accord with their Boston cousins in opposing British taxation. Today, a bronze teapot at the west side of the Courthouse Green commemorates the historic event.

Chicken Stuffed with Spinach and Feta Cheese

10 (6-ounce) boneless, skinless chicken breasts
½ (10-ounce) package frozen chopped spinach, thawed, drained
1½ cups cottage cheese
8 ounces feta cheese, crumbled
1¼ cups seasoned bread crumbs, divided

1 ounce grated Parmesan cheese
2 eggs, beaten
1 teaspoon oregano
½ teaspoon garlic powder
½ teaspoon pepper
¼ teaspoon nutmeg
6 tablespoons margarine, melted

Pound chicken between sheets of wax paper with a meat mallet until flattened. Press spinach to remove excess moisture. Combine spinach, cottage cheese, feta cheese, half the bread crumbs, Parmesan cheese, eggs, oregano, garlic powder, pepper, and nutmeg in a bowl and mix well. Spoon 3 ounces of spinach mixture in the center of each chicken breast. Fold chicken over to enclose filling.

Arrange chicken on a nonstick baking sheet. Brush with margarine. Sprinkle with remaining bread crumbs. Chill, covered, for 1 hour or longer. Bake at 325° for 30–40 minutes or until chicken is cooked through. Yields 10 servings.

Vintage Virginia (Virginia)

Chicken and Spinach Casserole

2 (10-ounce) packages frozen chopped spinach, defrosted, drained
4 whole chicken breasts, halved, skinned, boned, cooked
1 cup mayonnaise

2 (10¾-ounce) cans cream of chicken soup
1 tablespoon lemon juice
1 cup shredded sharp Cheddar cheese
½ cup buttered bread crumbs

Place drained spinach in a 9x13-inch ungreased baking dish. Place chicken breasts on top. Combine and mix mayonnaise, soup, and lemon juice. Spread over chicken. Sprinkle with cheese. Top with buttered crumbs. Bake at 350° for 30–40 minutes. Makes 8 servings.

The Enlightened Titan (Virginia)

Make Ahead Chicken Casserole

1 (6¼-ounce) package Uncle
  Ben's Long Grain and Wild Rice
4 whole chicken breasts, cooked
  and torn from bone
2 (10¾-ounce) cans mushroom
  soup
½ soup can water

1 cup chopped celery
1 cup chopped bell pepper
¾ cup mayonnaise
1 medium onion, chopped
1 can sliced water chestnuts,
  drained
1 large package slivered almonds

Prepare rice as directed on package. Spread evenly over bottom of large (9x13x2-inch) ovenproof baking dish. Place pieces of chicken breast over top of rice. Blend remaining ingredients, except almonds, and pour over chicken and rice. Refrigerate overnight. Remove from refrigerator and top with almonds; cover with foil and bake at 350° for 1½ hours. Sprinkle with paprika before serving.

Our Favorite Recipes (Maryland)

Best Ever Chicken

4 whole skinless, boneless,
  chicken breasts
½ pound sliced mushrooms, or
  more, if desired
1 (14½-ounce) can crushed
  tomatoes (can use stewed)

½ cup Italian Dressing or Russian
  Dressing
1 package dry onion soup mix
1 bay leaf

Place chicken breasts in a baking dish; top with sliced mushrooms. Add tomatoes. Mix dressing with onion soup mix and pour over. Toss in bay leaf. Bake, uncovered, one hour at 350°, basting frequently. Serve with rice or noodles. If too much liquid, drain some prior to serving. Remove bay leaf before serving. Serves 4–6.

Where There's a Will... (Maryland)

 Virginia is one of four states technically designated as commonwealths (sharing the title with Massachusetts, Pennsylvania, and Kentucky). The word commonwealth dates from the fifteenth century. The original phrase "common-wealth" or "the common weal" comes from the old meaning of "wealth," which is "well-being." The term literally meant "common well-being." Thus commonwealth originally meant a state or nation-state governed for the common good as opposed to an authoritarian state governed for the benefit of a given class of owners.

Italian Chicken
(Savory Chicken Italiano)

2½ pounds frying chicken	1 (10¾-ounce) can chicken broth
Salt and pepper	1 tablespoon parsley
3 tablespoons cooking oil	1 teaspoon garlic powder
2 cups spaghetti sauce	¼ cup shredded mozzarella

Cut up chicken; sprinkle chicken pieces with salt and pepper. Then brown chicken in oil in frying pan. After it is browned, drain off fat. Add spaghetti sauce, chicken broth, parsley, and garlic powder. Simmer, covered, for 40 minutes. After it has finished cooking, top with shredded mozzarella cheese. Makes 4 servings.

A Taste of Heaven (New Jersey)

Death by Garlic Chicken

Some people may find it hard to believe that anything made with 40 cloves of garlic would be edible, but this dish is delicious and delicately flavored. The long, slow cooking tames the garlic. The dish is juicy when done, and goes well over mashed potatoes or rice.

8 chicken legs and thighs, skinned and separated	1 teaspoon dried tarragon
2 tablespoons oil	½ cup dry vermouth
1 large onion, coarsely chopped	½ teaspoon salt
4 ribs celery, sliced into ¼-inch pieces	¼ teaspoon freshly ground black pepper
2 tablespoons minced fresh parsley, or 2 teaspoons dried parsley flakes	Dash of nutmeg
	40 cloves garlic, separated but not peeled

Brush chicken pieces on all sides with oil. In a large casserole or 5- to 6-quart heavy Dutch oven, combine onion, celery, parsley, and tarragon. Place chicken pieces over vegetables and herbs and pour vermouth over chicken. Sprinkle chicken with salt, pepper, and nutmeg. Distribute unpeeled garlic cloves throughout the casserole, tucking them under chicken pieces. Cover casserole tightly (you might fit a piece of foil around the top under the lid). Bake chicken in preheated 325° oven 1½ hours. Do not uncover casserole until after this time has elapsed. Serve chicken with garlic, advising the diners to squeeze flesh from papery coat. The garlic is especially tasty when eaten on crusty bread. Serves 8.

Sun-Sational Southern Cuisine (North Carolina)

Hot Chicken

2 cups cooked, diced chicken
1 cup Uncle Ben's Long Grain &
   Wild Rice
1 cup water chestnuts
2 tablespoons onion
½ cup mayonnaise

2 cups French-style green beans,
   drained
1 (10¾-ounce) can cream of celery
   soup
2 tablespoons pimento
Salt and pepper to taste

Mix all ingredients. Bake in large, greased baking dish in 350° oven for about 50 minutes. Serve hot.

What's Cookin' (Maryland)

Chicken Croquettes

SAUCE:

4 tablespoons butter
4 tablespoons flour
1½ cups chicken stock

½ cup heavy cream
Curry powder to taste
Salt and pepper to taste

Melt butter in a small heavy saucepan. Stir in flour. Blend well, cooking slowly over low heat. Slowly stir in chicken stock and cream. Stirring constantly, bring mixture slowly to a boil and cook for about 2 minutes or until Sauce has thickened. Season Sauce to taste with curry powder and salt and pepper. Cool one cup of the Sauce and hold the remaining cup warm, covered.

2 cups chopped, cooked chicken
½ teaspoon salt
¼ teaspoon celery salt
Cayenne pepper to taste
1 teaspoon lemon juice

¼ teaspoon onion juice
1 teaspoon chopped fresh parsley
2 eggs, beaten
½ cup bread crumbs

Mix together chicken, salt, celery salt, pepper, lemon juice, onion juice, parsley, and enough of the cooled Sauce to keep mixture soft but stiff enough to hold its shape. Chill mixture; then shape into 8 croquettes. Heat vegetable oil to 375°–385°. Dip croquettes into beaten eggs, roll in bread crumbs, and fry for 2–4 minutes. Serve croquettes with hot cream Sauce. Serves 4.

The Great Chefs of Virginia Cookbook (Virginia)

North Carolina Chicken

8 ounces butter or margarine
2 envelopes Italian Salad Dressing
  mix
½ cup lime juice
1 teaspoon salt
5 pounds chicken pieces

Melt butter in saucepan. Stir in salad dressing mix, lime juice, and salt. Marinate chicken 3–4 hours or overnight. Bake at 350° for 1 hour or until done. Or cook on outdoor grill for 1 hour turning and basting every 10–15 minutes. Serves 6.

Ship to Shore I (North Carolina)

Garden Chicken Pie

4 tablespoons butter
½ cup finely chopped onion
6 tablespoons flour
2 teaspoons instant chicken
  bouillon
½ teaspoon salt
½ teaspoon pepper
1½ cups half-and-half
½ cup water
4 cups chopped cooked chicken
1 cup thinly sliced carrots
1 (9-ounce) package frozen peas,
  thawed
1 (4-ounce) jar sliced mushrooms,
  drained
1 stick butter, melted
10 sheets phyllo pastry

Preheat oven to 375°. Melt butter in a saucepan. Add onion and sauté until wilted. Blend in flour, chicken bouillon, salt, pepper, half-and-half, and water. Cool, stirring, until slightly thickened. Add chicken, carrots, peas, and mushrooms. Stir to combine. Remove from heat.

Brush baking dish lightly with melted butter. Layer 5 sheets of phyllo in baking dish, brushing each sheet with butter. Keep phyllo sheets that you are not working with under a damp cloth to keep from drying out. Spread chicken filling over pastry sheets. Layer remaining 5 sheets of phyllo over chicken, brushing each sheet with butter. Bake pie 25–35 minutes or until golden. Serve. Makes 10–12 servings.

Note: If phyllo sheets are 14 x18 inches, only use 5 sheets and cut each sheet in half.

Stirring Performances (North Carolina)

Favorite Chicken Casserole

A real favorite of everyone and so easy to prepare.

2 cups diced, cooked chicken
1 (10¾-ounce) can cream of
  chicken soup
½ cup milk
1–1¼ cups chicken broth
½ cup chopped celery
¼ cup chopped onion

1 egg, beaten
½ bag (2 cups) Pepperidge Farm
  Herb Stuffing
1 tablespoon parsley flakes
  (optional)
Paprika

Spread chicken in bottom of a 2-quart flat casserole dish. Dilute soup with milk. Pour over top of chicken. Cook celery and onion in broth until tender (if you don't have broth, substitute 1 cup water with ½ stick butter and 1 chicken bouillon cube). Make dressing by combining broth, celery, onion, egg, stuffing, and parsley flakes. Spread dressing on top of soup. Sprinkle with paprika. Bake at 350° for 35–40 minutes or until bubbly and brown.

Granny's Kitchen (Virginia)

Creamed Chicken and Biscuits

1½ teaspoons margarine
½ large onion, chopped
4 cups chopped cooked chicken
1 (10¾-ounce) can cream of
  chicken soup (undiluted)

1 cup sour cream
½ cup milk
1 cup shredded mild Cheddar
  cheese, divided
6 frozen biscuits, thawed

Preheat oven to 350°. Grease bottom and sides of 7x11-inch baking dish. Heat margarine in a small nonstick skillet over medium-high heat until melted. Stir in onion; sauté until tender. Combine onion, chicken, soup, sour cream, and milk in a medium bowl; mix well. Spoon mixture into prepared baking dish. Bake 15 minutes. Remove from oven. Sprinkle baked layer with ¾ cup Cheddar cheese. Arrange biscuits in a single layer over top. Sprinkle with remaining Cheddar cheese. Bake until biscuits are golden brown and the sauce is bubbly, about 20 minutes. Serve immediately. Yields 6 servings.

Loving, Caring and Sharing (Virginia)

Crunchy Turkey Casserole

3 cups chopped cooked turkey
1 cup cooked rice
1 (8-ounce) can sliced
   water chestnuts, drained
2 tablespoons chopped onion
1 cup chopped celery

½ cup sliced almonds
1 (10¾-ounce) can cream
   of chicken soup
½ cup mayonnaise
1 cup crushed cornflakes

Combine turkey, rice, water chestnuts, onion, celery, almonds, soup, and mayonnaise, mixing thoroughly. Spread mixture in slightly greased 2-quart casserole. Bake at 350º for 30 minutes, sprinkle cornflakes on top of mixture, and bake an additional 15 minutes.

Carolina Sunshine, Then & Now (North Carolina)

Turkey and Leek Shepherd's Pie

This is a great recipe for using up Thanksgiving leftovers.

2 teaspoons olive oil
2 large leeks (white and light
   green parts only), washed and
   thinly sliced
1½ cups thinly sliced carrots
   (2–3 carrots)
1 tablespoon minced garlic
⅓ cup dry white wine
3 tablespoons flour
2 teaspoons fresh sage or ½
   teaspoon dried rubbed sage

2 cups chicken broth or leftover
   gravy
2 cups diced cooked turkey or
   chicken
1 cup frozen peas
Salt and pepper to taste
3 cups mashed potatoes (leftover
   or frozen)
1 large egg, beaten
1 tablespoon olive oil

Heat 2 teaspoons oil over medium heat. Add leeks and carrots and cook, stirring until the leeks soften, about 7 minutes. Add garlic and cook, stirring 1 minute more. Pour in wine and stir until most liquid is evaporated; add flour and sage, stirring constantly until flour starts to turn light brown, about 2 minutes. Stir in broth, bring to simmer; stir constantly, until sauce thickens and carrots are barely tender about 5 minutes. Add turkey and peas, salt and pepper. Transfer to a deep 10-inch pan or 2-quart dish. Mix potatoes with egg and 1 tablespoon oil. Spread potato mixture over turkey mixture. Set on baking sheet and bake 25–30 minutes at 425°, until the potatoes and filling are heated through and the top is golden brown. Serves 6.

Around the Table (New Jersey)

Seafood

North Carolina boasts more than 300 waterfalls, including the highest on the East Coast, Whitewater Falls, a 411-foot, two-tiered cascade located in Transylvania County in western North Carolina, 30 miles southwest of Asheville. There are more than 250 waterfalls and 200 miles of mountain streams in Transylvania County alone!

Fish Fillets with Sweet Sour Sauce

1 pound fish fillets (white sole,
   bass, haddock, or sturgeon)
¼ cup corn oil, divided
Salt to taste
½ cup chopped onion
1 green bell pepper, cut in thin
   strips
¼ cup firmly packed brown sugar
¼ teaspoon dry mustard
2 tablespoons water
1 tablespoon cornstarch
1 tablespoon soy sauce
⅓ cup lemon juice

Brush fillets with 2 tablespoons corn oil, sprinkle with salt. Cook until done under broiler. Arrange on warm platter and keep warm. Meanwhile cook onion in 2 tablespoons corn oil in skillet until light golden brown. Stir in green pepper. Mix together remaining ingredients, add to mixture in skillet. Cook until sauce is thick. Spoon over fish.

Centenary Cookbook (North Carolina)

Blackened Catfish

1 tablespoon paprika
1 teaspoon onion powder
1 teaspoon garlic powder
¾ teaspoon freshly ground
   black pepper
1 teaspoon cayenne pepper
¾ teaspoon white pepper
½ teaspoon thyme
½ teaspoon oregano
6 (8-ounce) skinless catfish fillets
6 tablespoons margarine, melted

Combine paprika, onion powder, garlic powder, black pepper, cayenne pepper, white pepper, thyme, and oregano in shallow dish. Dip fillet sin margarine; coat well with seasoning mixture. Heat large cast-iron skillet over very high heat for 10 minutes or until it is beyond the smoking stage and has a white ash in the bottom. Place fillets in single layer in skillet. Cook over high heat for 2 minutes on each side or until fish is blackened and flakes easily with fork. (Unless you have a very good exhaust fan for blackening fish, cook it outside.) Yields 6 servings.

Goodness Grows in North Carolina (North Carolina)

Catfish Fillets in Veggie Sauce

¼ cup chopped onion
¼ cup chopped green bell
  pepper
1 small clove garlic, minced
1 teaspoon olive oil
1 (7½-ounce) can chopped
  tomatoes, drained
¼ teaspoon sugar
¼ teaspoon dill weed

¼ teaspoon salt
Pinch of pepper
4 (1-pound) catfish fillets
2 tablespoons cold water
2 teaspoons cornstarch
2 tablespoons chopped parsley
¼ cup slivered almonds
  (optional)

In a large skillet over medium-high heat, sauté onion, pepper, and garlic in olive oil 4–5 minutes, until tender. Stir in tomatoes, sugar, dill weed, salt, and pepper. Bring to a boil. Reduce heat, cover and simmer 15 minutes, stirring often. Cut each catfish fillet into 4 portions (measure thickness). Add fillets to skillet; spoon sauce over fillets. Bring mixture to a boil. Reduce heat, cover, and simmer until fish flakes easily with a fork. Allow 4–6 minutes each ½-inch thickness of fish. Remove fish from skillet, but cover to keep warm.

In a small bowl, combine cold water and cornstarch. Stir cornstarch mixture into sauce in skillet. Cook over medium heat, stirring until bubbly. Add fresh chopped parsley and cook, stirring occasionally, for an additional 2 minutes. Serve sauce over fish portions. If desired, top with slivered almonds. Makes 4 servings.

Down Home Cooking Done Right (North Carolina)

Atlantic Stuffed Flounder Supreme

24 Ritz Crackers
4 tablespoons butter
Tabasco to taste
Garlic powder to taste
3 onions, sliced
1 green bell pepper, sliced
6 mushrooms, sliced
½ cup water
2 tablespoons vegetable oil
1 (8-ounce) package cream cheese
8 slices toast
2 pounds flounder fillets
1 lemon

Crumble Ritz Crackers by hand or with a food processor. Melt butter and stir into crackers. Season well with Tabasco and garlic powder; stir.

Place sliced onions, bell pepper, and mushrooms in skillet. Add water and boil until most of the water is gone and vegetables begin to stick to surface of pan. Reduce heat, add vegetable oil, and stir-fry until vegetables have browned. Turn off heat, add cream cheese, and stir until well mixed. Slice or tear toast into pieces, add to pan, and stir until well mixed.

Preheat oven to 425°. Grease an 8x12-inch pan and spread stuffing evenly upon it. Layer flounder fillets over stuffing. Sprinkle topping evenly over fillets. Bake 20 minutes or until topping begins to brown. Putting pan under broiler very briefly will result in a nicely browned top. Serve with lemon wedges as an entrée or as a meal-in-itself. Other fish may be substituted for the flounder. Do not overcook! Yields 4 servings.

The Great Taste of Virginia Seafood Cookbook (Virginia)

Harrison's Chesapeake House's Broiled Sea Trout

⅔ cup butter
2 teaspoons lemon juice
Salt and pepper to taste
1 medium onion, sliced
2 strips bacon, cut in half
2 sea trout fillets
2 dashes paprika

Melt butter and simmer with lemon juice, salt and pepper. Place 3 slices of onion and 2 half-strips of bacon on each fillet. Pour lemon butter over trout and cook under broiler until lightly browned. Sprinkle with paprika and serve immediately. Serves 2.

Recipe from Harrison's Chesapeake House, Tilghman Island, Maryland
Maryland's Historic Restaurants and their Recipes (Maryland)

Vegetable Stuffed Rainbow Trout

6 pan-dressed rainbow trout,
  fresh or frozen
2 teaspoons salt

Vegetable Stuffing
6 slices bacon, cut in thirds
Paprika

Thaw frozen fish. Sprinkle inside and out with salt. Stuff fish and place in a well-greased 11x14-inch baking pan. Place 3 pieces of bacon on each fish. Sprinkle with paprika. Bake at 350° for 25–30 minutes or until fish flakes easily when tested with fork. Turn oven control to broil. Place fish about 3 inches from source of heat and broil 2–3 minutes or until bacon is crisp. Yields 6 servings.

VEGETABLE STUFFING:

1 cup grated carrot
¾ cup chopped celery
½ cup chopped onion
⅓ cup vegetable oil
2 cups soft bread crumbs

1 tablespoon lemon juice
½ teaspoon salt
¼ teaspoon white pepper
¼ teaspoon thyme

Cook vegetables in oil until tender, stirring occasionally. Add remaining ingredients and mix lightly.

Heart of the Mountains (North Carolina)

Pecan-Crusted Trout

1 cup shelled pecans
¼ cup flour
1 teaspoon cayenne pepper
4 trout fillets

Salt and pepper to taste
½ cup milk
¼ cup peanut oil

Place pecans, flour, and cayenne pepper in food processor and process until nuts are finely chopped. Place nut mixture in a shallow bowl.

  Season trout fillets with salt and pepper. Dip fillets into milk and then into pecan flour. Heat oil in heavy skillet or nonstick pan. Place fillets skin side up in pan, and sauté 2 minutes until fish look nice and brown. Turn fillets and cook 2 minutes longer. Serve immediately. Serves 4.

A Taste of the Outer Banks III (North Carolina)

Rockfish Chesapeake

1 pound rockfish fillets
¼ teaspoon Worcestershire
½ teaspoon lemon juice
½ teaspoon seafood seasoning
1 teaspoon white wine
2 tablespoons mayonnaise

Heat oven to 450°. Place fillets on foil-lined baking dish. Mix remaining ingredients. Spread mayonnaise mixture thinly and evenly over the fillets. Bake at 450° for 6–8 minutes. Fish is done when it flakes. Makes 4 servings.

More Favorites from the Melting Pot (Maryland)

Boiled Rockfish with Sauce

SAUCE:

1½–2 cups white sauce
1 teaspoon lemon juice, or
   to taste
Dash of red pepper
¼ cup capers
½ teaspoon Worcestershire
   (optional)
¾ teaspoon salt and pepper

Mix all ingredients together and set aside.

1 (2- or 3-pound) rockfish,
   cleaned
1 onion slice
2 whole cloves
1 carrot
1 bay leaf
2 peppercorns
4 hard-boiled eggs, sliced
Lemon wedges, for garnish
Parsley, for garnish

Place cleaned rockfish in cheese cloth, tie closed, and drop in boiling salted water to which has been added a slice of onion, 2 whole cloves, carrot, bay leaf, and 2 peppercorns. Boil 6–10 minutes per pound. Lift out of water carefully and place on large platter before removing cheesecloth.

Pour Sauce over fish and garnish with slices of hard-boiled eggs, lemon wedges, and parsley. Another garnish to use with rock is to render 6–8 slices of bacon which have been diced into small pieces, and pour the hot bacon grease and rendered bacon over the boiled rockfish. This recipe serves 4.

A Cook's Tour of the Eastern Shore (Maryland)

Tilapia Veracruz

4 (6- to 8-ounce) Tilapia or other
  firm whitefish fillets
Olive oil plus 1 tablespoon,
  divided
Lemon or lime juice plus
  3 tablespoons, divided
Salt and pepper
Dried oregano
1 small green pepper, seeded
  and chopped
1 large onion, chopped

3 cloves garlic, minced
4 tablespoons water
1 (4-ounce) can diced green chiles
¼ cup sliced pimento-stuffed
  green olives
1 teaspoon ground cinnamon
¼ teaspoon ground white pepper
1 (14½-ounce) can stewed
  tomatoes
1 tablespoon drained capers

Rinse fish, pat dry, and arrange on lightly oiled 9x13-inch baking dish. Brush with olive oil and lemon or lime juice, salt and pepper, and sprinkle with oregano. Refrigerate while making sauce.

Heat 1 tablespoon oil in nonstick frying pan over medium-high heat. Add green pepper, onion, garlic, and water; cook, stirring often, until vegetables are tender-crisp (about 3–5 minutes). Add chiles, olives, 3 tablespoons lemon or lime juice, cinnamon, and white pepper; cook for 1 minute. Add tomatoes to pan and bring mixture to a boil. Boil, uncovered, stirring often, until sauce is slightly thickened (about 5 minutes).

Remove fish fillets from the refrigerator. Pour sauce over fish. Bake in a 350° oven until fish is just opaque but still moist in the thickest part (about 10–15 minutes); cut to test .

To serve, transfer fish and sauce to individual serving plates and sprinkle with capers. Serves 4.

Restaurant Recipes from the Shore and More... (Maryland)

It is believed that Francis Scott Key, a Maryland lawyer, wrote America's national anthem on September 14, 1814, while watching the bombardment of Fort McHenry in Baltimore Harbor. Congress adopted his song, "The Star-Spangled Banner," as the national anthem of the United States in 1931.

Salmon Steaks in Lemon/Dill Sauce

1 pound (1-inch-thick) salmon steaks	**1 tablespoon fresh lemon juice**
1 tablespoon butter	**¼ teaspoon dill**
	1 lemon, sliced thin

Place salmon steaks in a microwave-safe dish that has been lined with paper towels. Cover with a paper towel and microwave on HIGH 3½–4½ minutes (rotate dish once) or until salmon flakes apart with ease. Remove steaks from oven and set aside.

In a 1-cup glass measuring cup, microwave butter on HIGH setting 30–45 seconds or until butter is melted. Stir in lemon juice and dill. Place steaks on serving platter and spoon sauce over all. Garnish with lemon slices. Serves 4.

Historic Lexington Cooks (Virginia)

Grilled Salmon with Five-Roasted Pepper Salsa

The Omega-3 fatty acids in salmon have received praise from the scientific community for their possible role in the reduction of cholesterol. Teamed here with an easy-to-prepare, low-fat, very colorful salsa, the result is a healthy meal.

4 (6-ounce) salmon fillets	**1 tablespoon chopped opal basil**
Olive oil vegetable spray	**1 teaspoon extra virgin olive oil**
1 (6-ounce) red bell pepper	**(or V8 juice)**
1 (6-ounce) yellow bell pepper	**1 shallot, chopped**
1 (6-ounce) green bell pepper	**Juice of 1 lime**
2 tablespoons chopped red onion	**Salt and cracked black pepper to taste**

Grill salmon over hot coals using nonstick olive oil vegetable spray on grill. Roast peppers until black on all sides. Cover with plastic wrap for 5 minutes. Rinse off charred skin and remove seeds. Dice. Mix with remaining ingredients and season salsa to taste. Yields 4 servings.

Chef's Note: Salmon should be removed from the grill when the middle is still reddish. It will continue to cook somewhat and will remain moist.

Recipe by Jim Makinson, Kingsmill Resort, Williamsburg
Culinary Secrets of Great Virginia Chefs (Virginia)

Salmon Cakes

1 (16-ounce) can pink salmon
1 egg, beaten
1 (5-ounce) can evaporated milk
1 small onion, minced
½ cup minced green bell
  pepper

½ teaspoon salt
¼ teaspoon black pepper
3–4 slices fresh bread, torn into
  small bits
1 cup all-purpose flour
Oil to fry cakes in a 10-inch skillet

Drain and pick over salmon, removing skin and bones. In a large bowl, mix together all ingredients except flour and oil. Shape into hamburger-size patties, about ½-inch thick; dip in flour and fry in oil over medium heat until lightly browned. Drain on paper towels. Yields 4–6 servings.

Seafood Sorcery (North Carolina)

Salmon Croquettes

1 pound salmon fillets
¾ teaspoon seasoned salt,
  divided
¼ plus ⅛ teaspoon freshly
  ground pepper, divided
1 large potato, peeled and
  cut into 1-inch chunks
1 tablespoon milk

1 tablespoon butter
½ cup finely chopped onion
⅓ cup seeded and finely chopped
  green pepper
1 large egg, lightly beaten
½ cup dried bread crumbs
½ cup vegetable oil
Lemon wedges

Season salmon with ½ teaspoon salt and ⅛ teaspoon pepper. Place in large skillet and add enough cold water to barely cover. Simmer until salmon looks opaque when flaked in center, about 10 minutes. Transfer salmon to plate.

Boil potato in salted water until done. Drain well. Add milk and butter to potato and mash. Cool completely. Remove skin and bones from salmon. Place salmon in bowl and add mashed potato, onion, green pepper, and egg. Season with remaining ¼ teaspoon salt and ¼ teaspoon pepper.

Place bread crumbs in shallow dish. Using about ⅓ cup for each, form salmon mixture into 8 patties. Coat with crumbs, shaking off excess. Heat oil in skillet over medium-high heat. Add croquettes and cook until underside is golden brown, about 3 minutes. Turn and cook other side about 3 more minutes. Drain on paper towel briefly. Serve hot with lemon wedges.

DAPI's Delectable Delights (Delaware)

Ice House's Shrimp Scampi

4 teaspoons butter
2 ounces oil (olive or peanut)
2–3 garlic cloves, sliced
1 pound medium shrimp, shelled
½ teaspoon lemon juice
½ medium onion, chopped

1 tomato, chopped
½ green bell pepper, chopped
1 teaspoon black pepper
1 teaspoon salt
1 tablespoon chopped fresh parsley
¼ cup white wine

In skillet, melt butter, add oil and sauté garlic lightly. Add shrimp, cooking until it turns pink and begins to curl. Add lemon juice, onion, tomato, green pepper, black pepper, salt, parsley, and wine. Cook only a minute or so until tender. Remove shrimp and pour sauce from skillet over top. Serves 4.

Virginia's Historic Restaurants and Their Recipes (Virginia)

Shrimp Scampi Sensation

4 pounds jumbo shrimp, shelled
4 ounces butter, melted

1 cup fresh bread crumbs

Split shrimp down middle, and arrange on a baking tray. Brush with butter, sprinkle with bread crumbs. Broil 5 minutes. Arrange on a platter and pour Sauce over.

SAUCE:

4 scallions
1 clove garlic
1 tablespoon Worcestershire
1 cup lemon juice

Salt to taste
¾ cup cream sherry
3 stick butter
¾ cup Dijon mustard

Chop scallions finely, and press garlic. Add Worcestershire, lemon juice, salt, and sherry. Mix butter with mustard until soft and smooth. Add to rest of sauce. Boil 5 minutes, stirring constantly. This sauce is also excellent over chicken breasts and all fish. Serves 8.

Ship to Shore II (North Carolina)

 In Virginia, more people work for the U.S. Government than any other industry—about one-quarter of the state's workforce.

Shrimp in Lemon Butter

1 cup butter
¼ cup lemon juice
1 clove garlic, minced
1 teaspoon parsley flakes
1 teaspoon Worcestershire
1 teaspoon soy sauce

½ teaspoon coarsely ground black
   pepper
¼ teaspoon salt
2 pounds large shrimp, peeled,
   deveined
Lemon wedges (optional)

Melt butter in large skillet. Add next 7 ingredients; bring to a boil. Add shrimp. Cook over medium heat 5 minutes, stirring occasionally. Garnish shrimp with lemon wedges, if desired. Yields 4–6 servings.

Knollwood's Cooking (North Carolina)

All-Time Favorite Shrimp
with Artichokes

1 (20-ounce) can artichoke
   hearts
¾ pound shrimp, boiled,
   peeled, deveined
¼ pound fresh or canned
   mushrooms, sliced
5 tablespoons butter
¼ cup chopped onion

4 tablespoons flour
1½ cups half-and-half
1 tablespoon Worcestershire
Salt and pepper to taste
3 tablespoons dry sherry
¼ cup grated Parmesan cheese
Paprika

Drain artichokes, slice in half and arrange in buttered 9x13-inch baking dish. Spread cooked shrimp over these. Sauté mushrooms in butter for about 5 minutes, lift out and sprinkle over shrimp and artichokes. Cook onions in same butter until transparent. Add flour and cook a minute or two longer. Add half-and-half and stir until thickened. Add Worcestershire, salt lightly, as Parmesan cheese is salty), pepper, and sherry to cream sauce and pour over contents of baking dish. Sprinkle with Parmesan cheese and paprika. Bake at 375° for 20 minutes. Serves 6.

Christmas Favorites (North Carolina)

Sam's Spicy Grilled Shrimp

½ cup light olive oil
5 teaspoons Cajun seasoning
  mix
¼ cup oriental sesame oil
¼ cup fresh lemon juice
2 tablespoons minced fresh
  ginger

2 teaspoons dry mustard
2 teaspoons Tabasco
3 pounds large, uncooked shrimp,
  peeled and deveined (tails
  intact)

Whisk together all but shrimp in a large bowl. Add shrimp to the mix, stir to coat. Let stand for only 30 minutes, no more, no less. Start grill 10 minutes before putting the shrimp on. Use grill basket or skewers. Grill 2–3 minutes on each side.

Bountiful Blessings (Maryland)

Baked Stuffed Shrimp

Great company dish! Can be prepared earlier in the day and refrigerated. Large shrimp do just as well as jumbo.

24 raw jumbo shrimp, shelled,
  deveined
2 tablespoons plus 1 stick butter,
  divided
1 small onion, minced
¼ cup minced celery
½ green bell pepper, minced
1 tablespoon chopped parsley
1 pound backfin crabmeat

1 teaspoon salt
¼ teaspoon thyme
Dash of Tabasco
1 tablespoon Worcestershire
½ cup seasoned bread crumbs
1 egg, beaten
1 cup light cream or milk
1 stick butter
Paprika

Split shrimp lengthwise so they can be opened flat, but do not cut all the way through. Spread flat in buttered shallow baking dish, and set aside. In 2 tablespoons butter, sauté onion, celery, and green pepper until onion is just transparent. Remove from heat. Add parsley. Toss vegetable mixture with crabmeat. Add seasonings, bread crumbs, egg, and cream. Toss gently. Mound crab mixture on shrimp. Melt stick of butter, and pour over shrimp. Sprinkle with paprika, and bake at 400° for 15 minutes. This can be prepared early in the day. If so, pour butter over shrimp just before baking. Makes 6 servings.

Food, Family, and Friendships (Virginia)

Shrimp and Grits

LOW COUNTRY SPICE MIXTURE:

2 tablespoons white pepper
2 tablespoons black pepper
2 tablespoons chili powder

2 tablespoons sweet paprika
2 tablespoons dried parsley

Stir together, adjust seasonings to taste, and store in airtight container.

1 cup dry grits
1 cup grated white Cheddar
1 teaspoon salt
½ cup flour
Oil for frying
8 ounces kielbasa sausage,
   sliced ¼ inch
1 teaspoon Low Country
   Spice Mixture

2 cups sliced mushrooms
1 pound fresh shrimp, peeled
   and deveined
½ cup white wine
1 tablespoon butter,
   margarine, or oil
1 cup chopped scallions

Cook dry grits according to package directions. Mix cooked grits, grated cheese, and salt. Pour into greased 8x8-inch pan. Chill overnight in refrigerator.

   Slice 8 diagonal wedges; dust with flour mixed with Low Country Spice Mixture to taste. Deep-fry chilled grits wedges until brown and crusty. Place 2 wedges on each plate. In a pan with a little bit of oil, sauté sausage, mushrooms, and a teaspoon of Low Country Spices for 5 minutes. Add shrimp and cook until pink in color. Top grits wedges with shrimp mixture. Add wine and butter to pan drippings, stirring with wooden spoon. Pour wine sauce over shrimp and grits and garnish with chopped scallions. Serves 4.

Recipe from the Pilot House Restaurant
Modern Recipes from Historic Wilmington (North Carolina)

Southern Shrimp and Grits

1 pound shrimp, peeled	4 teaspoons fresh lemon juice
6 slices bacon	Salt and pepper to taste
Peanut oil	Hot sauce to taste
2 cups sliced fresh mushrooms	Chopped fresh parsley to taste
1 cup sliced green onions	Cheesy Grits
1 garlic clove, crushed	

Rinse shrimp, pat dry, and set aside. Chop bacon into small pieces. Cook bacon in large heavy skillet until browned at the edges. Remove bacon from skillet; set aside. Add enough peanut oil to bacon drippings in skillet to cover bottom of pan. Heat mixture over medium-high heat. Add shrimp. Sauté until shrimp begin to turn pink. Add mushrooms, green onions, garlic, and bacon. Cook until shrimp are pink and bacon is crisp. Add lemon juice, salt and pepper, hot sauce, and parsley and mix well.

Divide Cheesy Grits among 4 warm plates. Spoon shrimp mixture over grits and serve immediately.

CHEESY GRITS:

4 cups cooked grits	White pepper to taste
1 cup shredded sharp Cheddar cheese	Nutmeg to taste
½ cup grated Parmesan cheese	Hot sauce to taste

Prepare enough grits according to package directions to yield 4 cups. Add Cheddar and Parmesan cheeses to hot grits and stir until cheeses melt. Season with white pepper, nutmeg, and hot sauce, mix well, and set aside. Keep grits warm.

In Good Company (Virginia)

To settle a dispute between the colonies of Pennsylvania and Maryland, a survey was begun in 1762 by British astronomers Charles Mason and Jeremiah Dixon. The Mason-Dixon Line, a straight line between the 39° and 40° parallel, is now used as a regional boundary between the north and the south.

Annapolis Harbor Boil

¾ cup (6 ounces) Chesapeake-style seafood seasoning

8 lemons, 4 thinly sliced, 4 wedged for condiments

1 large yellow onion, sliced in rings and separated

1 large bell pepper (any color) sliced lengthwise in ½-inch strips

5 pounds red potatoes, scrubbed and halved, if necessary, to make no larger than 4-inch circumference

1½ pounds smoked sausage, cut into 3-inch lengths and browned

2 pounds medium unshelled shrimp, deheaded and rinsed

8 small ears of corn, halved

1 pound drawn butter or margarine

1½ cups cocktail sauce

Fill a 5-gallon crab pot ¾ full with hot water; add Chesapeake-style seafood seasoning and the 4 sliced lemons, and bring to a rolling boil. Add onion, pepper, and potatoes and boil for 20 minutes. Add sausage and boil an additional 20 minutes. Add shrimp and corn and allow to boil for 4 minutes, then turn off heat and leave for an additional 5 minutes in the water. Drain the entire mixture and ladle all items into 1 or 2 very large serving bowls. Serve immediately with butter and cocktail sauce. Serves 8–10.

Note: Chesapeake seafood seasoning is a regional specialty used in everything from seafood dishes to poultry and vegetables. The two most famous brands are Old Bay Seasoning and Wye River Seasoning.

Of Tide & Thyme (Maryland)

Sautéed Shrimp
with Red Harper Sauce

1 (14-ounce) jar roasted red
 peppers, rinsed and drained
1 tablespoon balsamic vinegar
¾ cup olive oil, divided
1 tablespoon sugar
Salt and pepper to taste
3 tablespoons butter, divided

½ cup cream
2 cloves garlic, finely chopped
 or pressed
3 pounds shrimp, peeled and
 deveined
¼ cup chopped parsley
Rice or pasta, cooked

Purée peppers with vinegar in food processor, adding ½ cup oil in thin stream. Stir in sugar, salt, and pepper. Bring to a simmer in saucepan. Stir in 2 tablespoons butter in pieces. (Can be made ahead to this point.) Stir in cream until just heated through. Do not boil.

Warm remaining ¼ cup olive oil with remaining 1 tablespoon butter in sauté pan. Add garlic. In single layer, sauté shrimp in batches. Salt to taste. Do not overcook. Mix shrimp with sauce and serve over rice or pasta. May use fewer shrimp and serve over baked grouper or other fish. Garnish with chopped parsley. Serves 6–8.
Recipe from Harper House

Modern Recipes from Historic Wilmington (North Carolina)

Virginia's Crabmeat

1 pound backfin crabmeat
1 tablespoon horseradish
1 teaspoon grated lemon rind
½ teaspoon Ac'cent

Dash of hot sauce
1 tablespoon grated onion
1½ cups mayonnaise
¾ cup sharp Cheddar cheese

Mix first 7 ingredients in baking dish. Sprinkle grated cheese on top and bake in 350° oven for 25 minutes. Serves 4.

The Boar's Head Cookbook (Virginia)

Mammaw's Steamed Crabs

First of all, the best crabs in the world are the ones you catch yourself. That's a whole 'nother story though, about catching crabs. But now that you have the crabs, about a bushel, fill the bathtub half full of water and dump them in. Now you can see what you have. Don't take too long to get the pot and stove ready or the crabs will drown for lack of oxygen.

1 (12-ounce) can beer
2 tablespoons Old Bay
  Seasoning
6 ounces vinegar
Water

A bushel of fresh crabs
Old Bay Seasoning for additional
  seasoning
Butter, melted

Get a big pot with a tray inside the bottom to keep crabs out of the fluids. Remember you're steaming them, not boiling them. Into the pot, pour a can of beer, 2 tablespoons Old Bay Seasoning, and vinegar, and fill to the bottom of the raised tray with water. (Somehow my grandmother always had a can of beer around, although I never saw her drink one.)

Fill the pot to the top with crabs; be careful, they'll cut your fingers with their sharp claws. Maybe use some tongs or heavy gloves. Pour some more Old Bay on top of crabs (but don't let them jump out of the pot). Turn on the heat and steam 'em up. Stay close by because when it starts getting hot in the pot, the crabs may try to push the top off and jump out. When they've just turned red, they're done.

Spread out some newspapers on the table and pour crabs (not the sauce) out. Have some large-handled butter knives or small wooden mallets to help (with breaking the shells). Maybe some melted butter in bowls and a few piles of Old Bay Seasoning out on the table. Some people like crackers to go with their Coca-Colas or beer. Now, picking and eating them crabs is another story, too....

Celebrate Virginia! (Virginia)

The olive-green and white "blue crab"—named for its vivid blue claws—is abundant in estuaries and coastal habitats of the Western Atlantic. The blue crab is a crustacean, like its cousins, the shrimp and the crayfish, and has ten legs. It walks sideways using the three middle pairs, uses its front pincer claws for defending itself and securing food, but earns its scientific name from the remaining pair. Callinectes, in Greek, means "beautiful swimmer," and its hind legs, shaped like paddles, make the crab a remarkable swimmer.

Soft-Shell Crabs

Soft-shell crabs are abundant and cheap almost all summer long. Most people don't cook them at home because they don't know how to clean the crabs. It is real easy to do right in your kitchen sink. Crabs must be alive when you clean them. You can wrap them in plastic and freeze them in a zip-lock bag if you want to have some crabs in the winter.

TO CLEAN CRABS:

Lift each side of crab's shell and pull off "dead man" (gills). Remove crab's apron. Squeeze crab firmly in middle to force out all innards. Do not leave any yellow or green stuff, as it can be bitter. Rinse cavity. Drain on paper towels.

1 egg
¼ cup water
Peanut oil for frying
Seafood breading mix (any brand you like)

2 teaspoons Old Bay Seasoning
Soft-shell crabs (2 per person)

Mix egg with water. Beat until frothy. Heat 2–3 inches of peanut oil in big iron frying pan. Mix generous amount of seafood breading mix with Old Bay Seasoning in a big zip-lock bag. Dip each crab in egg/water, drop into breading mix, and shake until thoroughly coated. Fry until golden brown. Don't let your oil get too hot or coating will burn. When you drop crabs in pan, put cover on pan immediately, as they will spatter and pop at first.

Note: If you cook a lot of crabs, of course you will have to increase quantities of ingredients accordingly.

Our Best to You! (North Carolina)

Crab Melt

1 pound crabmeat
¼ cup diced celery
¼ cup diced red onion
4 hard-boiled eggs, diced
½ teaspoon Old Bay Seasoning
¼ teaspoon dill weed

½ cup mayonnaise
¼ cup sour cream
4 English muffins
8 slices tomato
8 slices Cheddar cheese

Combine first 8 ingredients in a medium bowl. Separate muffins. Top each muffin half with 1 slice of tomato, crab mixture, and 1 slice of Cheddar. Broil in oven just until cheese melts. Serves 4.

Recipe from The Main Street Mill Pub & Grill, Fort Royal
A Taste of Virginia History (Virginia)

Aunt Hattie's Deviled Crab

Hattie Midgett started her cooking career by packing lunches for the Wright Brothers. Each day Orville and Wilbur would leave the Tranquil House and stop at Midgett's Store on the Manteo waterfront. There they would pick up their lunches before departing by boat for Kill Devil Hills.

1 pound claw crabmeat
½ jar Durkee's Famous Sauce
3 tablespoons mayonnaise

1 tablespoon Worcestershire
A shake of parsley flakes

Mix all ingredients together. Put into individual baking dishes. Bake at 350° a few minutes until brown.

A Taste of the Outer Banks (North Carolina)

PHOTO © PAUL CAMPBELL

On December 17, 1903, Wilbur and Orville Wright made the first successful sustained powered flight near Kitty Hawk, North Carolina. The Wright Brothers National Memorial, a 60-foot-high granite monument perched atop 90-foot-tall Kill Devil Hill, commemorates the visionary brothers.

Eastern Shore Crab Cakes

This is an old receipt from the Eastern Shore of Maryland.

1 pound crabmeat	**1 hard-boiled egg**
Salt and pepper to taste	**1 tablespoon Worcestershire**
1 egg	**Bread crumbs (from 2–3 slices**
¼ pound butter	**bread)**
1 tablespoon lemon juice	

Put crabmeat in a bowl and season to taste with salt and pepper. Add slightly beaten egg, melted butter, lemon juice, cut up hard-boiled egg, and Worcestershire. Then add just enough soft bread crumbs to make it into cakes (2 or 3 slices of bread). Fry the cakes a golden brown.

Maryland's Way (Maryland)

Best Maryland Crab Cakes

Best tasting crab cakes ever!

4 slices white bread with crusts trimmed, or ½ cup dry bread crumbs, or 6 saltines, crumbled	**1 egg, beaten**
	½ cup mayonnaise
½ teaspoon dry mustard	**½ teaspoon lemon juice**
½ teaspoon Chesapeake-style seafood seasoning	**½ teaspoon Worcestershire**
	1 pound crabmeat, shell and cartilage removed
¼ teaspoon Ac'cent	

Mix bread crumbs, mustard, seafood seasoning, and Ac'cent together and set aside.

In another bowl, gently fold together egg, mayonnaise, lemon juice, Worcestershire, and bread crumb mixture. Add crabmeat, and shape into individual cakes. Refrigerate for at least 2 hours to avoid breaking apart when cooked.

Place under broiler and broil until brown, or fry in oil until brown and drain on paper towels before serving. Serves 4–6.

Of Tide & Thyme (Maryland)

Edge Hill Crab Cakes

½ cup milk
1 pound crabmeat
1 egg, slightly beaten
1 teaspoon dry mustard
2 teaspoons mayonnaise
⅛ teaspoon pepper

1 teaspoon Worcestershire
1 teaspoon bitters
1 teaspoon chopped parsley
1 teaspoon salt
Milk
Cracker crumbs

Mix all ingredients except milk and cracker crumbs. Make into cakes. Dip in milk and then in cracker crumbs. Place on lightly greased baking sheet in 375° oven for 20 minutes. Serve with Caper Sauce. Makes 8 crab cakes

CAPER SAUCE:
1 tablespoon butter
2 tablespoons flour
1½ cups chicken broth

½ teaspoon salt
½ cup capers

Melt butter. Add flour and broth slowly. Add salt and capers.

Favorite Recipes of the Lower Cape Fear (North Carolina)

Imperial Crab Casserole

1 pound crabmeat
2 tablespoons chopped onion
2 tablespoons chopped green
   pepper
2 tablespoons flour
½ cup milk

½ teaspoon salt
Dash of pepper
¼ teaspoon Worcestershire
1 teaspoon lemon juice
2 tablespoons margarine, melted
2 hard-boiled eggs, chopped

Check crabmeat for pieces of shell and remove. Sauté onion and green pepper until tender; blend in flour and add milk gradually, stirring. Cook until thick, stirring. Add seasonings, Worcestershire, lemon juice, and margarine. Stir some of hot mixture into eggs to prevent curdling and add to remaining sauce. Add crabmeat; put in a greased casserole (or may use individual ramekins or cleaned crab shells). Bake in 350° oven for 25–30 minutes, or until top is browned.

Bread of Life (Maryland)

Deviled Crab Morattico

2 tablespoons Hellmann's
  mayonnaise
2 tablespoons prepared mustard
2 tablespoons vinegar

Dash of Worcestershire
Dash of Tabasco
Salt and pepper to taste
1 pound crabmeat

TOPPING:

½ cup bread crumbs
Paprika

4 pats butter

Mix all stuffing ingredients together, adding crabmeat last. Toss gently. Place in shells. Do not pack. Top with bread crumbs, paprika, and a large pat of butter on each. Bake at 350° for 30 minutes. Makes 4 large servings for dinner.

The Rappahannock Seafood Cookbook (Virginia)

Fresh Sea Scallops
in White Wine Sauce

1 large clove garlic, crushed
12 tablespoons butter, divided
1 pound fresh sea scallops
3 teaspoons flour
½ cup Johannisberg Riesling
2 teaspoons minced parsley

⅛ teaspoon white pepper
⅛ teaspoon paprika
Salt to taste
½ pound thin vermicelli, cooked al
  dente

In a large skillet heat 6 tablespoons butter and sauté until tender. Remove scallops from pan and save butter and juices in a separate container. Melt remaining 6 tablespoons butter in the same pan. Whisk in flour, stir and cook 2–3 minutes. Add wine, parsley, seasonings, and juices from scallop cooking. Cook until thickened. Add more wine if too thick. Return scallops to sauce and heat. Serve over cooked vermicelli. Serves 4.

Virginia Wine Country (Virginia)

Tarragon Scallops

1 pound fresh scallops
¼ cup milk
¼ cup flour
Fresh ground pepper
6 tablespoons vegetable oil
4 tablespoons butter

Juice of ½ lemon
3 tablespoons finely chopped
 tarragon
2 tablespoons finely chopped
 parsley

Put scallops in a bowl and add milk. Let scallops soak in milk for a few minutes. Put flour on a plate. Season flour with pepper. Lightly dredge scallops in flour, shaking off the excess. Sauté scallops in oil in a skillet until browned. Remove scallops from skillet and set aside. Discard oil from skillet. Add butter to skillet, then add lemon juice, tarragon, and parsley. Cook until butter begins to bubble. Return scallops to skillet and heat through. Serve over cooked pasta or rice. Serves 2.

Lambertville Community Cookbook (New Jersey)

Simply Scrumptious Virginia Bay Scallops in Wine Sauce

¾ cup bread crumbs
¼ cup grated Parmesan cheese
4 tablespoons butter
2 tablespoons margarine
2 stalks celery, leaves
 removed, sliced
1½ medium onions, chopped

6 tablespoons flour
1 cup milk
½ cup white wine
4 ounces medium sharp
 Cheddar, sliced
1 pound Virginia bay scallops

Preheat oven to 350°. Prepare topping by combining bread crumbs and Parmesan cheese in a small bowl. Melt butter and margarine in a medium (2-quart) saucepan. Sauté celery and onions in melted butter and margarine. Blend in flour to make a paste; cook one full minute over medium heat. Gradually add milk, stirring after each addition. Stir wine into sauce. Add cheese and let it melt into sauce, stirring frequently. Fold in scallops. Pour into a greased 2-quart casserole dish. Sprinkle on topping. Bake for 20–30 minutes until bubbly. Serve over noodles or rice. Yields 5 servings.

The Great Taste of Virginia Seafood Cookbook (Virginia)

Seafood au Gratin

½ lemon, sliced
½ small onion, sliced
3 cups water
1 tablespoon fresh basil
2½ pounds rockfish
1 pound scallops

½ small onion, minced
¼ cup chopped green pepper
2 tablespoons butter
½ pound sliced mushrooms
¼ cup bread crumbs

Boil lemon and onion slices in water. Add basil and cook for 5 minutes. Add rockfish and scallops and poach for 5 minutes. Remove and break apart the fish, reserving the liquid, but discarding the lemon and onion. In a saucepan, sauté the minced onion and pepper in butter, then add mushrooms.

SAUCE:

1 cup butter
1 cup flour
2 cups cream
2 cups fish stock
½ teaspoon dry mustard

½ cup shredded Swiss cheese or
   Gruyère
¼ cup dry white wine or ¼ cup
   sherry
Salt and pepper to taste

Melt butter in a saucepan and slowly add the flour. Then add the cream and stock until thickened. Add the mustard, cheese, wine, salt and pepper. Combine the fish, vegetables, and sauce. Pour into a baking dish. Cover with bread crumbs. Bake for 35 minutes at 350°.

Chesapeake's Bounty (Maryland)

Fresh Fried Oysters

1 pint fresh oysters
2 eggs, beaten
2 cups cornmeal
2 teaspoons salt

1 teaspoon pepper
2 tablespoons flour
Shortening for frying

Rinse and drain oysters; soak in eggs. Mix cornmeal, salt, pepper, and flour. Dip oysters in flour mixture and fry in deep shortening until golden brown. Drain on paper towels; enjoy.

Cooking with Love & Memories (North Carolina)

Oyster Fritters

1 cup flour
1 teaspoon baking powder
1 teaspoon salt
¼ teaspoon pepper
2 eggs

1 cup milk
1 quart oysters
Oil
Tartar or seafood sauce

Combine flour, baking powder, salt and pepper in a bowl. In another bowl, beat together eggs and milk. Stir in dry ingredients. Stir oysters into the batter. Pour about 1 inch of oil into a skillet. Heat until bubbly. Using a large spoon, drop about 3 oysters into oil. Fry until golden brown on each side. Remove and put on paper towels. Keep warm in a 200° oven. Serve with tartar or seafood sauce.

Chesapeake's Bounty (Maryland)

Native Americans created great mounds of leftover oyster shells, feeding heavily upon them for centuries without destroying the oyster bars in the Chesapeake Bay. Early English settlers were also able to harvest oysters in great quantities without reducing the ability of the species to recover. The Constitution of Virginia states that the natural oyster beds, rocks, and shoals in the waters of the Commonwealth shall not be leased, rented, or sold but shall be held in trust for the benefit of the people of the Commonwealth. America's only oyster museum is on Chincoteague Island, where the Oyster and Maritime Museum documents the island's oystering and seafood history.

Oysters Parmesan

½ pint oysters, drained
1 tablespoon chopped onion
1 cup milk, divided
1½ tablespoons butter
2 tablespoons flour
¼ teaspoon salt

Dash of pepper
¼ teaspoon celery salt
¼ cup Parmesan cheese
1 teaspoon chopped parsley
3 English muffins, split, or patty
   shells, or toast points

Combine oysters, onion, and ½ cup milk and cook over medium heat 15 minutes (Do NOT overcook oysters.) Melt butter and blend in flour and seasonings and rest of milk; cook until thick, stirring constantly. Add Parmesan and parsley and stir well. Add oyster mixture and cook 5 minutes. Serve over lightly toasted and buttered muffins, toast points or patty shells. You may also serve oysters in a chafing dish for added elegance.

A Taste of History (North Carolina)

CAKES

On April 9, 1865, General Robert E. Lee (Confederate) surrendered to Lt. General Ulysses S. Grant (Union) at the home of Wilmer McLean in the village of Appomattox Court House, Virginia, bringing an end to the Civil War.

Homemade Strawberry Shortcake

The contrast of hot and cold makes this simple dessert outstanding.

1 quart strawberries, hulled and cut in half	1½ sticks unsalted butter
2 tablespoons orange liqueur (optional)	1 cup light cream or milk
½ cup granulated sugar, divided	Additional sugar for sprinkling over shortcakes
3 cups sifted all-purpose flour	1 cup heavy cream
4 teaspoons baking powder	¼ cup confectioners' sugar
½ teaspoon salt	1 teaspoon vanilla

Mix halved berries with liqueur and ¼ cup granulated sugar. Chill several hours. Sift flour with baking powder, salt, and remaining ¼ cup sugar. Cut in butter until particles are size of small peas. Add light cream or milk all at once. Stir just enough to moisten dry particles. Turn dough out on lightly floured board and knead just a few times to shape into smooth ball.

With rolling pin or with fingers, shape dough into a rectangle about 6x9 inches. With sharp knife, cut oblong into 6 (3-inch) or 12 (1½-inch) squares. Put biscuits on a lightly greased cookie sheet. Sprinkle additional granulated sugar over top of shortcakes and bake in preheated 425° oven 15–20 minutes or until biscuits are deeply browned.

While biscuits are baking, whip heavy cream with confectioners' sugar and vanilla until stiff. When biscuits are ready, split them while hot into halves. Spoon berries over bottom half. Top with second half of biscuit. Add more berries and top with whipped cream. Serve immediately.

Someone's in the Kitchen with Melanie (North Carolina)

Velvet Cake

This recipe came from a woman 90 years old who said it belonged to her mother. It is the moist crumbly-type cake that really does just disappear in the mouth. There is no better cake recipe in my book. I like to bake it in a large pan about two inches deep and then frost it with chocolate frosting and cut it into squares.

1 cup butter, softened	1 cup buttermilk
2 cups sugar	¾ teaspoon baking soda
2 egg yolks	2½ cups sifted flour
2 whole eggs	1 teaspoon vanilla

Cream butter. Add sugar and cream and mix well. Beat in egg yolks; mix well. Add whole eggs, one at a time, beating well after each. Stir soda into buttermilk and add to creamed mixture alternately with flour, blending well. Add vanilla.

Pour into 3 greased layer cake pans and bake at 375° for 20–25 minutes or until done. Cool and frost with white frosting made from egg whites left from the 2 yolks used in the recipe. If baked in a loaf, bake at 325° until done.

North Carolina and Old Salem Cookery (North Carolina)

Italian Cream Cake

1 stick margarine, softened	1 teaspoon baking powder
½ cup shortening	1 teaspoon vanilla
2 cups sugar	1 (3½-ounce) can coconut
5 eggs	1 cup chopped nuts
2 cups plain flour	1 cup buttermilk
1 teaspoon soda	

Cream margarine, shortening, and sugar well. Add remaining ingredients. Cream all together and bake in 3 greased (8-inch) cake pans at 350° for 25 minutes. Cool and frost layers with the following frosting. Makes 3 layers.

FROSTING:

1 (8-ounce) package cream cheese, softened	1 (1-pound) box powdered sugar
1 stick margarine, softened	Chopped nuts for sprinkling
1 teaspoon vanilla	

Mix all but nuts and spread on layers. Sprinkle top with chopped nuts.

The Special Occasion Cookbook (North Carolina)

Lemon Mousse Cake

1 yellow cake, baked in Bundt
  pan
1 envelope unflavored gelatin
¾ cup water
1 (14-ounce) can sweetened
  condensed milk

1 teaspoon grated lemon rind
½ cup lemon juice
2 cups stiffly whipped cream
Fresh blueberries for garnish
  (optional)

Line bottom and sides of an 8- or 9-inch springform pan with slices of baked cake. Trim edges neatly to fit pan, especially along the top; set aside. Sprinkle gelatin over water in a small saucepan. Let stand 1 minute. Cook over low heat, stirring constantly 1 minute or until dissolved. Set aside.

Combine condensed milk, lemon rind, and lemon juice, stirring well. Add reserved gelatin mixture, stirring well. Fold in whipped cream. Pour mixture into prepared springform pan. Cover and refrigerate overnight or until set. Remove sides of springform pan when ready to serve. May garnish top with fresh blueberries, if desired.

My Table at Brightwood (Virginia)

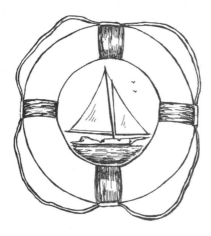

Carolyn's Coconut Cake

2 cake layers, baked and cooled
   (Duncan Hines Butter Cake is
   good)
¼ cup coconut milk (optional)
2 cups sugar

16 ounces sour cream
1 (12-ounce) package coconut (or
   fresh), divided
1 (8-ounce) container Cool Whip

Split cake layers. Sprinkle layers with coconut milk, if desired. Mix sugar, sour cream, and coconut (save ½ cup for topping). Chill. Keep 1 cup of this mixture for frosting. Spread remaining portion between layers. Combine Cool Whip with reserved 1 cup of frosting mixture. Pile frosting on top and sides of cake and sprinkle with reserved ½ cup coconut. Cover with cake saver and refrigerate 3 days. Yields 12 or more servings.

South Coastal Cuisine (Delaware)

Rave Review

CAKE:

1 (18¼-ounce) package yellow
   cake mix
1 (3-ounce) package coconut
   instant pudding
1⅓ cups water

4 eggs
¼ cup oil
2 cups flaked coconut
1 cup chopped nuts, toasted

Combine all and mix well. Put into 3 greased and floured pans. Bake 35 minutes at 350°.

COCONUT ICING:

4 tablespoons butter, softened
1 (8-ounce) package cream
   cheese, softened
1 box powdered sugar

2 cups flaked coconut
2 teaspoons milk
1 teaspoon vanilla

Cream butter and cream cheese. Add sugar, coconut, milk, and vanilla. Mix well and ice between layers.

Ship to Shore I (North Carolina)

Spice Cake

1 cup quick oatmeal
1¼ cups boiling water
½ cup shortening
1 cup brown sugar
1 cup sugar
2 eggs

1⅓ cups flour
1 teaspoon baking soda
½ teaspoon salt
½ teaspoon cinnamon
½ teaspoon nutmeg
1 teaspoon vanilla

Pour boiling water over oatmeal. Let stand 10 minutes. Cream shortening, brown sugar, and white sugar. Add to oatmeal mixture. Add eggs one at a time. Sift flour, soda, salt, cinnamon, nutmeg, and add to mixture. Stir just enough to mix. Add vanilla. Pour into greased 9x13-inch pan and bake in 325° oven 35–40 minutes. Yields 18 servings.

TOPPING:

1 stick margarine, softened
1 cup brown sugar
2 egg yolks

1 cup well-drained crushed
   pineapple
1 cup chopped nuts

Cream margarine, sugar, and egg yolks together. Add pineapple and nuts (if desired, use one or the other). Spread on cooled cake. Brown under broiler. Serve warm.

Recipes from Our Front Porch (North Carolina)

Favorite Carrot Cake

1 cup white sugar
1 cup brown sugar
1 cup vegetable oil
4 eggs
2 (4½-ounce) jars baby
  food carrots

1 teaspoon vanilla
2 cups flour
1½ teaspoons baking soda
½ teaspoon salt
2 teaspoons cinnamon
¾ cup finely chopped walnuts

Preheat oven to 350°. In mixer bowl, beat sugars and oil together. Add eggs, carrots, and vanilla, beating until smooth. Add flour, baking soda, salt, cinnamon, and nuts, beating well. Pour into a greased springform pan with 4-inch sides. Bake 1 hour. Cool 10 minutes and release cake from springform. Frost by cutting cake into 2 layers.

FROSTING:

1 (3-ounce) package cream
  cheese, softened
½ stick butter, softened
1 (1-pound) box confectioners'
  sugar

2 teaspoons vanilla
2 teaspoons lemon juice

Beat cream cheese and butter together until fluffy. Gradually add sugar until thoroughly blended. Add vanilla and lemon juice. If needed, add drops of milk to frosting until of spreading consistency. Makes enough frosting for filling, top, and sides of cake.

The Curran Connection Cookbook (North Carolina)

Pocahontas' life has formed the basis of many legends. Because she never learned to write, the thoughts, feelings, and motives of the historical Pocahontas remain largely unknown. Her story became the source of much romantic myth-making in the centuries following her death. The Walt Disney Company's 1995 animated feature Pocahontas presents a highly-romanticized and fictional view of a love affair between Pocahontas and John Smith, in which Pocahontas teaches Smith the value of respect for nature. However, the records of the Jamestown, Virginia, indicate that Pocahontas had only a friendship with Captain John Smith (having saved his life more than once), and actually married John Rolfe. The marriage helped to establish peaceful relations between the Indians and the English, and therefore played a significant role in American history.

Carrot-Pineapple Cake

I guarantee that this is the moistest carrot cake you'll ever eat.

1 cup shortening	**1 teaspoon cinnamon**
2 cups sugar	**¼ teaspoon salt**
3 eggs	**1 cup crushed pineapple**
3 cups sifted flour	**2 cups grated carrots**
2 teaspoons baking soda	**1 cup pecans (optional)**

Cream shortening and sugar. Add eggs, one at a time. Sift flour, soda, cinnamon, and salt together. Add pineapple, grated carrots, and pecans. Bake at 350° for about one hour in a tube pan.

TOPPING:

1 stick butter	**1 box powdered sugar**
1 (8-ounce) package cream cheese, softened	**2 teaspoons vanilla**
	1 cup chopped pecans

Combine butter and cream cheese. Add powdered sugar, mixing until smooth. Add vanilla and nuts. Spread on cake.

Our Favorite Recipes (Maryland)

Old Southern Orange Slice Cake

2 cups sugar	**1 tablespoon orange juice**
½ pound butter, softened	**2 cups pecans**
4 eggs, beaten	**½ pound dates, cut up**
3½ cups sifted cake flour (reserve 1 cup to dredge pecans, dates, and candy)	**1 pound orange slice candy, cut in half**
½ teaspoon baking soda	**1 can coconut**
½ cup buttermilk (or ½ cup milk and 1 tablespoon vinegar)	

Cream sugar and butter until light and fluffy. Add eggs. Add flour and baking soda alternately with buttermilk. Add orange juice. Fold in pecans, dates, and candy orange slices that have been dredged in the reserved flour (also add the reserved flour). Fold in coconut. Bake at 250° in a greased and floured tube pan 1½ hours, or until cake tester comes out clean.

GLAZE (OPTIONAL):

½ cup orange juice	**½ cup sugar**

Boil until sugar is dissolved.

A Second Helping (New Jersey)

Punch Bowl Cake

A North Carolina Christmas favorite. Put this cake in a glass bowl; you want the layers to show.

1 (18¼-ounce) package
  yellow cake mix
2 (3.4-ounce) packages vanilla
  instant pudding mix, divided
1 (20-ounce) can fruit cocktail,
  drained, divided
2 (8-ounce) cans crushed
  pineapple, with juice,
  divided

1 (21-ounce) can cherry pie
  filling, divided
2 cups chopped pecans, divided
2 (7-ounce) packages flaked
  coconut, divided
2 (8-ounce) containers frozen
  Cool Whip, thawed, divided
Maraschino cherries for garnish
  (optional)

Prepare cake mix according to package directions. Cool layers and break into 1-inch pieces. Prepare 1 box pudding mix as directed on package. Place pieces of 1 cake layer in bottom of large glass bowl. Spoon prepared pudding mix evenly over cake pieces; top with half of fruit cocktail, 1 can pineapple with juice, ½ of the cherry pie filling, 1 cup pecans, and 1 package coconut. Spread 1 container Cool Whip on top.

Repeat the layers, ending with Cool Whip on top. Garnish with maraschino cherries. Chill until ready to serve. Refrigerate any leftovers. Makes about 36 servings.

Granny's Taste of Christmas (North Carolina)

North Carolina is home to the National Association for Stock Car Auto Racing (NASCAR) Hall of Fame, as well as NASCAR legend Richard Petty, who was born in Level Cross on June 2, 1937. Petty has seen motorsports racing grow from dirt tracks in North Carolina to high-tech speedways across the country, becoming the fastest-growing sport in the nation. NASCAR maintains offices in four North Carolina cities: Charlotte, Mooresville, Concord, and Conover. Additionally, owing to its roots, all but a handful of NASCAR teams are still based in North Carolina, especially near Charlotte. The first NASCAR "Strictly Stock" race ever was held at Charlotte Speedway (not the Charlotte Motor Speedway) on June 19, 1949.

Do-Nothing-Cake

2 cups all-purpose flour
2 cups sugar
2 eggs
1 teaspoon baking soda

½ teaspoon salt
1 teaspoon vanilla
1 (20-ounce) can crushed
   pineapple, undrained

Put all ingredients in large bowl and mix with spoon (not mixer). Pour into 9x13-inch pan. Bake at 350° for 30–40 minutes or until center is done. Spoon Topping on cake while hot. So easy.

TOPPING:

1 stick butter or margarine
1 cup sugar
1 (5-ounce) can evaporated milk

1 cup chopped nuts
1 cup flaked coconut

Combine butter, sugar, and milk in small saucepan. Cook 5 minutes. Add nuts and coconut. Spoon on cake while hot. Yummy!

Granny's Kitchen (Virginia)

Mountain Dew Cake

1 (18¼-ounce) box orange cake
   mix
1 (3-ounce) box instant coconut
   cream pie filling

1 cup vegetable oil
4 eggs
1 cup Mountain Dew beverage

Mix ingredients and pour into 3 floured and greased layer pans. Bake at 350° for 30 minutes. Test at 25 minutes.

FILLING AND FROSTING:

1 (16-ounce) can crushed
   pineapple
1½ cups sugar

1 stick margarine
2 tablespoons flour
1 (7-ounce) can flaked coconut

Bring ingredients, except coconut, to a boil over medium heat. Remove from heat and stir in coconut. Let cool 15 minutes. Spread between layers and on top of cake.

Recipes from Home (Virginia)

Cherry "Upside-Down" Cake

½ cup firmly packed brown
  sugar
1 (20-ounce) can sour pie
  cherries, drained; reserve juice
1¾ cups sifted all-purpose
  flour
2 teaspoons baking powder

½ teaspoon salt
1 cup sugar
⅓ cup oil
¾ cup milk
1 teaspoon vanilla
1 egg

Have all ingredients at room temperature. Grease a 8x12-inch pan with butter. Sprinkle brown sugar on bottom of pan. Add drained cherries. Sift together flour, baking powder, salt, and sugar. Add to shortening and milk and vanilla. Beat 1½ minutes until batter is well blended. Add egg, unbeaten, and beat another 1½ minutes. Pour over cherries in pan. Bake in moderate 350° oven 35–45 minutes.

A Taste of History (North Carolina)

Apple Pie Cake

¼ cup butter, softened
1 cup sugar
1 teaspoon baking soda
2 tablespoons hot water
1 egg
1 cup all-purpose flour

1 teaspoon cinnamon
1 teaspoon vanilla
¼ teaspoon nutmeg
½ cup chopped nuts
2 cups diced apples

Cream together butter and sugar. Dissolve baking soda in hot water and add to creamed mixture. Stir in all other ingredients. Pour into greased 9-inch pie pan. Bake at 350° for 35–40 minutes. Serve warm with ice cream or sweetened whipped cream.

Variation: For an easy/lazy brunch, double recipe and bake in a 9x13-inch pan; cut into squares for easy serving. Serve with slices of Cheddar cheese and tiny sausage links. Fresh yogurt or whipped cream cheese is good with it, too.

Vesuvius, Virginia: Then and Now (Virginia)

Cranberry Cake

FROSTING:

5 tablespoons flour	**½ cup butter**
1 cup sugar	**½ cup cream cheese**
1 cup milk	**1 teaspoon vanilla**

Mix flour and sugar in saucepan. Whisk in milk and cook until thickened. Cool. Cream butter and cream cheese until smooth. Beat in flour mixture and vanilla. Chill until cake is cool. Beat occasionally until thick enough to spread.

1½ cups cranberries	**Grated rind from 1 orange**
¼ cup chopped walnuts	**2½ cups sifted flour**
¼ cup water	**1 teaspoon baking soda**
½ cup butter or shortening	**1 teaspoon salt**
1½ cups sugar	**3 tablespoons cocoa**
2 eggs, beaten	**1 teaspoon vinegar**
1 teaspoon red food coloring	**1 cup buttermilk**

Grease and flour 2 (8-inch) cake pans. Cook cranberries with walnuts in water until skins pop and berries are soft. Cool. Cream butter and sugar; add eggs, food coloring, and orange rind. Sift together flour, baking soda, salt, and cocoa. Add vinegar to buttermilk. Mix sifted ingredients alternately with buttermilk into the egg mixture. Fold in cranberries and walnuts mixture. Bake at 325° for 25–30 minutes. Cool and frost. Serves 10–12.

Cape May Fare (New Jersey)

Strawberry Delight Cake

This is truly a light and refreshing dessert to be served on a hot summer day, or after a heavy meal.

2 small packages strawberry Jell-O
2 cups hot water
2 small packages frozen
   strawberries

2 (8-ounce) containers Cool Whip
1 angel food cake

Dissolve Jell-O in hot water. Add frozen strawberries. When cool, add Cool Whip and stir until smooth. Pinch angel food cake into very small pieces and line the bottom of a 9x13-inch pan with half of the pieces. Spoon half the strawberry/Cool Whip mixture over the cake; repeat layers. Refrigerate until firm, about 2 hours.

Barineau-Williams Family Cookbook Vol. II (Delaware)

Orange Juice Cupcakes

These were a specialty of Miss Huyetts' Tea Room, a popular gathering place in downtown Charlottesville in the 1920's.

½ cup shortening or butter,
   softened
1 cup sugar
2 eggs
½ cup milk

1½ cups flour
½ teaspoon salt
2 scant teaspoons baking powder
1 teaspoon vanilla

Cream butter and sugar. Beat in eggs one at a time. Add milk alternately with mixture of flour, salt, and baking powder. Add vanilla. Bake at 425° until surface springs back to the touch (about 15 minutes).

   While cupcakes are still warm, dip (do not soak) them in Syrup. These keep well for several days. Yields 2 dozen.

SYRUP:
1 cup sugar
Juice and grated rind of 1 lemon

Juice and grated rind of 1
   orange

The Best of the Bushel (Virginia)

Mandarin Orange Cake

Great cake to take to covered dish suppers. In North Carolina, this is known as the "Pig Pickin' Cake."

**1 (18¼-ounce) package
    yellow cake mix
4 large eggs, beaten**

**½ cup vegetable oil
1 (11-ounce) can Mandarin
    oranges, with juice**

Preheat oven to 350°. Beat cake mix, eggs, oil, oranges, and juice together just until smooth. Pour into 3 well-greased and floured 9-inch cake pans. Bake in preheated oven 25 minutes. Cool about 5 minutes before removing from pans. Remove from pans and finish cooling on wire cake racks. Then frost with the Icing below.

ICING:

**1 (3.4-ounce) package vanilla
    instant pudding and pie
    filling mix
1 (20-ounce) can crushed
    pineapple, drained**

**1 (12-ounce) carton frozen
    Cool Whip, thawed**

Place pudding mix in a bowl; add drained pineapple and mix well. Fold in Cool Whip, mixing just until blended. Ice cake and then refrigerate. Keep cake refrigerated between servings.

Turnip Greens, Ham Hocks & Granny's Buns (North Carolina)

The Fiddler's Grove Ole Time Fiddler's & Bluegrass Festival, one of the most prestigious and authentic fiddling competitions in the United States, is held in Union Grove, North Carolina, over Memorial Day weekend every year. Striving to maintain a low-key, family feel, the festival limits ticket sales to the first 5,000 takers. The festival began in 1924 in the small rural community of Union Grove as a fund-raising venture by local teacher and musician H.P. Van Hoy and his wife Ada to raise money for school supplies.

Orange Blossoms

GLAZE:

2 oranges   1 box powdered sugar
2 lemons

Grate rind of oranges and lemons; squeeze juice from both. Sift sugar into mixture of peel and juice, saving enough of powdered sugar to dust over glazed cakes. If mixture is too dry, add small amount of additional orange juice. This mixture should be of glaze consistency.

CAKES:

1⅓ cups sugar   ½ teaspoon salt
3 eggs   1 teaspoon vanilla
1½ cups all-purpose flour   ½ cup water
1½ teaspoons baking powder

Grease and flour tea-cake pans (tiny muffin-size pans). Preheat oven at 350°. Cream sugar and eggs; add sifted flour, baking powder, and salt. Add vanilla and water. Fill tea-cake pans no more than half full. Bake 12–15 minutes. Take out of pan while hot; dip into Glaze mixture. Drain on rack; place wax paper under rack to catch Glaze dripping.

Note: This recipe is especially attractive on table when lightly dusted with powdered sugar and garnished with mint leaves. Great for spring weddings and parties. Yields 6 dozen.

Island Born and Bred (North Carolina)

Lemon Poppy Seed Cakes

These are very pretty cakes that mix up quickly. I made this for my husband's Army National Guard Family Day Picnic one year, and some of the soldiers are still talking about it. They loved it!

1 (18¼-ounce) box yellow
  cake mix
1 (3-ounce) box lemon or
  coconut instant pudding mix

¼ cup poppy seeds
4 eggs
½ cup vegetable oil
1 cup hot water

Mix all ingredients and pour into 2 greased (9x5-inch) bread pans. Bake at 350° for 40–50 minutes.

Variation: I like the combination of lemon and poppy seed, but coconut is also very good. You can leave out the poppy seeds and you will still have a great cake.

Gritslickers (North Carolina)

German Chocolate Upside-Down Cake

Easy and delicious—indulge and bulge!

1 cup flaked coconut
1 cup chopped pecans
1 (18¼-ounce) package
  German chocolate cake mix
1 stick butter or margarine

1 (8-ounce) package cream cheese,
  softened
1 (1-pound) box confectioners'
  sugar

Combine coconut and pecans; spread evenly on bottom of a greased 9x13-inch pan. Mix cake mix according to directions on package; pour over coconut-pecan mixture. Put butter and cream cheese into a saucepan; heat until mixture is warm enough to stir in confectioners' sugar. Spoon mixture over top of cake batter. (As cake bakes, the cream cheese mixture will settle to bottom with coconut and pecans, making a delicious "Frosting." Bake at 350° for 50–60 minutes, or until done. Serve from pan, do not cut until cake is cooled.

Holiday Treats (Virginia)

Sour Cream Chocolate Chip Cake

Who can ever resist a chocolate chip? this recipe for a sour cream cake with nut and chocolate chips is sure to please your family or guests as well. I bake it in a Bundt pan.

1 cup butter, softened
1¼ cup sugar
3 eggs, lightly beaten
½ pint sour cream
2 cups cake flour, sifted
1 teaspoon baking powder
½ teaspoon baking soda
1 teaspoon vanilla
1 (12-ounce) package chocolate chips
1 cup chopped pecans

Preheat oven to 350°. Grease and flour a 10-inch Bundt pan. Cream butter and sugar. Beat in eggs and sour cream. Sift together dry ingredients and add to sugar mixture. Add vanilla, chips, and pecans. Pour into pan. Bake 1 hour.

Taste Buds (North Carolina)

Self-Filling Chocolate Chip Cupcakes

1 (18¼-ounce) box chocolate or yellow cake mix

Make cake according to package directions. Spoon batter into 24 greased or paper-lined muffin tins, filling ⅔ full.

FILLING:

1 (8-ounce) package cream cheese, softened
1 egg, slightly beaten
⅓ cup sugar
1 cup semisweet chocolate chips

In mixing bowl, beat cream cheese, egg, and sugar until smooth. Fold in chips. Drop by tablespoonfuls into batter. Bake at 350° for 20 minutes or until tests done. Allow to sit for at least 10 minutes before removing from muffin tin.

From Our Home to Yours (North Carolina)

Chocolate Mousse Cake

There is no flour in this cake because it is really a chocolate mousse that when baked turns into a rich, fudgy cake. If the cake is baked the day before and chilled thoroughly, it will be easier to unmold and slice.

6 eggs
½ cup plus 2 tablespoons sugar, divided
16 ounces semisweet chocolate
¼ cup strong brewed coffee
¼ cup plus 1 tablespoon Grand Marnier or dark rum, divided

2 tablespoons vanilla extract
3 cups heavy cream, divided
2 tablespoons sugar
Shaved chocolate

Put eggs and ½ cup sugar into a bowl and begin to beat on high speed. Continue beating at least 5 minutes or until mixture is thick and creamy.

Put chocolate in top of a double boiler. Add coffee and Grand Marnier or rum and melt until smooth. Remove from heat. Add vanilla; set aside.

Whip 1 cup heavy cream until thick and stiff. Fold chocolate into the beaten egg mixture and then gently fold in whipped cream. Make sure batter is well mixed and then pour it into a 9-inch springform pan. Set pan into a larger pan and fill larger pan with about 2 inches of hot water. Bake cake in a preheated 350° oven 1 hour until center of cake seems firm to the touch. When cake is done, remove from oven and carefully lift it out of water bath. Set it on a rack to cool completely. Cover and chill at least 8 hours or overnight.

To serve cake, whip remaining 2 cups cream with 2 tablespoons sugar and 1 tablespoon Grand Marnier or rum. Whip until thick and stiff. Remove cake from refrigerator. Run a knife around side, and gently release sides of springform pan. Invert cake onto a serving platter and carefully lift off bottom. Frost top and sides of cake with whipped cream. Decorate with shaved chocolate. Surround cake with fresh fruit, if desired. Serves 8–10.

Virginia Wine Country (Virginia)

Chocoholic's Dream

True chocoholics will experience Nirvana when tasting this fabulous cake.

CAKE:

½ cup strong brewed coffee
8 ounces semisweet chocolate,
  cut into pieces

1 cup granulated sugar
1 cup unsalted butter
4 eggs

Preheat oven to 350°. Grease a 9x5x3-inch loaf pan. Line with parchment, and grease parchment well. In a small saucepan, combine coffee, chocolate, sugar, and butter. Cook over medium heat until butter and chocolate are melted. Stir occasionally. Remove from heat and stir in eggs. Blend well and pour into prepared pan. Bake at 350° for 55–65 minutes, or until cake cracks around sides and is crisp on top. Remove from oven and cool in pan. Cover with foil and refrigerate overnight or for up to one week.

At serving time, invert chilled cake on an oval serving platter; remove pan and carefully peel off the parchment.

TOPPING:

1 cup whipping cream
¼ cup confectioners' sugar
¼ teaspoon vanilla extract
2 tablespoons shaved semisweet
  chocolate

Fresh raspberries, for garnish
Fresh strawberries, for garnish
Candied violets, for garnish

Whip cream with sugar and vanilla until soft peaks hold their form. Frost the top of the cake with whipped cream mixture. Dust with grated chocolate. Mound berries at either end of the cake on the plate. Place a few berries on top of cake. Stud berry mounds with candied violets and place a few on the top of the cake. Yields 8–10 servings.

A Matter of Taste (New Jersey)

During the 1930s, Earl Hamner, Jr. wrote about his youth in Nelson County, Virginia, during the Depression. His writings were the basis for the television series *The Waltons*. John-Boy's bedroom and Ike Godsey's store are re-created at Walton's Mountain Museum in Schuyler, home of Earl Hamner, Jr.

Decadent Fudge Bundt Cake

1 cup butter or margarine,
  softened
1½ cups sugar
4 eggs
½ teaspoon baking soda
1 cup buttermilk
2½ cups all-purpose flour
1½ cups semisweet chocolate
  mini-morsels, divided

2 (4-ounce) bars sweet baking
  chocolate, melted and cooled
⅓ cup chocolate syrup
2 teaspoons vanilla extract
4 ounces white chocolate, chopped
2 tablespoons plus 2 teaspoons
  shortening, divided

Cream butter in a large mixing bowl; gradually add sugar, beating well at medium speed of an electric mixer. Add eggs, one at a time, beating after each addition. Dissolve soda in buttermilk, stirring well. Add to creamed mixture alternately with flour, beginning and ending with flour. Add 1 cup mini-morsels, melted chocolate, chocolate syrup, and vanilla, stirring just until blended. (Do not overbeat.)

Spoon batter into a heavily greased and floured 10-inch Bundt pan. Bake at 300° for 1 hour and 25–35 minutes, or until cake springs back when touched. Invert cake immediately onto a serving plate and let cool completely.

Combine white chocolate and 2 tablespoons shortening in top of a double boiler; bring water to a boil. Reduce heat to low; cook until mixture is melted and smooth. Remove from heat. Drizzle melted white chocolate mixture over cooled cake. Melt remaining ½ cup mini-morsels and 2 teaspoons shortening in a small saucepan over low heat, stirring until smooth. Remove from heat and let cool; drizzle over white chocolate.

Country Chic's Home Cookin (Maryland)

Lewes, Delaware, is situated where the Delaware Bay and Atlantic Ocean meet at Cape Henlopen. Founded as a whaling station by Dutch settlers in 1631, Lewes also holds the distinction of being "the first town in the first state."

Edna's Old-Fashioned Pound Cake

1 cup butter, softened
1 cup vegetable shortening
3 cups sugar
6 eggs
4 cups cake flour

¼ teaspoon salt
1 teaspoon baking powder
1 cup milk
1 teaspoon almond or vanilla
   flavoring

Preheat oven to 300°. Grease and flour a 10-inch tube pan. Set aside. In large bowl, cream butter and shortening until well-blended. Add sugar gradually until fluffy. Add eggs, one at a time, beating well after each addition. In a separate bowl, sift then measure flour. Add salt and baking powder.

Combine milk and flavoring in a measuring cup. With mixer on low speed, add flour mixture alternately with milk to butter mixture. Begin and end with flour. Pour batter into pan. Bake 1½ hours or until a tester inserted in cake comes out clean. Remove from oven and cool in pan on wire rack before inverting on plate to serve. Yields 12–16 servings.

Red Pepper Fudge and Blue Ribbon Biscuits (North Carolina)

Three Chocolate Cake

1 (18½-ounce) package devil's
   food cake mix
1 (4⅛-ounce) package instant
   chocolate pudding mix
½ cup brewed coffee

4 large eggs, beaten
1 cup sour cream
½ cup vegetable oil
½ cup dark rum
2 cups semisweet chocolate chips

Preheat oven to 350°. Combine all ingredients, except chocolate chips. With electric mixer, blend on low speed. Beat on medium speed for one minute. Scrape sides of bowl, and beat for one minute longer. Fold in chocolate chips. Pour into a greased and floured Bundt pan. Bake for 55–60 minutes. Turn out of pan and cool.

Flavors of Cape Henlopen (Delaware)

5-Flavor Pound Cake

CAKE:

2 sticks butter, softened
½ cup vegetable shortening
3 cups sugar
5 eggs, well beaten
3 cups all-purpose flour
½ teaspoon baking powder

1 cup milk
1 teaspoon coconut extract
1 teaspoon rum extract
1 teaspoon lemon extract
1 teaspoon vanilla extract
1 teaspoon butter extract

Cream butter, shortening, and sugar until lightly fluffy. Add eggs which have been beaten until lemon colored. Combine flour and baking powder and add to creamed mixture alternately with milk. Stir in flavorings. Spoon into a greased and papered 10-inch tube pan and bake at 325° for 1 hour and 30 minutes.

GLAZE:

1 cup sugar
½ cup water
1 teaspoon coconut extract
1 teaspoon rum extract

1 teaspoon butter extract
1 teaspoon lemon extract
1 teaspoon vanilla extract
1 teaspoon almond extract

Combine ingredients in heavy saucepan. Bring to a boil and stir until sugar is melted; pour over cake just out of oven. Let sit in pan until cake is cool. Can freeze. Serves 12–15.

Mountain Elegance (North Carolina)

Crusty Cream Cheese Pound Cake

1 cup butter or margarine,
   softened
½ cup shortening
3 cups sugar
1 (8-ounce) package cream
   cheese, softened

3 cups sifted cake flour, or 2¾
   cups all-purpose flour
6 eggs, beaten
1 tablespoon vanilla extract

Cream butter and shortening. Gradually add sugar, beating well at medium speed of mixer. Add cream cheese, beating well until light and fluffy. Alternately add flour and eggs, beginning and ending with flour. Stir in vanilla. Grease and flour 10-inch tube pan. Bake at 325° for 1 hour and 15 minutes.

Restaurant Recipes from the Shore and More... (Maryland)

Best Ever Butter Pecan Pound Cake

¾ pound butter
2 teaspoons baking powder
1 pound cake flour
3½ cups coarsely ground
   pecans
12 large eggs (10 jumbo)

1 pound very fine granulated
   sugar
⅔ cup firmly packed light
   brown sugar
1 tablespoon vanilla

Beat butter until fluffy. Add baking powder to flour. Add ⅓ of flour mixture to butter and beat until creamy. Set aside. Add ground nuts to remaining ⅔ flour mixture. Set this aside, too. In a separate bowl beat eggs, sugars and vanilla. Set aside. Stir nut mixture into flour mixture. Batter will be very stiff. Then add egg mixture a little at a time blending well after each addition. Pour into a greased and floured 10-inch tube pan or Bundt pan and bake at 300° until cake tests done in the middle.

Note: Be sure to weigh accurately. And grind, not chop the nuts. The success of this recipe depends on exact amounts of ingredients. It has taken many failures to finally come up with the perfect recipe to duplicate the old south version of nut cake. Enjoy!

Mrs. Claus' Favorite Recipes (North Carolina)

Chocolate Chip Pound Cake

1 (18¼-ounce) package yellow
  cake mix
1 (3-ounce) package vanilla
  instant pudding
⅔ cup oil
⅔ cup water

4 eggs
1 (6-ounce) package semisweet
  chocolate chips
½ square German chocolate,
  grated

Beat cake mix, pudding, oil, water, and eggs until well blended. Stir in by hand the chocolate chips and German chocolate. Bake in greased tube pan 1 hour at 300°. Test for doneness at end of 1 hour. May need cooking 10–15 minutes longer. Cool in pan 15 minutes.

Church Family Favorites

Coffee Toffee Ice Cream Cake

28 Oreo cookies
6 large Heath candy bars
  (coffee-toffee bars)
½ gallon chocolate ice cream

8 ounces Hershey's chocolate
  syrup, divided
½ gallon coffee ice cream

Put 14 Oreo cookies in one plastic bag and 14 in another plastic bag. Crush with a rolling pin or mallet. do nut use food processor. Place 6 Heath candy bars in a plastic bag and crush. Lightly oil a 10-inch springform pan. Sprinkle bottom of pan with one bag of cookies. Add ½ gallon softened chocolate ice cream. Drizzle 4 ounces of Hershey's syrup over ice cream. Sprinkle second bag of cookies over syrup. Add ½ gallon softened coffee ice cream. Drizzle with remaining 4 ounces Hershey's syrup. Sprinkle top with crushed Heath bars. Cover with foil. Freeze until hard. Serves 25.

Bravo (North Carolina)

Turtle Pecan Cheesecake

2 cups cookie crumbs
¼ cup butter, softened
2½ (8-ounce) packages
   cream cheese, softened
1 cup sugar
1½ tablespoons flour

1 teaspoon vanilla
¼ teaspoon salt
3 eggs
2 tablespoons whipping cream
1 cup chopped, toasted pecans

Combine cookie crumbs and butter; press onto bottom of a 9-inch springform pan. Beat cream cheese until creamy. Add sugar, flour, vanilla, and salt; mix well. Add eggs, beating well. Blend in cream. Pour over crust. Bake in a preheated 450° oven 10 minutes; reduce temperature to 200°. Continue baking 35–40 minutes or until set. Loosen sides. Cool completely. Drizzle with ½ Caramel Topping, ½ Chocolate Topping, pecans, remaining ½ Caramel Topping, and remaining Chocolate Topping. Store in refrigerator.

CARAMEL TOPPING:

½ (14-ounce) package
   caramels, unwrapped

⅓ cup whipping cream

Combine over low heat; stir until melted and smooth.

CHOCOLATE TOPPING:

4 (1-ounce) squares German
   chocolate, chopped

1 teaspoon butter
2 tablespoons whipping cream

Combine over low heat; stir until melted and smooth.

Recipes for the House that Love Built (North Carolina)

 Five of the seven species of sea turtles existing in the world today—all on the endangered species list—can be found in North Carolina's coastal waters. The most commonly seen turtle is the loggerhead, which nests on the state's beaches from May through August.

Amaretto Mousse Cheesecake

2 cups graham cracker crumbs
½ cup butter, softened
1 (¼-ounce) package gelatin
  powder, unsweetened
½ cup water
¾ cup light whipping cream
3 (8-ounce) packages cream
  cheese, softened

1¼ cups sugar
1 (5-ounce) can evaporated milk
1 teaspoon lemon juice
⅓ cup amaretto
1 teaspoon vanilla extract
Melted chocolate (optional)
Sliced almonds (optional)

Combine graham cracker crumbs with butter. Press in bottom and up sides of 9-inch springform pan; chill. In small saucepan, sprinkle gelatin over cold water. Let stand 1 minute. Stir over low heat until completely dissolved, about 3 minutes. Set aside. Whip cream; keep chilled.

In large bowl of mixer, cream cheese with sugar until fluffy, about 3 minutes. Gradually add milk and lemon juice; beat at medium-high speed about 2 minutes, until very fluffy. Gradually beat in gelatin mixture, amaretto, and vanilla until thoroughly blended. Fold in whipped cream. Pour into crust; chill 8 hours or overnight. Garnish with melted chocolate and/or sliced almonds, if desired.

Secret Recipes (North Carolina)

No-Bake Easy Cheesecake

2 packages ladyfingers
2 packages Jell-O No-Bake
  Cheesecake Mix (take out
  crumbs)
1 (8-ounce) package cream
  cheese, softened

3 cups milk
1 (12-ounce) container Cool Whip
1 can blueberry pie filling or
  your favorite fruit topping

Separate ladyfingers and place around sides and on bottom of springform pan. Mix cheesecake mix and cream cheese with milk until blended. Add container of Cool Whip and blend for 3 minutes at low speed. Pour mixture into pan. Refrigerate for 2 hours. Top with blueberry pie filling or fruit topping, or serve on side.

The Great Gourmet (New Jersey)

Strawberry Glazed Cream Cheesecake

CRUST:

¾ cup coarsely ground walnuts

¾ cup finely ground graham
  crackers

3 tablespoons unsalted butter,
  melted

Preheat oven to 350°. Place rack in center of oven. Lightly butter a 9-inch or 10-inch springform pan. Combine above ingredients and press into bottom of springform pan.

FILLING:

4 (8-ounce) packages cream
  cheese, softened

4 eggs

1¼ cups sugar

1 tablespoon lemon juice

2 teaspoons vanilla

Beat cream cheese by electric mixer or processor until smooth. Add eggs, sugar, lemon juice, and vanilla. Beat thoroughly. Spoon over crust. Set pan on baking sheet to catch any butter that may drip out. Bake 10-inch cake 40–45 minutes or 9-inch cake 50–55 minutes. Remove from oven. Let stand at room temperature 15 minutes.

TOPPING:

2 cups sour cream

¼ cup sugar

1 teaspoon vanilla

Combine above ingredients and blend well. Cover and refrigerate. When cake finishes baking, spoon Topping over, return to oven and bake 5 minutes longer. Let cool and refrigerate cake at least 24 hours or preferably 2–3 days.

GLAZE:

1 quart strawberries

1 (12-ounce) jar raspberry jelly

1 tablespoon cornstarch

¼ cup orange liqueur

¼ cup water

Wash and dry strawberries. Combine a little jelly with cornstarch in saucepan and mix well. Add remaining jelly, orange liqueur, and water and cook over medium heat, stirring until thickened and clear—about 5 minutes. Cool to lukewarm. Loosen cake from pan. Remove springform. Arrange berries on top, pointed end up. Spoon Glaze over. Return to refrigerator until Glaze is set. Yields 10–12 servings.

Nothing Could Be Finer (North Carolina)

Blueberry Swirl Cheesecake

This is the easiest cheesecake I have ever found. It tastes like a traditional recipe, but it's not as time-consuming. You don't need a springform pan for this cheesecake, and the swirls of fruit make this beautiful as well as delicious.

2 (8-ounce) packages cream
  cheese, softened
½ cup sugar
¼ teaspoon vanilla

2 eggs, beaten
1 graham cracker crust
1 (21-ounce) can blueberry
  pie filling, divided

Beat cream cheese, sugar, and vanilla until smooth. Add eggs and mix. Pour into crust. Drop several tablespoonfuls of pie filling onto top of cream cheese mixture. Swirl blueberries with a knife. Bake at 350° for 35–40 minutes. Cool on wire rack. Chill for at least 2 hours. Serve with remaining blueberry pie filling.

Gritslickers (North Carolina)

Seafoam Frosting

Seafoam Frosting is often used on spice or devil's food cake. This is the best recipe I have ever tried.

2 egg whites
1½ cups brown sugar, firmly
  packed

Dash of salt
⅓ cup of water
1 teaspoon vanilla

Combine egg whites, sugar, salt, and water in top of double boiler. Place over rapidly boiling water and beat at high speed for 7 minutes, or until mixture will stand in stiff peaks. Add vanilla and beat until thick enough to spread.

North Carolina and Old Salem Cookery (North Carolina)

COOKIES and CANDIES

Originally gray, which was the color of the sandstone it was built out of, the White House in Washington DC was painted white to cover smoke stains caused by having been burned during the War of 1812.

Benne Cookies

1 cup benne (sesame) seeds
10 tablespoons butter, softened
10 tablespoons margarine,
  softened
1½ cups sugar
3 cups all-purpose flour

6 tablespoons milk
2 cups flaked coconut
½ cup chopped almonds
2 teaspoons vanilla
Dash of salt

Toast benne seeds until light brown; do not burn seeds. Cream butter, margarine, and sugar together until fluffy. Add flour and milk, stir until just combined. Add benne seeds, coconut, almonds, vanilla, and salt. Mix well.

Preheat oven to 325°. Take up about 1 tablespoon of dough for each cookie and roll into a 1-inch ball. Flatten slightly and place 1 inch apart on lightly greased cookie sheet. Bake at 325° for 15–20 minutes. Cool on racks. Makes about 6 dozen cookies.

Vegetarian Masterpieces (North Carolina)

Tryon Palace Ginger Crinkle Cookies

This recipe was provided in answer to many requests.

⅔ cup Wesson oil
1 cup sugar
1 egg
4 tablespoons molasses
2 cups sifted all-purpose flour

2 teaspoons baking soda
½ teaspoon salt
1 teaspoon cinnamon
1 teaspoon ginger
¼ cup sugar for dipping

Preheat oven to 350°. Mix oil and sugar thoroughly. Add egg and beat well. Stir in molasses. Sift dry ingredients together and add. Drop by teaspoonfuls into sugar and form into balls coated with sugar. Place on ungreased cookie sheet 3 inches apart. Bake for 15 minutes. Cookies will flatten and crinkle. Remove to wire rack. Yields 5 dozen.

Pass the Plate (North Carolina)

Jelly Topped Almond Bites

2 sticks butter, softened
1 cup sugar
1 egg
1 teaspoon almond extract
2 cups all-purpose flour
½ teaspoon baking soda
½ teaspoon salt
½ teaspoon nutmeg
1 cup quick-cooking or
    old-fashioned oatmeal, uncooked
1 (8-ounce) jar cherry jelly (or
    other tart red jelly, such as
    currant)
1 package chopped almonds

Preheat oven to 375°. Beat butter and sugar together until light and fluffy. Add egg and almond extract and beat until blended. Sift together flour, soda, salt, and nutmeg. Gradually add to creamed mixture and beat well. Stir in oatmeal. Shape dough into 1¼-inch balls. Place on ungreased cookie sheets and make a hollow in each ball. Bake for about 12 minutes. Cool on racks. Then place a small amount of jelly in each hollow and sprinkle with chopped almonds. Yields about 3½ dozen.

Note: Any flavor jam or jelly you prefer can be used instead of cherry.

The Other Side of the House (Virginia)

Almond Biscotti

Delicious with a warm drink; great for dunking!

1¼ cups whole almonds
2¼ cups flour
1½ teaspoons baking powder
¼ teaspoon almond extract
¼ teaspoon nutmeg
2 eggs
¾ cup sugar
¼ teaspoon salt
1½ teaspoons vanilla
¼ pound salted butter, softened

Preheat oven to 350°. Coarsely chop almonds and toast lightly. Let cool. Mix all ingredients well. Batter will be very thick. Divide into 5 logs; shape evenly. Bake for 45 minutes. Remove from oven and slice each log diagonally into strips. Put back in oven for 5–10 minutes until crispy.

Fair Haven Fare (New Jersey)

Unique Date Cookies

1 cup butter, softened
1 cup sugar
1 cup brown sugar
3 eggs

1 tablespoon vanilla
4 cups all-purpose flour
1 teaspoon salt
1 teaspoon baking soda

Cream together butter and sugars. Add eggs and beat until fluffy. Add vanilla. Sift together flour, salt, and baking soda and add to mixture. Mix well and chill. Before taking dough out of refrigerator, combine Filling ingredients. Roll out dough on floured board and spread with Filling. Roll up like a jellyroll and chill overnight. Slice into 1/8-inch thick pieces and place on lightly greased baking sheets. Bake at 375° for 12 minutes.

FILLING:

1 pound dates, chopped
1/2 cup sugar

1/2 cup water

Combine filling ingredients in saucepan and boil for 1 minute. Set aside to cool. Spread dough with cooled Filling.

A Cookbook of Pinehurst Courses (North Carolina)

Black Walnut Drop Cookies

These squares are rich but make luscious use of Carolina's full-flavored black walnuts.

1/2 cup shortening
1/2 cup butter, softened
2 1/2 cups dark brown sugar
2 eggs
2 1/2 cups sifted all-purpose
   flour

1/4 teaspoon salt
1/2 teaspoon baking soda
1/8 teaspoon walnut flavoring
1 cup crushed black walnuts

Cream shortening and butter. Add sugar and mix well. Add eggs and mix. Sift flour with salt and soda and add to creamed mixture with flavoring and nuts. Don't add any more flavoring because 1/8 teaspoon gives a fine walnut taste.

Drop by half teaspoons onto a greased cookie sheet. Bake in a moderate (350°) oven for about 10 minutes or until lightly browned. Makes about 5 dozen.

North Carolina and Old Salem Cookery (North Carolina)

3-C Cookies

(Chocolate, Cherries, and Coconut)

¾ cup butter, softened
1 cup packed brown sugar
1 egg
1 teaspoon vanilla
2¼ cups all-purpose flour
½ teaspoon salt
1 teaspoon baking powder
¾ cup chopped maraschino
  cherries
½ cup shredded, sweetened
  coconut
1 cup semisweet chocolate chips

Preheat oven to 350°. Cream butter and sugar together. Add egg and vanilla. Beat until fluffy. Blend in flour, salt, and baking powder. Add chopped cherries, coconut, and chocolate chips. Blend just until mixed. Drop onto ungreased cookie sheets and bake 9–11 minutes, depending on size of cookie and type of cookie sheet used. Remove to wire rack and cool.

Tried and True Recipes (Virginia)

Nannie White's Potato Chip Crunch Cookies

Delicious and crunchy. A dainty party cookie.

1 cup butter or margarine,
  softened
½ cup sugar
1 teaspoon vanilla
1½ cups crushed potato chips
½ cup chopped pecans
2 cups sifted all-purpose flour

Cream together butter or margarine, sugar, and vanilla. Add crushed potato chips and chopped pecans. Sift in flour. Form into small balls, using about 1 teaspoon dough for each. Place on ungreased cookie sheet. Press balls flat with bottom of a tumbler dipped in sugar. Bake at 350° for 16–18 minutes, or until cookies are lightly browned. If desired, sprinkle with colored sugar crystals and top each cookie with pecan half or candied cherry half. Makes 3½ dozen cookies.

Granny's Kitchen (Virginia)

Sandies

1 cup butter, softened
1¼ cups confectioners' sugar,
 divided
2 teaspoons vanilla

1 tablespoon water
2 cups sifted all-purpose flour
1 cup chopped pecans

Preheat oven to 300°. Cream butter and ¼ cup confectioners' sugar together. Add vanilla and water. Add flour. Mix well and add chopped pecans. Form small balls, and place on ungreased cookie sheet. Bake at 300° for 20–25 minutes or until slightly brown. While still warm, roll in remaining confectioners' sugar. Makes 3 dozen.

Cooking with Grace (Virginia)

Chocolate Marshmallow Cookies

These cookies will become everyone's favorites.

1¾ cups sifted cake flour
½ teaspoon salt
½ teaspoon baking soda
½ cup unsweetened cocoa
½ cup shortening
1 cup sugar

1 egg
1 teaspoon vanilla
¼ cup milk
18 large marshmallows, halved
36 pecan halves

Sift together cake flour, salt, soda, and cocoa and set aside. In a mixing bowl, cream shortening and sugar. Add the egg, vanilla, and milk; mix well. Add dry ingredients and mix well. Drop by heaping teaspoonfuls about 2 inches apart onto greased cookie sheet. Bake in preheated 350° oven for 8 minutes. Do not overbake. Remove from oven and top each cookie with a marshmallow half. Return to oven for 2 minutes. Remove cookies to wire racks to cool. Meanwhile, make frosting and spread on each cookie; top with a pecan half. Makes 3 dozen.

FROSTING:

2 cups sifted confectioners'
 sugar
5 tablespoons unsweetened
 cocoa

⅛ teaspoon salt
3 tablespoons butter, softened
4–5 tablespoons light cream or
 milk

Beat all ingredients until smooth and of spreading consistency and frost cookies.

Country Chic's Home Cookin (Maryland)

Opie's Trick or Treat Cookies

The best trick is to treat yourself to these.

½ cup butter or margarine, softened
1 cup sugar
1 cup plus 2 tablespoons firmly packed brown sugar
3 eggs
2 cups peanut butter
¾ teaspoon light corn syrup

¼ teaspoon vanilla extract
4½ cups regular oats, uncooked
2 teaspoons baking soda
¼ teaspoon salt
1 cup M&M candies
6 ounces semisweet chocolate chips

Cream butter; gradually add sugar. Beat well with an electric mixer at medium speed. Add eggs, peanut butter, syrup, and vanilla. Beat well. Add oats, soda, and salt; stir well. Stir in remaining ingredients (dough will be stiff). Pack dough into a ¼ cup measure. Drop dough, 4 inches apart, onto lightly greased cookie sheets. Lightly press each cookie into a 3½-inch circle with fingertips. Bake at 350° for 12–15 minutes (centers of cookies will be slightly soft). Cool slightly on cookie sheets; remove to wire racks and cool completely. Makes 2½ dozen.

Aunt Bee's Delightful Desserts (North Carolina)

The Andy Griffith Show writers came up with various names for its characters and locations from the small towns surrounding Mount Airy, North Carolina, where Andy Griffith was born in 1926. Among the obvious are: Mulberry (Mayberry), Pilot Mountain (Mount Pilot), Taylorsville (Andy Taylor), Lawsonville (Floyd Lawson), Crumpler (Helen Crump), Walkertown (Ellie Walker), Jonesville (Sam Jones), Warrensville (Warren Ferguson), and Stoneville (Mayor Stoner). All these towns are less than twenty-five miles from where Andy grew up.

Chocolate Kiss Macaroons

⅓ cup butter or margarine, softened
1 (3-ounce) package cream cheese, softened
¾ cup sugar
1 egg yolk
2 teaspoons almond extract
2 teaspoons orange juice

1¼ cups all-purpose flour
2 teaspoons baking powder
¼ teaspoon salt
1 (14-ounce) container flaked coconut
1 (9-ounce) package chocolate kiss candies, wrappers removed

One hour before baking, in a large mixing bowl, cream together butter, cream cheese, and sugar until fluffy. Add egg yolk, almond extract, and orange juice, and beat well.

In another bowl, combine flour, baking powder, and salt; add gradually to creamed mixture. Stir in all but ¾ cup coconut. Set remainder aside. Cover and chill dough 1 hour, or until it can be handled easily.

Preheat oven to 350°. Shape dough into balls 1 inch in diameter, then roll in remaining coconut. Place on an ungreased cookie sheet. Bake 10–12 minutes, or until lightly browned (watch to make sure coconut doesn't burn). Remove from oven; before cookies begin to cool, press an unwrapped chocolate kiss on top of each. Cool 1 minute, then remove to a wire rack to finish cooling. Yields 4–5 dozen cookies.

Red Pepper Fudge and Blue Ribbon Biscuits (North Carolina)

Thomasville, North Carolina, appropriately dubbed "Chair City," named its most conspicuous landmark, a thirty-foot replica of a Duncan Phyfe armchair, as its first official local historic landmark. The chair is located in the heart of downtown Thomasville, and is symbolic of the furniture industry's presence in the area.

Lemon Crispies

Great for a children's tea party.

1 box lemon cake mix
½ cup butter, melted

1 egg
1 cup Rice Krispies

Combine cake mix, butter, and egg in a mixing bowl. Gently stir in Rice Krispies. Roll dough into 1½-inch balls. Place 2 inches apart on an ungreased cookie sheet. Bake in a preheated 350° oven for 9 minutes or until edges are golden. Cool on cookie sheet for 1 minute. Remove and cool on a wire rack. Yields 25–30 cookies.

Capital Celebrations (Washington, DC)

Layer Cookies

FIRST LAYER:

½ cup Crisco
1 cup sugar
2 eggs

½ teaspoon salt
1½ cups all-purpose flour
1 teaspoon baking powder

Cream Crisco and sugar and eggs well-beaten. Add salt and vanilla. Sift baking powder with flour and add to egg mixture. Spread in long shallow pan and cover with Second Layer.

SECOND LAYER:

1 cup brown sugar
½ teaspoon vanilla

2 egg whites, beaten stiff
¾ cup chopped nuts

Spread this mixture over First Layer and bake in medium oven. Cut into squares when cool. They freeze well.

High Hampton Hospitality (North Carolina)

Marble Squares

1 (8-ounce) package cream
  cheese, softened
2⅓ cups sugar, divided
3 eggs, divided
¾ cup water
½ cup butter
1½ ounces unsweetened baking
  chocolate

2 cups all-purpose flour
½ cup sour cream
1 teaspoon baking soda
½ teaspoon salt
1 cup (6 ounces) semisweet
  chocolate chips

In a mixing bowl, beat cream cheese and ⅓ cup sugar until light and fluffy. Beat in 1 egg; set aside. In a saucepan, bring water, butter, and chocolate to a boil, stirring occasionally. Remove from heat. Mix in flour and remaining sugar. Stir in sour cream, baking soda, salt, and remaining 2 eggs until smooth. Pour into a greased and floured 10x15x1-inch baking pan. Dollop cream cheese mixture over the top; cut through batter to create a marbled effect. Sprinkle with chocolate chips. Bake at 375° for 30–35 minutes, or until a toothpick comes out clean. Cool. Yields about 5 dozen squares.

Bountiful Blessings (Maryland)

Cheesecake Bars

. . . a hit with everyone!

⅓ cup butter, softened
⅓ cup brown sugar

1 cup all-purpose flour
½ cup chopped nuts

Cream butter with brown sugar in small mixing bowl, add flour and nuts. Mix to make a crumb mixture. Reserve 1 cup for topping. Press remainder into bottom of 8-inch square pan.

FILLING:

¼ cup sugar
1 egg
1 (8-ounce) package cream
  cheese, softened

½ teaspoon vanilla
2 tablespoons milk
1 tablespoon lemon juice

Mix well and beat until creamy. Pour over crumb mixture. Sprinkle remaining crumbs over Filling. Bake at 350° for 12–15 minutes.

Mountain Potpourri (North Carolina)

Pecan Pie Squares

FILLING:

4 eggs, slightly beaten   **3 tablespoons margarine, melted**
1½ cups sugar   **1½ teaspoons vanilla**
1½ cups Karo syrup   **2½ cups chopped pecans**

Mix all ingredients, except pecans, until well blended. Stir in pecans.

3 cups all-purpose flour   **¾ cup margarine, softened**
¼ cup plus 2 tablespoons sugar   **Dash of salt**

Heat oven to 350°. Grease a jellyroll pan. Combine ingredients until crumbly. Press firmly in pan. Bake 20 minutes. Pour Filling over baked layer; spread evenly. Bake 25 minutes. Cool. Cut in 1½-inch squares. Makes 36 squares.

Think Healthy (Virginia)

Pecan Caramel Cream Squares

16 vanilla caramels   **1 cup heavy cream, whipped**
24 large marshmallows   **1 cup graham cracker crumbs**
½ cup milk   **4 tablespoons butter, melted**
1 cup chopped pecan pieces,
  toasted

In top of double boiler place caramels, marshmallows, and milk, being careful not to let the bottom touch the boiling water. Cook, stirring occasionally until all is melted and smooth (about 25 minutes). Remove and cool. Stir in pecans. Carefully fold in whipped cream. Combine graham cracker crumbs and butter. Reserve ¼ cup. Press remainder into a greased 6x10-inch pan. Pour caramel mixture over. Sprinkle with remaining graham cracker crumbs. Chill overnight. Serves 6–8.

A Taste of History (North Carolina)

Sinful Caramel Squares

Rich, sweet squares layered with chocolate, caramel, and pecans.

1 (14-ounce) package caramels,
  unwrapped
⅔ cup evaporated milk, divided
1 (18¼-ounce) box German
  chocolate cake mix

¾ cup butter, melted
1 cup chopped pecans, divided
2 cups (about 12 ounces)
  semisweet chocolate chips

Preheat oven to 350°. Melt caramels with ⅓ cup evaporated milk over low heat, stirring until smooth. Keep warm. Combine remaining ⅓ cup evaporated milk, cake mix, and melted butter. Mix well. Press half of cake mixture into bottom of greased and floured 9x13-inch baking pan. Bake in center of oven for 6 minutes. Sprinkle ¾ cup pecans and chocolate chips over crust. Top with caramel mixture, spreading to edges of pan. Drop teaspoons of remaining cake mixture over top of caramel. Press gently to spread. Sprinkle with remaining ¼ cup pecans. Bake for 20 additional minutes. Cool completely. Cut into 2-inch squares. Yields 24 squares.

You're Invited (North Carolina)

Butterscotch Krispie Treats

½ cup butterscotch pieces
2 tablespoons butter

2½ cups mini marshmallows
2½ cups Rice Krispies

Combine butterscotch pieces and butter in a large microwaveable bowl. Cook uncovered 2 minutes at #7 POWER, or until melted. Stir in marshmallows. Cook uncovered 2 minutes or until marshmallows are softened, stirring 2 times. Stir until smooth. Stir cereal into mixture and with back of spoon sprayed with cooking spray, press into greased 8-inch-square dish. Cut into squares.

Turnip Greens, Ham Hocks & Granny's Buns (North Carolina)

Delaware became the first state by ratifying the U.S. Constitution on December 7, 1787, the first of the colonies to do so. In addition to being called the First State, Delaware is also known as the Diamond State, the Blue Hen State, and Small Wonder.

Cornflake Treats

1¼ cups white Karo syrup
1 cup sugar
1 cup peanut butter

4 cups cornflakes
2 cups peanuts

Bring syrup and sugar to a rolling boil. Then take off heat and add peanut butter. Mix well. Pour over cornflakes and peanuts. Mix well; then pour into a 9x13-inch dish. Press smooth. Cut into squares.

Recipes from Jeffersonville Woman's Club (Virginia)

Choco-Chewies

FILLING:
1 (12-ounce) package semisweet
   chocolate bits
2 tablespoons butter

1 (14-ounce) can sweetened
   condensed milk

DOUGH:
1 cup butter, melted
1 pound brown sugar
½ cup chopped nuts
2 eggs

2 cups all-purpose flour
1 teaspoon salt
1 teaspoon vanilla

Melt Filling ingredients in top of a double boiler. In a large bowl, mix remaining ingredients. Spread half the Dough on a greased 10x15-inch cookie sheet; drizzle Filling over it, and top with remaining Dough. Bake at 350° for 30–35 minutes. Cut squares before cooling. May be frozen. Do not double.

The Belle Grove Plantation Cookbook (Virginia)

Chinese Chews

¾ cup all-purpose flour
1 cup sugar
1 (8-ounce) box chopped dates

2 cups chopped pecans
2 eggs
Confectioners' sugar

Mix flour, sugar, dates, and nuts together. Add well-beaten eggs to mixture and mix well. Pat out in pan about 12x14 inches. Bake at 375° about 30 minutes or until golden brown. Cool. Cut into squares and coat with confectioners' sugar.

Gather 'Round Our Table (Virginia)

Chocolate Bars

3 squares unsweetened chocolate	1½ cups sugar
1½ sticks butter	¾ cup all-purpose flour
3 eggs	¾ cup chopped pecans

Preheat oven to 350°. Melt chocolate and butter over very low heat. Cool. Beat eggs and sugar together and add to chocolate mixture. Add flour and nuts. Mix well. Spread into a 9x13-inch pan and bake 20 minutes, no more. Cool.

ICING:

6 tablespoons butter, softened	3 tablespoons evaporated milk
3 cups powdered sugar	1 teaspoon vanilla

Mix ingredients; spread over cool cake.

GLAZE:

1 square unsweetened chocolate	1 tablespoon butter

Melt chocolate; add butter, stir well. Drizzle over cake. Refrigerate. Makes 15 squares.

A Cook's Tour of the Azalea Coast (North Carolina)

Sour Cream Apple Squares

2 cups all-purpose flour	1 teaspoon baking soda
½ cup butter or margarine, softened	1 teaspoon salt
2 cups firmly packed light brown sugar	1 cup sour cream
	1 teaspoon vanilla
1 cup chopped nuts	1 egg
2 teaspoons cinnamon	2 cups peeled, finely chopped apples (about 2)

Preheat oven to 350°. Blend together flour, butter, and sugar until crumbly. Stir in nuts. Press 2¾ cups mixture into an ungreased 9x13-inch pan.

To remaining mixture add cinnamon, soda, salt, sour cream, vanilla, and egg. Blend well. Stir in apples. Spoon evenly over base. Bake 30–40 minutes until a toothpick inserted in center comes out clean. Cut into squares. Yields 18–24 squares.

Red Pepper Fudge and Blue Ribbon Biscuits (North Carolina)

Fresh Apple Blondies

Fresh apples add a special touch to these treats! Serve them with vanilla ice cream and Butterscotch Sauce.

2½ cups all-purpose flour
2 teaspoons baking powder
1 teaspoon baking soda
1 teaspoon cinnamon
1 teaspoon salt
2 cups sugar
1 cup vegetable oil

2 eggs
2 teaspoons vanilla extract
3 cups chopped apples
1 cup chopped nuts (optional)
1 (12-ounce) package (2 cups)
   butterscotch chips

Sift flour, baking powder, baking soda, cinnamon, and salt together. Combine sugar and oil in mixing bowl and beat until smooth. Add eggs and beat until thickened. Add dry ingredients and vanilla and mix well. Fold in apples and nuts, if desired.

Spoon into a 9x13-inch baking pan sprayed with nonstick cooking spray. Sprinkle with butterscotch chips and press chips down lightly with a spatula. Bake at 350° for 50–60 minutes or until a wooden pick inserted into center comes out clean. Cool on a wire rack, and cut into squares. Serve with Butterscotch Sauce. Serves 15.

BUTTERSCOTCH SAUCE:
2 cups packed brown sugar
⅔ cup light corn syrup
¼ cup butter

½ cup light cream
1 teaspoon vanilla

Combine brown sugar, corn syrup, and butter in saucepan and bring to a boil. Boil 5 minutes, then stir in cream and vanilla. Cool to room temperature and store in refrigerator. Also good served over ice cream or cake.

Oh My Stars! Recipes that Shine (Virginia)

Peanut Butter Bites

BAR:

½ cup creamy or crunchy
  peanut butter
¼ cup unsalted butter,
  softened
1¼ cups granulated sugar
2 large eggs, lightly beaten

1 teaspoon vanilla extract
2 cups all-purpose flour
1 teaspoon baking powder
½ teaspoon salt
1 cup chopped peanuts, plus
  more for garnish

Heat oven to 350°. Line a 9x13-inch baking pan with foil; generously coat with nonstick cooking spray.

In medium-size bowl, beat together peanut butter and butter. Beat in sugar until well blended; beat in eggs and vanilla. Stir in flour, baking powder, and salt. Add peanuts (mixture will be stiff). Press batter evenly into prepared pan. Bake in 350° oven 30 minutes or until bar pulls away from sides of pan. Let cool completely in pan on wire rack.

FROSTING:

½ cup creamy peanut butter
¼ cup unsalted butter,
  softened

½ cup confectioners' sugar

In medium-size bowl, beat together peanut butter, butter, and confectioners' sugar until smooth and fluffy. Spread over top of cooled Bar. Sprinkle with chopped peanuts, if desired, and cut into 36 rectangles.

Cooking with Love & Memories (North Carolina)

Peanut Butter Crunch Bars

1 stick butter
1 (16-ounce) jar peanut butter
3¾ cups powdered sugar

3 cups crispy cereal or cornflakes
1 (16-ounce) package semisweet
  chocolate chips

Melt butter over low heat in a saucepan. In mixing bowl, blend peanut butter and sugar. Add melted butter and continue to blend. Stir in cereal. Pile mixture into a lightly greased 9x13-inch pan and spread evenly over bottom of pan.

In a separate saucepan, melt chocolate chips over low heat. Spread melted chocolate evenly over cereal layer. Refrigerate to cool. Cut into bars. Makes approximately 30 bars.

Delightfully Seasoned Recipes (Virginia)

Dream Bars

1 (18¼-ounce) package
  chocolate cake mix
1 large egg
½ cup butter or margarine,
  melted
1 (6-ounce) package chocolate
  chips

1 (7-ounce) package walnut pieces
6 ounces flaked coconut
1 (14-ounce) can sweetened
  condensed milk

Grease a 9x13-inch pan. Preheat oven to 350°. Mix cake mix, egg, and butter together in bowl. (Mixture will be very stiff.) Spread mixture evenly in pan. Top with layers of chocolate chips, coconut, and walnuts sprinkled evenly over mixture. Pour condensed milk over all, as evenly as possible. Bake 30–35 minutes. Let cool completely before cutting into bars.

Secret Recipes (North Carolina)

Raspberry Brownies

24 ounces chocolate chips,
  divided
¼ cup margarine
11 ounces cream cheese,
  divided
1½ cups sugar

6 eggs, divided
2 teaspoons vanilla
1½ cups flour
¾ teaspoon baking powder
1 cup heavy cream, divided
⅓ cup raspberry preserves

Heat and stir 12 ounces chocolate chips and margarine until melted and blended; set aside. Beat 8 ounces cream cheese with sugar; beat in 3 eggs. Mix in vanilla, melted chocolate, flour, and baking powder. Pour into greased 9x13-inch pan; set aside.

Heat and stir 6 ounces chocolate chips with ⅔ cup cream until blended; set aside. Beat 3 ounces cream cheese with preserves. Add remaining 3 eggs and melted chocolate; pour over mixture in pan. Bake 50 minutes at 350°. Cool on wire rack. Heat and stir 6 ounces chocolate chips with ⅓ cup cream until blended. Spread over cooled brownies. Chill to set. Store in refrigerator. Makes 2½ dozen.

Sealed with a Knish (Maryland)

Special Brownies

A little bite goes a long way.

4 ounces unsweetened chocolate, divided
½ cup plus 2 tablespoons butter, divided

1 cup sugar
2 eggs, beaten
½ cup self-rising flour
½ cup chopped pecans

Combine 2 ounces unsweetened chocolate and ½ cup butter in a 4-cup microwave-safe bowl. Microwave on High until melted. Add sugar, eggs, and flour, and mix well. Stir in pecans. Spoon into a greased 9x13-inch glass baking dish. Bake at 350° for 20 minutes or until brownies pull away from side of dish. Let stand until cool. Spread Buttercream Frosting over the top. Chill in refrigerator.

Melt remaining 2 ounces unsweetened chocolate and 2 tablespoons butter in a saucepan, stirring to mix well. Pour over Buttercream Frosting, tilting the pan so the chocolate mixture will spread evenly. Let stand until cool. Cut into bite-size pieces. Yields 9–10 dozen.

BUTTERCREAM FROSTING:

¼ cup butter, softened
2 cups confectioners' sugar

2 tablespoons milk
½ teaspoon vanilla extract

Beat butter in mixer bowl until fluffy. Add confectioners' sugar, milk, and vanilla, and beat until smooth.

Seaboard to Sideboard (North Carolina)

 The Cape Hatteras Lighthouse, built in 1870 in North Carolina, is the tallest brick lighthouse (208 feet) in North America. The lighthouse was relocated in 1999, and moved away from the ocean to protect against beach erosion. Now located 1,600 feet from the shore, as it did at the time it was built, Cape Hatteras is the largest lighthouse ever to be moved due to erosion problems.

White Chocolate Brownies

1 cup unsalted butter
10 ounces white chocolate,
  broken in small pieces
1¼ cups sugar
4 large eggs

1 tablespoon vanilla
2 cups unbleached all-purpose flour
½ teaspoon salt
1 cup coarsely chopped pecans

Preheat oven to 325°. Line a 9x11-inch pan with aluminum foil, leaving a little overhang around the edges of the pan; butter the foil. (No aluminum foil necessary if disposable aluminum pan is used.) Heat 1 cup unsalted butter and chocolate, stirring frequently, in a large saucepan over low heat until melted and smooth. Remove from heat.

Using a wooden spoon, stir sugar into melted chocolate; then stir in eggs and vanilla. (The mixture will look curdled.) Add flour, salt, and chopped pecans, and quickly stir just until mixed. Pour batter into the pan. Bake the brownies until the top is lightly golden but the center is somewhat soft when pressed lightly, 30–35 minutes. Let cool to room temperature. Refrigerate the brownies at least 3 hours. Using the foil, lift the brownies from the pan. Cut into 20–25 squares, although larger portions are usually requested!

Recipe by John Tierney, Representative from Massachusetts
The Congressional Club Cookbook (Washington, DC)

Cape Hatteras
Lighthouse

Cape Lookout
Lighthouse

Bodie Island
Lighthouse

Chocolate Cookie Pizza

½ cup plus 2 tablespoons
   butter, softened, divided
½ cup brown sugar
¼ cup sugar
1 teaspoon vanilla
1 egg
1¼ cups all-purpose flour
½ teaspoon baking soda
3 tablespoons milk

1 (6-ounce) package chocolate
   chips
1 cup powdered sugar
½ cup pecan halves
½ cup M&M's
¼ cup shredded coconut
2 ounces white chocolate,
   melted

Preheat oven to 350°. In a large bowl, combine ½ cup butter, brown sugar, sugar, vanilla, and egg until well combined. Add flour and baking soda to make a stiff dough. Pat dough onto an ungreased 12-inch pizza pan or baking sheet. Bake in oven 15 minutes or until golden brown. Remove cookie from oven and let cool.

In a saucepan over very low heat, combine remaining 2 tablespoons butter, milk, and chocolate chips. Heat, stirring frequently, until chocolate is melted. Remove chocolate mixture from heat and stir in powdered sugar. Beat until smooth. If frosting is not glossy, stir in a few drops of hot water. Spread frosting over baked and cooled cookie. Immediately decorate with pecan halves, M&M's, and coconut. Press toppings lightly into frosting. Drizzle melted white chocolate over toppings. Let stand until set. If desired, remove from pan and cut into wedges. Makes 12–16 slices.

Down Home Cooking Done Right (North Carolina)

Norfolk, VIrginia, is the home base for the U.S. Navy's Atlantic Fleet. The U.S. Atlantic Fleet provides fully trained, combat-ready forces to support U.S. and NATO commanders in regions of conflict throughout the world.

Gobbler Goodies

¼ cup (½ stick) butter or
  margarine
4 cups miniature marshmallows
6 cups crisp rice cereal

28 chocolate sandwich cookies
1½ cups chocolate frosting
1 (12-ounce) package candy corn

Melt butter in saucepan. Add marshmallows. Cook over low heat until melted, stirring constantly. Stir in the cereal. Remove from heat and let cool for 10 minutes. With buttered hands, form cereal into 28 (1½-inch) balls. Twist apart the sandwich cookies. Spread frosting on each cookie half and use 28 halves as the base for each turkey.

Place each cereal ball on top of a frosted cookie half, pressing to adhere. Press 3 pieces of candy corn in a fan pattern on each remaining cookie half. Press each cookie half into a cereal ball to form a tail. Attach candy corn with frosting to form the turkey's head. Yields 28 Gobbler Goodies.

Beyond Peanut Butter and Jelly (New Jersey)

Goo Goo Clusters

2 tablespoons butter
1 (12-ounce) package chocolate
  chips
1 (14-ounce) can condensed
  milk

2 cups dry roasted peanuts
1 (16-ounce) package miniature
  marshmallows

In saucepan on medium to low heat, cook butter, chocolate chips and condensed milk about 10 minutes. Don't let it stick. Let cool, then stir in nuts and miniature marshmallows. Press into a buttered 9x13-inch pan. Refrigerate for 1 hour or more. Cut into squares.

If You Can't Stand the Heat... (North Carolina)

Lemon Bonbons

These would be very nice for a party because they are pretty as well as delicious.

1 cup butter, softened
⅓ cup confectioners' sugar
¾ cup cornstarch

1¼ cups sifted all-purpose
  flour
½ cup finely chopped pecans

Mix butter with sugar until light and fluffy. Add cornstarch and flour, mixing well. Refrigerate until easy to handle. Start oven at 350°. Shape dough into 1-inch balls. Place balls on nuts scattered on wax paper. Flatten with bottom of glass. Put cookies not-side-up on ungreased cookie sheet. Bake 15 minutes. Frost with Bonbon Frosting. Makes 4 dozen.

BONBON FROSTING:
1 cup confectioners' sugar
1 teaspoon butter, softened

2 tablespoons lemon juice

Blend sugar, butter, and lemon juice until smooth. Tint with desired food coloring.

Could I Have Your Recipe? (Virginia)

Tidewater Toffee

2 cups sugar
1 pound butter (do not substitute
  margarine)

1½ cups chopped pecans,
  toasted

Melt sugar and butter in a saucepan over medium heat. Bring to a boil, stirring often; bring temperature of mixture to hard-crack stage of 300°–310° (you must use a candy thermometer). Watch carefully and do not burn.

Stir chopped and toasted pecans into butter and sugar mixture; mix well. Pour quickly onto a lightly greased 10x15x1-inch baking pan. Cool to the touch; score top. Cool completely and crack into pieces. Serves 12.

Toast to Tidewater (Virginia)

Tiger Stripes

1 pound white chocolate
1 (12-ounce) jar chunky peanut
   butter

2 (8-ounce) packages semisweet
   chocolate, melted

Combine white chocolate and peanut butter in top of double boiler above water heated to boiling. Reduce heat and stir constantly until mixture is melted and well blended. Spread mixture onto a wax paper lined 10 x15-inch jellyroll pan. Pour semisweet chocolate over first layer and swirl through with a knife. Chill until firm. Cut into small squares. Store in refrigerator. Yields 6 dozen squares.

Heart of the Mountains (North Carolina)

Christmas Cheer Fudge

Superb! A must for Christmas, but you do not have to wait until Christmas to make this fudge, just omit the candied fruit.

2 cups sugar
1 cup half-and-half
⅓ cup white corn syrup
⅓ cup butter
¼ teaspoon salt
1 teaspoon vanilla

½ cup candied red cherries,
   halved
½ cup candied green pineapple,
   diced
1 cup broken walnuts
1 cup halved pecans

Combine sugar, cream, corn syrup, butter, and salt in a heavy saucepan. Cook and stir over medium heat until sugar is dissolved. Cover saucepan and boil 1 minute (this helps prevent sugar crystals from forming). Uncover, cook at medium steady boil to the soft-ball stage (236°) or until a soft ball forms in cold water. Remove from heat. Add vanilla and immediately beat with electric mixer at medium speed. Beat until mixture is creamy and begins to hold shape, about 10 minutes. Thoroughly mix in fruits and nuts. Pour into a greased 9-inch square pan. When firm enough, cut into squares. Let stand for 24 hours.

Holiday Treats (Virginia)

Chocolate Fudge

3 cups sugar
½ cup Hershey's cocoa
⅛ teaspoon salt
1 tablespoon white corn syrup

1½ cups milk
⅓ cup butter or margarine
1 teaspoon vanilla
1 cup chopped nuts

Butter a cookie sheet and set aside. Mix together sugar, cocoa, salt, corn syrup, and milk in a 4-quart saucepan. Over high heat, stir until mixture begins to boil. Clip candy thermometer to side of pan. Turn down heat to medium and cook without stirring until temperature on thermometer reaches 234°. Remove from heat. Add butter or margarine and vanilla. Do not stir. Let cool at room temperature 15 minutes.

Beat with a wooden spoon only until fudge begins to lose some of its gloss and starts to thicken. Add nuts and quickly spread into prepared pan. Cut into squares when cool. Store in an airtight container. Yields about 1½ pounds.

Hints:
(1) Be sure to use a pan large enough to prevent boiling over during cooking.
(2) Mixture will boil quickly, but will take 20–25 minutes to reach 234°; set timer for 20 minutes, then check temperature.
(3) Do not stir after mixture reaches boiling—it causes graininess.
(4) In hot weather, you may want to allow an extra degree of temperature (235°).
(5) Don't overbeat; it makes the fudge too hard.

Red Pepper Fudge and Blue Ribbon Biscuits (North Carolina)

The world's first synthetic fiber, Nylon, was discovered in Wilmington, Delaware, by DuPont researchers, led by Dr. Wallace H. Carothers in the 1930s. Although World War II dampened the initial excitement that surrounded this astonishing creation, the post–war consumer boom saw the explosion of many types of Nylon products. Toothbrushes, women's stockings, lingerie, brushes, shirts, rope, shoe laces, parachutes, and many more products that people use every day all incorporate the use of Nylon.

Spanish Gold Bricks

So easy and just delicious!

1 package graham crackers
½ cup finely chopped pecans
½ cup butter

½ cup margarine
½ cup sugar

Separate sections of graham crackers and line on ungreased jellyroll pan so that sides of graham crackers are touching. Sprinkle finely chopped pecans evenly over graham crackers. In a saucepan, melt together butter, margarine, and sugar. Boil and stir for 2 minutes. Pour slowly and evenly over the top of graham crackers and nuts until all are covered. Bake at 325° for 8–10 minutes. Cool in pan about 10 minutes. Separate with a knife. Store in an airtight container. These can be frozen.

Gourmet by the Bay (Virginia)

Pistachio Orange Drops

1 cup butter or margarine,
  softened
1 cup powdered sugar
1 teaspoon grated fresh orange
  peel
2 cups all-purpose flour

1 cup finely chopped pistachio nuts,
  divided
1 cup semisweet chocolate chips
2 tablespoons vegetable
  shortening

Preheat oven to 375°. In a large bowl, beat butter, sugar, and orange peel with electric mixer until fluffy. Stir in flour until well blended. Reserve 3 tablespoons pistachio nuts. Stir remainder into dough. Shape rounded teaspoonfuls into 1-inch balls. Arrange 1½ inches apart on cookie sheets. Bake 8–10 minutes until lightly browned. Remove to rack to cool. Melt chocolate and shortening in a small heavy saucepan over low heat; stir until smooth. Dip tops of cookies into chocolate mixture. Place cookies on rack; sprinkle with reserved nuts. Let stand until chocolate is set. Store in a cool place. Yields 72 cookies.

Cardinal Cuisine (Virginia)

Cherry Divinity

3 cups granulated sugar
½ cup light corn syrup
Dash of salt
½ cup cold water

2 egg whites
1 teaspoon vanilla
½ cup candied red cherries
½ cup chopped nuts

Place sugar, syrup, salt, and water in pan over low heat. Stir until sugar is dissolved. Cook until a small amount forms a soft ball in cold water—a candy thermometer takes the guesswork out of the job.

Beat egg whites until stiff and continue beating while pouring half the syrup in gradually. Cook remaining syrup until it forms a hard ball in cold water. Beat egg whites slowly until remaining syrup cooks. Add remaining syrup gradually. Continue beating until candy is thick enough to drop. Add vanilla, cherries, and nuts. A few drops of red vegetable coloring gives a prettier pink color. Drop on wax paper.

What Is It! What Do I Do with It! (North Carolina)

Pies and Other Desserts

PHOTO COURTESY OF NC DIVISION OF TOURISM, FILM AND SPORTS DEVELOPMENT. BILL RUSS, PHOTOGRAPHER.

America's largest privately owned home, Biltmore Estate, is nestled among 8,000 acres near Asheville, North Carolina. George Vanderbilt, son of industrialist Cornelius Vanderbilt, saw his 250-room chateau completed in 1895. This National Historic Landmark is one of the country's most visited historic residences.

Holly's "Best" Apple Pie

The best apple pie that you will ever eat. The secret is soaking the apples in melted butter. Serve warm to get the best rich butter flavor.

½ cup butter or margarine, melted	2 tablespoons flour
4 cups sliced apples	¾ teaspoon ground cinnamon
⅔ cup sugar	¼ teaspoon nutmeg
	1 (9-inch) pastry shell, unbaked

Pour melted butter over sliced apples and soak a few minutes. Combine sugar, flour, and spices. Remove apples from butter (reserve any that is left and use in Topping). Coat apples with sugar mixture; pour into pastry shell.

TOPPING:

½ cup all-purpose flour	¼ cup butter or margarine
¼ cup brown sugar	½ cup chopped pecans (optional)

Combine ingredients and crumble over apples. Bake at 400° for 40–45 minutes, or until brown and apples are tender. Serve warm with a scoop of vanilla ice cream.

Holiday Treats (Virginia)

Sour Cream Apple Pie

FILLING:

2 cups sliced Rome apples	1 egg (or substitute), beaten
1 (9-inch) pie shell	1 cup sour cream
¾ cup sugar	½ teaspoon vanilla
4 tablespoons flour	⅛ teaspoon salt

TOPPING:

⅓ cup sugar	¼ cup butter
⅓ cup flour	1 teaspoon cinnamon

Arrange apples (sliced and peeled) into unbaked pie shell. Mix remaining filling ingredients together and pour over apples. Bake at 350° for one hour. While pie is baking, blend topping ingredients together. Crumble this mixture over top of baked pie. Bake 15 minutes longer. Serve warm.

Note: Can use reduced-fat or fat-free sour cream or plain yogurt.

A Taste of GBMC (Maryland)

Berry Best Blueberry Pie

1 (9-inch) pie shell, baked
4 cups fresh blueberries,
    divided
1½ cups sugar
¼ teaspoon salt

3 tablespoons cornstarch
½ teaspoon grated lemon rind
¼ cup water
3 tablespoons butter
Whipped topping

Line a baked pie shell with 2 cups berries. Cook remaining 2 cups berries with sugar, salt, cornstarch, lemon rind, and water until thick. Remove from heat and add butter. Pour over the fresh berries. Cool. Serve with whipped topping.

Cabbage to Caviar (North Carolina)

Heavenly Pineapple Pie

1 (9-inch) pie crust
1 (20-ounce) can crushed
    pineapple with juice
Pineapple juice and water to
    make 1 cup
⅔ cup sugar, divided

1 envelope unflavored gelatin
¼ teaspoon salt
4 large eggs, separated
2 tablespoons lemon juice
½ teaspoon lemon rind

Prepare, bake, and cool pie crust. Drain and save juice from pineapple, pressing out excess juice with back of spoon. Add water to measure 1 cup. Mix ⅓ cup sugar with gelatin and salt in small saucepan. Beat egg yolks with 1 cup pineapple juice. Stir into gelatin-sugar mixture. Cook over very low heat, stirring constantly, about 10 minutes, until mix coats a spoon. Remove from heat. Stir in drained pineapple, lemon juice, and lemon rind. Cool until mix begins to jell. Beat egg whites to soft peaks. Gradually beat in remaining sugar (⅓ cup), beating to a stiff meringue. Gently fold into pineapple mix. Spoon into shell. Chill until firm. Makes 6 generous servings.

Atlantic Highlands (New Jersey)

In colonial times, pineapples were recognized as a symbol for hospitality. Sea captains would bring this exotic fruit home from their journeys and mount it on the fence post to indicate they were at home and available to receive visitors.

Tanglewood Manor House Restaurant's Tar Heel Pie

**12 ounces cream cheese,
  softened**
½ cup sugar
½ pint whipping cream

1½ medium bananas, sliced
**1 (9-inch) deep-dish pie shell,
  baked**

Mix softened cream cheese with sugar. Whip cream until stiff peaks form. Carefully fold cream into cheese mixture and mix until thoroughly blended. Slice bananas and place in bottom and sides of pie shell. Pour cheese mixture over bananas and chill until firm.

BLUEBERRY GLAZE:
1 package frozen blueberries
⅓ cup sugar

1 tablespoon cornstarch

Combine all ingredients and cook over low heat until thick. Be careful not to break up the berries. Cool to room temperature. Spoon Glaze evenly over cheese mixture and chill several hours or overnight.

North Carolina's Historic Restaurants (North Carolina)

Glazed Strawberry Pie

1½ quarts fresh strawberries
**1 (9-inch) pie crust, baked, or
  graham cracker pie crust**
1 cup sugar
2½ tablespoons cornstarch

Pinch of salt
½ cup water
1 tablespoon butter
Few drops of red food coloring
Whipped cream

Wash and hull berries. Put 1 quart of berries into prepared pie crust. Combine sugar, cornstarch, and salt in saucepan. Crush remaining ½ quart berries and place in saucepan with sugar and water. Bring mixture to a boil, stirring constantly and cook until thick and clear. Remove from heat; add butter and enough food coloring to make the color pronounced but not too red. Strain glaze and pour carefully over berries in pie shell. Cool before serving. Pipe edges around pie with whipped cream.

A Cookbook of Pinehurst Courses (North Carolina)

Sweet Potato Custard Pie

1 cup mashed sweet potatoes
1 cup sugar
2½ tablespoons butter, melted
2 eggs, separated
1 teaspoon vanilla
1½ cups scalded milk
1 pinch of nutmeg

Mix potatoes, sugar, and butter; beat well. Add egg yolks, vanilla, milk, and nutmeg; beat total mixture well. Beat egg whites stiff, and add them last; stir well. Pour into a 9-inch pie shell. Bake at 400° for 30 minutes, then reduce heat to 350° for 30 minutes. Test for doneness with a knife.

Come, Dine with Us! (Maryland)

I Would Kill for a Piece of Virginia Pie

1 (8-ounce) package cream cheese, softened
1 (14-ounce) can condensed milk
1 (16-ounce) carton frozen Cool Whip, thawed
1 stick margarine
½ cup flaked coconut
½ cup chopped pecans
½ cup caramel ice cream topping
2 pie crusts, baked

Combine cream cheese and condensed milk; fold in Cool Whip. Set aside. In frying pan, lightly brown margarine, coconut, and pecans. Let cool slightly. Divide cream cheese mixture into 4 parts. Divide caramel topping into 4 parts. Divide coconut-pecan mixture into 4 parts. Into each cooled pie crust, make a layer of cream cheese mixture, drizzle a layer of caramel topping over this layer; sprinkle a layer of coconut-pecan mixture over this. Repeat to make another layer of each in each crust. Chill until time to serve.

Pungo Strawberry Festival Cookbook (Virginia)

Born May 29, 1736, in Hanover County, VIrginia, Patrick Henry is perhaps best known for the speech he made in the House of Burgesses on March 23, 1775: "Is life so dear, or peace so sweet, as to be purchased at the price of chains and slavery? Forbid it, Almighty God! I know not what course others may take; but as for me, give me liberty or give me death!" This speech is credited by some with single-handedly instigating the Revolutionary War. Henry became the first governor of Virginia on July 29, 1776.

Coconut Crème Pie

4 tablespoons flour
¼ teaspoon salt
2 cups milk
2 eggs, separated
2 tablespoons butter

1 teaspoon vanilla
1 well-packed cup flaked coconut
½ cup sugar, honey or syrup
1 (9-inch) pie shell, baked

Mix flour and salt and add milk slowly, stirring well. Cook over medium heat, stirring constantly. When mixture has boiled and is thickened, remove from heat and add egg yolks, mixing thoroughly. Add butter, vanilla, coconut, and sugar, honey, or syrup. Cool and pour in baked pie shell. Prepare Meringue.

MERINGUE:
2 egg whites
¼ teaspoon cream of tartar

4 tablespoons sugar
1 teaspoon vanilla

Beat egg whites until peaks will hold. Add cream of tartar; slowly add sugar, beating well after each addition. Add vanilla. Seal pie with Meringue. Bake at 425° until lightly browned. Serve warm or cold.

Heavenly Dishes (North Carolina)

No-Bake Key Lime Pie
or Parfaits

2 cups crushed graham
  cracker crumbs
1 stick butter, melted
1 (14-ounce) can sweetened
  condensed milk

½ cup Key lime juice
Whipped cream
Fresh raspberries for garnish

Combine graham cracker crumbs and butter, and press into bottom of pie pan or parfait dishes. (You may use prepared graham cracker pie crust.)

In a bowl, mix condensed milk with Key lime juice until well blended. It will begin to thicken; pour into pie shell. Chill several hours before serving, then slice and top with whipped cream and garnish with raspberries. Yields 6 servings.

Hungry for Home (North Carolina)

Southern Nut Pie

2 (9-inch) unbaked pie shells
6 eggs
1¼ cups light brown sugar
2¼ cups light corn syrup
2 teaspoons vanilla, divided

3 tablespoons butter, melted
1½ cups finely ground peanuts
2 cups seedless raisins (optional)
1 cup whipping cream
¼ cup confectioners' sugar

Preheat the oven to 350° for 10 minutes before the pies are ready to be baked. Do not bake the shells.

Beat the eggs well. Add the brown sugar, corn syrup, and 1½ teaspoons of vanilla. Mix well. Add the melted butter and peanuts. Add the raisins, if desired. Pour the mixture into the pie crust shells. Bake at 350° for 40 minutes. Cool on a rack.

Whip the cream until stiff. Add the confectioners' sugar and ½ teaspoon of vanilla. Garnish the pies with the sweetened whipped cream. Makes 2 pies.

Favorite Meals from Williamsburg (Virginia)

Grasshopper Pie

32 large marshmallows, or
**   3 cups miniatures**
½ cup milk
¼ cup crème de menthe
3 tablespoons white crème de cacao
1½ cups chilled whipping cream

Few drops green food coloring (optional)
Chocolate cookie crust, homemade or prepared
Grated semisweet chocolate

Heat marshmallows and milk over medium heat, stirring constantly, just until marshmallows are melted. Refrigerate until thickened. Stir in liqueurs. Beat whipping cream in chilled bowl until stiff. Add food coloring. Fold marshmallow mixture into whipped cream. Pour into crust. Sprinkle with grated semisweet chocolate. Refrigerate at least 3 hours. Serves 6.

Cape May Fare (New Jersey)

German Chocolate Angel Pie

SHELL:

2 egg whites
⅛ teaspoon salt
⅛ teaspoon cream of tartar

½ cup sugar
⅛ teaspoon vanilla
½ cup finely chopped nuts

Beat egg whites with salt and cream of tartar until foamy. Add sugar, 2 tablespoons at a time, beating well after each addition; continue beating until stiff peaks form. Fold in vanilla and nuts. Spoon into lightly greased 8-inch pie pan to form nest-like shell, building sides up to ½ inch above edge of pan. Bake at 300° for 50–55 minutes. Cool.

CHOCOLATE CREAM FILLING:

1 (4-ounce) bar Baker's German
  sweet chocolate
3 tablespoons water

1 teaspoon vanilla
1 cup heavy cream, whipped

Stir chocolate in water over low heat until melted; cool until thick. Add vanilla. Fold whipped cream into chocolate mixture. Pile into cooled shell. Chill 2 hours. Serves 6–8.

Out of Our League (North Carolina)

Asheville, North Carolina-native Thomas Clayton Wolfe (1900–1938) is considered to be one of the great writers of the 20th century. Wolfe's first novel, *Look Homeward, Angel,* was inspired by a stone angel statue that stands in Oakdale Cemetery in Hendersonville. A classic of American literature, *Look Homeward, Angel* has never gone out of print since its 1929 publication.

Mud Pie

1½ cups crumbled chocolate
  wafer cookies
3 tablespoons butter, melted
½ gallon coffee ice cream,
  softened

1 (16-ounce) can fudge topping
Cool Whip or whipped cream
Chocolate sprinkles

Make a crust of crumbs and butter in deep-dish pie pan. Freeze. Spread softened ice cream over crust. Freeze. Top with Cool Whip or whipped cream. Freeze. Sprinkle with chocolate sprinkles at time of serving.

Thought for Food (Virginia)

White Chocolate Pecan Mousse Pie

1 (15-ounce) package refrigerated
  pie crusts, divided
1 teaspoon flour
2 tablespoons butter
2 cups chopped pecans
1 cup vanilla milk chips or white
  chocolate baking bar, chopped

¼ cup milk
2 cups whipping cream
⅓ cup sugar
1 teaspoon vanilla extract
Grated chocolate or
  chocolate-flavored syrup
  (optional)

Preheat oven to 450°. Prepare 1 pie crust according to package directions for unfilled crust. Refrigerate remaining crust for later use. Place prepared crust in a 10-inch springform pan or 9-inch pie pan; press in bottom and up sides of pan. Flute top edge of crust with fork dipped in flour. Generously prick bottom and sides of crust with fork dipped in flour. Bake in preheated oven until golden brown, 9–11 minutes. Cool completely.

In a 10-inch skillet over medium heat, melt butter. Stir in pecans; cook, stirring constantly, until pecans are golden brown, about 6 minutes. Cool completely, about 1 hour. In a small saucepan over low heat, stirring with a wire whisk, melt vanilla chips and milk. Cool completely, about 1 hour.

In a large bowl, beat whipping cream until stiff peaks form. Fold in sugar, vanilla, melted vanilla chips mixture, and pecans; blend well. Spoon mixture into cooled crust. Refrigerate 4 hours before serving. Just before serving, garnish with grated chocolate or chocolate syrup, if desired.

Virginia Traditions (Virginia)

Peach Cobbler

15 medium peaches, sliced
1 tablespoon lemon juice
⅓ cup all-purpose flour

2 cups sugar
2 teaspoons ground ginger
1 teaspoon salt

Combine ingredients, mix well, and set aside.

PASTRY:
3 cups sifted all-purpose flour
2 teaspoons salt
1 cup shortening

½ cup water
3 tablespoons butter

Combine flour and salt. Cut in shortening. Sprinkle with water. Press dough into a ball. Roll out ⅓ of the dough and cut into thin strips. Roll out remaining dough for top crust.

Pour ½ the peach filling into a buttered 9x13-inch baking dish. Cover with pastry strips. Add remaining filling. Dot with butter, and cover with top crust. Slit center of top crust several times. Bake in 350° oven 1 hour. Makes 12 servings.

Food, Family, and Friendships (Virginia)

Ellie's Apple Crisp

6 large apples, peeled and
    sliced
½ cup orange juice
½ cup sugar
½ teaspoon cinnamon

¾ cup sifted flour
½ cup packed light brown sugar
¼ teaspoon salt
6 tablespoons butter or margarine

Arrange apples in a greased baking dish. Pour orange juice over apples. Combine granulated sugar and cinnamon and sprinkle over apples. Combine flour, brown sugar, salt, and butter to make a crumbly mixture. Spread over apples. Bake at 350° until apples are tender and crust is lightly browned, about 45 minutes. Makes 6 servings.

Variation: For a nutty flavor, add ¼ cup rolled oats and an additional table-spoon butter to flour mixture.

Aunt Bee's Delightful Desserts (North Carolina)

Deluxe Apple Tart

CRUST:

1½ cups all-purpose flour
½ teaspoon baking powder
½ teaspoon salt

¼ cup cold butter
¼ cup shortening
3½–4 tablespoons milk

Combine flour, baking powder, and salt; cut in butter and shortening with pastry blender until mixture resembles coarse meal. Sprinkle milk over surface; stir with a fork until ingredients are moistened. Shape into a ball; chill at least an hour. Roll dough to ⅛-inch thickness on a lightly floured surface. Fit pastry into an 11x17x½-inch tart pan or an 11-inch round tart pan with a removable bottom. Set aside.

ALMOND MIXTURE:

½ cup, plus 2 tablespoons
    blanched slivered almonds
½ cup sugar

1 egg
1 tablespoon melted butter

Position knife blade in food processor bowl. Add almonds; process until finely ground. Add sugar, egg and butter; process until well mixed. Spread mixture evenly over the bottom of the pastry; set aside.

FILLING:

2 cups water
2 tablespoons lemon juice
4–5 golden delicious apples
¼ cup sugar
½ teaspoon ground cinnamon

¼ cup butter
½ cup peach preserves
2 tablespoons water
2 tablespoons apricot brandy

Combine water and lemon juice. Peel and core apples; cut into ¼-inch-thick slices. Dip apples in lemon juice mixture; drain well. Arrange apples so slices are overlapping on top of Almond Mixture. Sprinkle with sugar and cinnamon. Dot with butter. Bake at 400° approximately 1 hour.

Combine peach preserves and water; cook over low heat, stirring constantly, until melted. Press through a sieve; add the brandy. After removing tart from oven, carefully brush syrup over tart. Cool. Remove rim of pan before serving. Yields 10–12 servings.

Cooking Along the Susquehanna (Maryland)

Chocolate Mousse

When you want a dessert that is just a little bite of something . . . this one is extra easy and has the taste of mousses that take hours.

1 (6-ounce) package chocolate chips	1 egg
2 tablespoons granulated sugar	Pinch of salt
1 teaspoon vanilla	¾ cup milk
	Whipped cream or whipped topping

Put chocolate chips, sugar, vanilla, egg, and salt in container of electric blender. Heat milk just to boiling; pour into six demi-tasse cups. Chill and serve topped with whipped cream or topping. Makes 6 servings.

What Is It! What Do I Do with It! (North Carolina)

Banana Pudding

North Carolina natives think of banana pudding as a dessert served everywhere. It was not until I received a request for the recipe from New York City that I began to realize, it is distinctive to this section.

½ cup plus 6 tablespoons sugar, divided	4 eggs
Pinch of salt	2 cups milk
3 tablespoons flour	Vanilla wafers
	Bananas

Blend ½ cup sugar, salt, and flour. Add 1 whole egg and 3 yolks and mix together. Stir in milk. Cook over boiling water, stirring, until thickened. Remove from heat and cool.

In a baking dish, arrange a layer of whole vanilla wafers, a layer of sliced bananas, and a layer of custard. Continue, making 3 layers of each.

Make a meringue of remaining 3 egg whites and remaining 6 tablespoons sugar. Spread over banana mixture and brown in 375° oven. Makes 8 servings. Serve cold, not chilled.

North Carolina and Old Salem Cookery (North Carolina)

Old-Fashioned Cold Bread Pudding

4 eggs
4 cups milk, divided
1½ cups sugar
2 teaspoons vanilla

6–8 cold biscuits
½ stick butter or margarine
½ teaspoon nutmeg

Preheat oven to 350°. Beat eggs with 1 cup milk. Add sugar, and beat to dissolve. Then add remaining milk and vanilla. Beat well. Pour in greased 9x13-inch dish. Crumble biscuits into it; lightly press into milk. Dot with butter or margarine and sprinkle nutmeg over all. Bake at 350° for 50–60 minutes until as brown as you like it.

Note: Can be baked in 2 medium-size baking pans, or halved for 1 medium-size pan.

Grandma's Cookbook (Virginia)

Crème Brûlée

An easy gourmet dessert!

2 cups light cream
5 egg yolks
3½ tablespoons sugar

2 tablespoons vanilla
¼ cup dark brown sugar

Preheat oven to 325°. Heat cream in top of a double boiler until warm. Do not allow water in bottom of double boiler or the cream to boil!

Use electric mixer to beat egg yolks; gradually add sugar. Very slowly add warm cream to egg yolk mixture. Allow mixer to run slowly while adding cream; add vanilla and pour into an uncovered 1½-quart oven-proof dish. (Do not use a flat dish since the custard will be too thin.) Place dish in a pan of hot water and bake 40–45 minutes or until set. Remove baking dish and pan of water from oven and sift the brown sugar over custard immediately; place custard under boiler for 1 or 2 minutes or until the sugar melts. Do not scorch! Chill until very cold! Easy—yet sensational!! Serves 6.

Note: Do not allow sugar to be thicker in some places than in others or it won't melt completely.

Words Worth Eating (Virginia)

Chocolate Dipped Strawberries

1 quart strawberries, washed and
  unstemmed
2 tablespoons butter
1 (6-ounce) package semisweet
  chocolate morsels

1 teaspoon vanilla or orange extract
  (try it both ways!)
1 (14-ounce) can sweetened
  condensed milk

Arrange strawberries on doilied plate. Place remaining ingredients in top of double boiler, and stir until blended. Serve in bowl over hot water and let guests hand dip strawberries. If there is any sauce left over, freeze and re-use as fudge sauce for ice cream. Serves 4. Wonderfully easy—wonderfully delicious!

Ship to Shore II (North Carolina)

Strawberries Bourbonnaise

This deliciously simple recipe is too good to be true. Make it for no reason and it will be something nobody will forget. Make it for a special occasion and it will become a tradition.

2 cups sugar
¼ cup unsalted butter
½ cup heavy cream
½ cup bourbon

1½ quarts strawberries, stemmed
  (the fresher the better)
Whipped cream

Use a heavy cast aluminum or black iron skillet and make sure bottom of pan fits burners. Place on medium heat until you feel heat penetrate through bottom of pan to hand held over pan. When pan is hot, immediately add sugar. Stir with long-handled wooden spoon. As sugar starts to melt, stir gently until you have golden-colored syrup. Remove from heat and add butter. When butter is melted, add heavy cream a little at a time . . . very carefully. Stir in bourbon. Let sauce cool down and pour into a glass container. Cover and refrigerate. When cool, this wonderful sauce will be caramelized.

To serve: Place strawberries in individual stemmed glasses. Pour caramel sauce over strawberries. Top with a dollop of whipped cream. Sauce can be kept in refrigerator for several weeks. Yields 8 servings.

Food Fabulous Food (New Jersey)

Cream Puffs

Take one and a half pints water and put into a porcelain kettle, let it come to a boil; add quarter pound butter and let it melt; then stir in quickly three-quarters pound flour, and three teaspoonfuls Royal baking powder (sifted into flour three or four times), this forms a stiff dough; take from fire, let cool, then beat in six eggs, (two at a time); stir to a smooth paste; have baking pan greased, take one large tablespoonful at a time and lay in the pan, a little space between each; bake about twenty minutes, in hot oven, to a delicate brown.

FILLING:

Take one pint fresh milk, two tablespoonfuls cornstarch, mixed with a little milk; quarter pound pulverized sugar and two eggs; stir well together, and cook until it thickens, stirring all the time; flavor with vanilla, or any seasoning you prefer; split the cake at one side, and fill with this cream.

The Old Virginia Cook Book (Virginia)

Chocolate Intemperance

1 (19-ounce) package Duncan Hines Fudge Brownie Mix	½ cup strong coffee
2 tablespoons water	3 eggs, separated
3 eggs	½ cup Kahlúa (or less)
1 pound semisweet chocolate bits	2 tablespoons sugar
	1 cup whipped cream

Mix brownie mix with water and 3 eggs. Bake in 2 foil-lined 9-inch cake pans until done, 350° for 15–18 minutes. Set aside to cool. Melt chocolate with coffee in top of double boiler. Remove from heat. Beat 3 egg yolks until pale yellow. Stir into cooled chocolate mixture. Gradually stir in Kahlúa.

In separate bowl beat egg whites, gradually adding sugar until stiff. Whip cream. Gently fold whipped cream into cooled chocolate and then fold in egg whites. Place one brownie layer in springform pan. Pour chocolate mixture over. Top with remaining brownie layer. Chill. This dessert serves about 20 people and freezes nicely.

Culinary Contentment (Virginia)

Chocolate Torte

1 stick butter
1 cup all-purpose flour
¾ cup chopped pecans
1 (8-ounce) package cream
  cheese, softened
1 cup powdered sugar

1 (9-ounce) carton prepared
  whipped topping
1 (6-ounce) package chocolate
  instant pudding mix
1 teaspoon almond flavoring

Melt butter in 9x13-inch baking dish. Sprinkle flour and nuts and spread until smooth with spoon. Bake in 350° oven for 15 minutes. Let cool. Cream cheese and sugar. Mix together 1 cup whipped topping and cheese mixture. Spread over crust as first layer. Prepare pudding as directed on box and add flavoring. Spread over first layer. Top with remaining whipped topping. Yields 12 servings.

Recipes from Our Front Porch (North Carolina)

Pumpkin Pie Dessert Squares

BOTTOM LAYER:

1 box yellow cake mix, divided
½ cup melted butter

1 egg

Grease bottom of 9x12x2-inch pan. Reserve 1 cup cake mix for topping. Combine remaining cake mix, butter, and 1 egg. Press into pan.

FILLING:

1 pound can solid-packed
  pumpkin
2½ teaspoons pumpkin pie spice

½ cup brown sugar, firmly packed
2 eggs, beaten
⅔ cup milk

Combine all ingredients until smooth. Pour over crust.

TOPPING:

1 cup reserved cake mix
¼ cup sugar

1 teaspoon cinnamon
¼ cup butter, softened

Combine all ingredients and sprinkle over filling. Bake at 350° for 40–45 minutes; or until knife inserted in center comes out clean. If desired, serve with whipped topping.

A Taste of Catholicism (Maryland)

Fruit and Cheese Pizza

1 (20-ounce) package refrigerated
  sugar cookie dough
1½ (8-ounce) packages
  cream cheese, softened
⅓ cup plus 2 tablespoons
  sugar

3 tablespoons brandy or orange
  juice, divided
1 teaspoon vanilla extract
4 cups thinly sliced fruit
¼ cup berries
½ cup fruit preserves (any flavor)

Preheat oven to 375°. Lightly spray a 14-inch pizza pan with vegetable spray. Cut cookie dough into ¼-inch thick rounds. Arrange in slightly overlapping pattern on prepared pan, covering pan completely. (Flour your hands before you start working with the dough to make this all go much easier.) Press dough together to seal. Make a ridge on edges of crust with your fingers (to hold the filling). Bake until puffed and golden, about 10 minutes. Cool completely.

Combine cream cheese, sugar, 1 tablespoon brandy, and vanilla in bowl. Spread evenly over crust. Arrange fruit in circular pattern over filling. Put berries in center. Melt preserves with remaining 2 tablespoons brandy in small saucepan over low heat. Brush over fruit. Chill for at least an hour before serving.

Angel Food (North Carolina)

More than half of the Atlantic coast's breeding population of great blue herons nests in Chesapeake Bay. The bay, the nation's largest estuary, and surrounding areas provide both the ideal food and habitat necessary for great blue heron survival. As a result, the great blue heron is rivaled only by the blue crab as the symbol of Chesapeake Bay wildlife.

Banana Split Trifle

1 (3-ounce) package vanilla
   instant pudding mix
4 cups milk, divided
60 vanilla wafers, divided
3 bananas, sliced
6 tablespoons chocolate syrup,
   divided
1 (15-ounce) can crushed
   pineapple, drained

1 (3-ounce) package chocolate
   instant pudding mix
1 (8-ounce) carton frozen
   whipped topping, thawed
10 maraschino cherries, halved
   and drained
¼ cup chopped pecans or
   walnuts

Prepare vanilla pudding according to package directions using 2 cups milk. Let stand 30 seconds to thicken. Arrange 30 wafers in bottom of a 3-quart glass, straight-sided bowl. Spoon vanilla pudding over wafers. Arrange sliced bananas over pudding. Drizzle bananas with 3 tablespoons chocolate syrup. Arrange remaining 30 wafers over chocolate and bananas. Spoon pineapple evenly over wafers.

Prepare chocolate pudding according to package directions using remaining 2 cups milk. Let stand 30 seconds to thicken. Spoon chocolate pudding over pineapple. Spread whipped topping over chocolate pudding, spreading to edges of bowl to seal. Cover with plastic wrap and refrigerate overnight. Before serving, arrange cherries over whipped topping; sprinkle with nuts. Drizzle remaining 3 tablespoons chocolate syrup over top. Makes 8–10 servings.

A Taste of Heaven—Haven of Hope and Healing (North Carolina)

Nicknamed the Queen City, Charlotte, North Carolina, was named in honor of Queen Charlotte, wife of King George III of England. A dessert called a "charlotte," which had its beginnings around the turn of the 17th century, was a British invention, served hot and probably also named after Queen Charlotte. But as adaptations were made, famed French chef Antonin Careme made the first cold charlotte (charlotte russe), which consisted of a mold lined with cake and filled with a custard.

Sleeping Meringue

1 angel food cake, sliced
  horizontally into halves
6 egg whites
¼ teaspoon salt
½ teaspoon cream of tartar
1½ cups sugar

1 teaspoon vanilla
1 cup whipping cream
2 cups sliced fruit, such as
  strawberries, peaches,
  blueberries, or a combination

Preheat oven to 450°. Place half the angel food cake in a buttered deep-dish springform pan with a hole. Beat egg whites in a large bowl until stiff peaks form; add salt and cream of tartar while beating. Add sugar and vanilla gradually, and beat 15 minutes. Pour meringue over cake half in pan. Place in oven. Turn off the heat, and go to bed (8–10 hours). Remove dessert from pan to a serving plate just before serving time. Whip whipping cream in a bowl, and spread over top of dessert. Garnish with fruit. Makes 8–10 servings.

Note: There is half a cake left over, so you can double the recipe and make two desserts, or just nibble on that extra half of the cake. I consider that a cook's benefit.

Celebrate Virginia! (Virginia)

Coffee Charlotte

A beautiful and delicious dessert, this is especially good for a dinner party. Prepare a day in advance of serving.

12 plain ladyfingers
2 tablespoons instant coffee
  granules
¼ teaspoon salt
⅔ cup sugar
2 packets unflavored gelatin

3 cups milk
¼ cup cognac
2 cups whipping cream, whipped
Grated semisweet chocolate
  for garnish

Split ladyfingers in halves and line bottom and sides of a 9- or 10-inch springform pan with cut surfaces inward. Combine coffee, salt, sugar, and gelatin in saucepan. Add milk and simmer until sugar and gelatin are dissolved. Remove from heat and stir in cognac. Chill until spoonful of filling mounds slightly. Fold whipped cream into filling and pour into prepared pan. Chill until firm. Remove sides of pan and garnish with chocolate. Yields 10 servings.

Carolina Sunshine, Then & Now (North Carolina)

Pecan Tassies

Nutty rich—a real favorite.

PASTRY:

1 (3-ounce) package cream
  cheese, softened
1 stick margarine, softened

1 cup all-purpose flour
Dash of salt

Blend together cream cheese, margarine, flour, and salt. Shape into 24 balls; press each ball into 1¾-inch muffin tins (press dough in bottom and sides with fingers, do not leave any holes).

FILLING:

2 eggs, beaten
1 cup brown sugar
2 tablespoons margarine, melted

1 teaspoon vanilla
Dash of salt
1 cup chopped pecans

Combine eggs, brown sugar, margarine, vanilla, and salt. Mix well (do not beat with beater, or tops will be crusty instead of nutty). Divide pecans evenly in pastry shells. Pour Filling in shells, filling ⅔ full. Bake at 350° for 20–25 minutes. Cool slightly before removing from pans. Cool on wire rack. Makes 24.

Variation: Lemon Tassies, substitute white sugar for brown; omit pecans and add 2 tablespoons lemon juice and 1 teaspoon lemon rind.

Granny's Kitchen (Virginia)

Cherry Holiday Dessert

1½ cups boiling water
1 (6-ounce) package or
    2 (3-ounce) packages
    sugar-free cherry Jell-O
1½ cups cold water
1 (21-ounce) can sugar-free
    cherry pie filling

4 cups cubed sugar-free angel food
    cake
3 cups cold milk
2 (3-ounce) packages sugar-free
    vanilla pudding
1 (8-ounce) carton whipped
    topping, divided

Stir boiling water into gelatin in large bowl at least 2 minutes until completely dissolved. Stir in cold water and sugar-free cherry pie filling. Refrigerate 1 hour or until slightly thickened and consistency of unbeaten egg whites.

Place cake cubes in 3-quart serving bowl. Spoon gelatin mixture over cake. Refrigerate about 45 minutes or until set but not firm (gelatin should stick to finger when touched and should mound). Pour milk into large bowl. Add pudding mixes. Beat with wire whisk 1 minute. Gently stir in 2 cups whipped topping. Spoon over gelatin mixture in bowl. Refrigerate 2 hours or until set. Top with remaining whipped topping and garnish as desired.

Editor's Extra: Can also be layered in a glass trifle dish for a beautiful presentation.

Favorite Recipes: Bayside Baptist Church (Virginia)

One of the world's most famous inventors was Thomas A. Edison, who invented the movie camera and phonograph in his labs in West Orange and Menlo Park, New Jersey. Also, the first incandescent lamp was made by Edison in 1879 in Menlo Park; Roselle, New Jersey, became the first town in the nation to be lighted by electricity in 1883. (The New Jersey town of Edison is named after him.)

Aunt Bee's Homemade Strawberry Ice Cream

6 cups sliced strawberries,
  fresh or frozen
2 cups sugar, divided
3 cups light cream

3 cups heavy cream
½ teaspoon vanilla extract
½ teaspoon almond extract
⅛ teaspoon salt

Sprinkle strawberries with half the sugar. Mix creams and remaining sugar, extracts, and salt. Freeze until partially frozen. Stir in sugared fruit and continue to freeze.

Thelma Lou could use this recipe with peaches instead of strawberries, and it would turn out just peachy. Makes 1 gallon.

Aunt Bee's Delightful Desserts (North Carolina)

Ice Cream Flower Pot

2 tablespoons chocolate cookie
  crumbs, divided
1 scoop chocolate ice cream
Green sprinkles

Gumdrops
Cookies or peanut butter cups
Candy spearmint leaf

To make the "dirt," place 1 tablespoon chocolate crumbs into bottom of a small clear plastic cup. Add a scoop of softened chocolate ice cream, followed by a second layer of cookie crumbs. For grass, put green sprinkles on top. Place a cut straw into center of flowerpot and freeze.

Meanwhile make a "flower" by sticking gumdrops into sides of a cookie or peanut butter cup with toothpicks. To serve, press the flower into the straw. Add a candy spearmint leaf. Makes 1 pot.

All American Recipes

List of Contributors

PHOTO ©DOUG WILSON / VIRGINIA TOURISM CORPORATION.

The Tomb of the Unknowns (a.k.a. Tomb of the Unknown Soldier) in Arlington National Cemetery, Virginia, is dedicated to American soldiers from World Wars I and II, the Korean Conflict, and the Vietnam War who died without their remains being identified. The Tomb is guarded 24 hours a day by specially trained members of the 3rd Infantry Division, U.S. Army.

Listed below are the cookbooks that have contributed recipes to this book, along with copyright, author, publisher, city, and state, when applicable.

Angel Food, Norma Johnson, Pinehurst, NC

Apron Strings ©1983 The Women's Committee of the Richmond Symphony, Richmond, VA

Around the Table, Mothers' Center of Monmouth County, Little Silver, NJ

Atlantic Highlands, Atlantic Highlands Historical Society, Atlantic Highlands, NJ

Aunt Bee's Delightful Desserts ©1996 Ken Beck and Jim Clark, Rutledge Hill Press, Nashville, TN

Barineau-Williams Family Cookbook, Vol. II, Barineau-Williams Family, DE

The Belle Grove Plantation Cookbook ©1986 Belle Grove, Inc., Middletown, VA

The Best of the Bushel ©1987 The Junior League of Charlottesville, VA

The Best of Mayberry ©1996 Betty Conley Lyerly, Mount Airy, NC

Best of Friends ©2000 Friends of Baltimore Parent's Association, Baltimore, MD

Beyond Peanut Butter and Jelly ©2000 International Nanny Association, Collingswood, NJ

Bill Neal's Southern Cooking ©1989 William F. Neal, The University of North Carolina Press, Chapel Hill, NC

Blackened Mountain Seasonings, Kemper Bornman, Linda Warren, and Suzanne Goodell, Bayou Ladies, Black Mountain, NC

The Boar's Head Cookbook, Felicia Rogan, Boar's Head Inn, Charlottesville, VA

Bountiful Blessings, St. John Lutheran Church, Linthicum, MD

Bravo ©1984 The Greensboro Symphony Guild, Greensboro, NC

Bread of Life, Joy Circle of the Christian Women's Fellowship, Silver Spring, MD

Breakfast at Nine, Tea at Four ©1998 Callawind Publications, Inc., Sue Carroll, Cape May, NJ

Cabbage to Caviar, Ellen Powell, Reidsville, NC

Cape May Fare, Mid-Atlantic Center for the Arts, Cape May, NJ

Capital Celebrations ©1997 The Junior League of Washington, DC

Capital Classics ©1989 Junior League of Washington, DC

Cardinal Cuisine, Mount Vernon Hospital Auxiliary, Alexandria, VA

Carolina Sunshine, Then & Now ©1996 Charity League of Charlotte, NC

Celebrate Virginia! ©2002 James A. Cruchfield, Rowena Fullinwider, and Winette Sparkman Jeffrey, Norfolk, VA

Celebrations...Food, Family, and Fun ©1999 The Fayetteville Academy, Fayetteville, NC

Centenary Cookbook, United Methodist Women, Centenary United Methodist Church, Winston-Salem, NC

Chesapeake Bay Country ©1987 W.C. (Bill) Snyder, The Donning Company Publishers, Atglen, PA

Chesapeake's Bounty ©2000 Conduit Presse, Katie Moose, Annapolis, MD

Children's Party Book ©1984 The Junior League of Hampton Roads, Inc., Newport News, VA

Christmas Favorites, Mary Ann Crouch and Jan Stedman, Charlotte, NC

Coastal Cuisine ©1999 Connie Correia Fisher with Joanne Correia, Small Potatoes Press, Collingswood, NJ

Collected Recipes ©1995 Linda D. Channell, Allamuchy, NJ

Come, Dine with Us, The Gravenor's, Salisbury, MD

Command Performances ©1989 Friends of the Opera, Southwest Virginia Opera Society, Inc., Roanoke, VA

The Congressional Club Cookbook ©1998 The Congressional Club, Washington, DC

Cook's Tour of the Eastern Shore ©1948 Easton Maryland Memorial Hospital Junior Auxiliary, Centreville, MD

A Cook's Tour of the Azalea Coast ©1982 The Auxiliary to the Medical Society of New Hanover, Wilmington, NC

A Cookbook of Pinehurst Courses ©1980 Moore Regional Hospital Auxiliary, Moore Regional Hospital Auxiliary, Pinehurst, NC

A Cookbook of Treasures, Trinity Presbyterian Church, Claymont, DE

Cookin' for the Cure, Relay for Life Team "Shining Stars for a Cure", Salem, VA

Cooking with the Allenhurst Garden Club, The Allenhurst Garden Club, Allenhurst, NJ

Cooking with Heart in Hand ©1987 Suzanne Winningham Worsham, Clifton, VA

Cooking Along the Susquehanna, Susquehanna Museum of Havre de Grace, Havre de Grace, MD

Cooking with the Sandhills Woman's Exchange, Sandhills Woman's Exchange, Pinehurst, NC

Cooking with Grace ©2005 Grace and Holy Trinity Episcopal Church Women, Richmond, VA

Cooking with Love & Memories, Corinth Baptist Church WOM, Monroe, NC

Cooking with Class, Volume II ©1990 Union Baptist Church, Ruth Bible Class, Chincoteague, VA

Cooking Through the Years, Clara Maass Medical Center Auxiliary, Belleville, NJ

Could I Have Your Recipe? ©1981 Janice Porter, Reston, VA

Country Treasures, Virginia Farm Bureau, Richmond, VA

Country Chic's Home Cookin, Christine C. Milligan, Preston, MD

Country Home Favorites ©2004 Peggy Gebauer, Vinton, VA

Culinary Secrets of Great Virginia Chefs ©1995 Martha Hollis Robinson, Thomas Nelson Publishers, Nashville, TN

Culinary Contentment ©1984 Virginia Tech Faculty Women's Club, Blacksburg, VA

The Curran Connection Cookbook, Carol (Cammy) Curran, Pinehurst, NC

Dan River Family Cookbook ©1982 Dan River, Inc., DBA Dan River Outlet, Danville, VA

DAPI's Delectable Delights, Delaware Adolescent Program, Inc., Camden, DE

A Dash of Down East ©1986 The Junior Guild of Rocky Mount, Inc., Rocky Mount, NC

Davie County Extension and Community Association Cookbook, Davie County ECA, Inc., Mocksville, NC

Delectable Cookery of Alexandria ©1973 Polly Norment and Anne Mudd Cabaniss, Alexandria, VA

Delightfully Seasoned Recipes, 911 Emergency Communications Center, Virginia Beach, VA

Dining by Fireflies ©1994 Junior League of Charlotte, Inc., Charlotte, NC

Discovery Tour 2006 Cookbook, Breaks District Boy Scouts, Gundy, VA

Down Home Cooking Done Right, New Life Women's Leadership Project, Williamston, NC

The Enlightened Titan ©1988 The Patrons Association of Trinity Episcopal School, Richmond, VA

Even More Special ©1986 The Junior League of Durham and Orange Counties, Inc., Durham, NC

Fair Haven Fare, Fair Haven PTA, Fair Haven, NJ

Favorite Recipes: Bayside Baptist Church ©2004 Bayside Baptist Church, Bayside Baptist Church Women's Ministry, Virginia Beach, VA

Favorite Recipes of the Lower Cape Fear, The Ministering Circle, Wilmington, NC

Favorite Meals from Williamsburg ©1982 Colonial Williamsburg Foundation, Williamsburg, VA

Favorite Recipes: Barbara's Best Volume II, Barbara D. Boothe, Lottsburg, VA

The Fearington House Cookbook ©1987 Jenny Fitch, Jenny Fitch, Ventana Press, Chapel Hill, NC

Feeding the Flock, First Baptist Church, Southport, NC

The Fine Art of Dining, Muscarelle Museum of Art, Williamsburg, VA

Flavors of Cape Henlopen, Village Improvement Association, Rehoboth Beach, DE

Food, Family, and Friendships ©1996 Mary M. Darden and Margaret T. Proffitt, Virginia Beach, VA

Food Fabulous Food ©1997 The Women's Board to Cooper Health System, Camden, NJ

Frantic Elegance ©1989 Arendell Parrott Academy, Kinston, NC

From Our Home to Yours ©2003 Lisa Shively Cookbooks, Lisa Lofton Shively, Eden, NC

From Ham to Jam, Mary Baldwin Alumnae Association, Staunton, VA

Frugal Family Recipes ©2005 BlueRidgePublishing.com, Michelle Jones, King, NC

Gardeners in the Kitchen, New Market Garden Club, New Market, MD

Gather 'Round Our Table ©2005 Edith Vick Farris, Massanutten, VA

The Glen Afton Cookbook ©1999 The Glen Afton Women's Club, Trenton, NJ

God & Country Cookbook ©2002 First United Methodist Church, Forest City, NC

Goodness Grows in North Carolina ©1989 North Carolina Department of Agriculture, Marketing Division, Raleigh, NC

Gourmet by the Bay ©1989 Dolphin Circle of the King's Daughters and Sons, Virginia Beach, VA

Grandma's Cookbook, Don Hopkins, Hopkins Enterprises, Spencer, VA

Granny's Taste of Christmas ©2006 Dianne C. Evans, EvanCraft, Inc., Charlotte, NC

Granny's Kitchen, Theone L. Neel, Bastian, VA

The Great Gourmet, St. Gregory the Great PTA, Hamilton Square, NJ

The Great Taste of Virginia Seafood Cookbook ©1984 Mary Reid Barrow and Public Relations Institute, Inc., Mary Reid Barrow with Robin Browder, The Donning Company Publishers, Atglen, PA

The Great Chefs of Virginia Cookbook ©1987 Virginia Chefs Association, The Donning Company Publishers, Atglen, PA

Gritslickers ©2005 Lisa Shively Cookbooks, Lisa Lofton Shively, Eden, NC,

The Ham Book ©1987 Monette R. Harrell and Robert W. Harrell, The Donning Company Publishers, Smithfield, VA

Have Fun Cooking with Me, Lela J. Clarke, Statesville, NC

Have Fun Cooking with Me Again and Again ©1999 Lela J. Clarke, Statesville, NC

Heart of the Mountains ©1987 Buncombe County Extension Homemakers, Asheville, NC

Hearthside Cooking ©1986 Nancy Carter Crump, McLean, VA

A Heavenly Taste You Can't Miss, Dreama Dee Robinson, Graham, NC

Heavenly Dishes, Sandy Plains WMU, New Life Pregnancy Services, Gastonia, NC

High Hampton Hospitality ©1970 Lily Byrd, Cashiers, NC

Historic Lexington Cooks ©1989 Historic Lexington Foundation, Lexington, VA

Holiday Treats, Theone L. Neel, Bastian, VA

Holiday Fare ©2004 The Colonial Williamsburg Foundation, John R. Gonzales, Colonial Williamsburg Foundation, Williamsburg, VA

Hungry for Home ©2003 Amy Rogers, John F. Blair, Publisher, Winston-Salem, NC

The Hunt Country Cookbook ©1963 Warrenton Antiquarium Society, Warrenton, VA

I Remember ©1988 Hank Kellner, Simmer Pot Press, Boone, NC

If You Can't Stand the Heat..., Volunteer Fire Department/Ladies Auxiliary, New Bern, NC

In the Kitchen with Kendi, Volume 1 ©1999 Kendi O'Neill, Diversions Publications, Frederick, MD

In Good Company ©1999 Junior League of Lynchburg, VA

In Good Taste ©1983 Department of Nutrition, School of Public Health of the University of North Carolina, Chapel Hill, NC

Island Born and Bred ©1987 Harkers Island United Methodist Women, Harkers Island, NC

It's Delicious! ©2003 Hospitality House of Richmond, Inc., Richmond, VA

Jarrett House Potpourri, The Jarrett House, Dillsboro, NC

Jaycee Cookin', Annapolis Maryland Jaycees Cookbook Committee, Annapolis, MD

Just Like Mama's, Judy Hensley, Gate City, VA

Kids in the Kitchen, O. T. Bonner Middle School, Danville, VA

Knollwood's Cooking, Knollwood Baptist Church, Winston-Salem, NC

Korner's Folly Cookbook ©1977 Beth Tartan and Fran Parker, TarPar Ltd., Kernersville, NC

Lambertville Community Cookbook ©1996 Kalmia Club of Lambertville, NJ

A Laugh & A Glass of Wine, Bonnie L. DeLelys, Fredericksburg, VA

Let Us Keep the Feast in Historic Beaufort ©2001 St. Paul's Episcopal Church Women, Beaufort, NC

Love Yourself Cookbook ©1987 Edie Low, Charlotte, NC

Loving, Caring and Sharing, Cordelia Higgins, Crewe, VA

Making Time ©1998 Arendell Parrott Academy, Kinston, NC

Mama Dip's Family Cookbook ©2005 Mildred Council, University of North Carolina Press, Chapel Hill, NC

Marion Brown's Southern Cook Book ©1980 The University of North Carolina Press, Marion Brown, Chapel Hill, NC

Market to Market ©1983 The Service League of Hickory, NC

Mary B's Recipes, Mary Anne Fritts, Burlington, NC

Maryland's Way ©1963 Hammond-Harwood House Association, The Hammond-Harwood House, Annapolis, MD

Maryland's Historic Restaurants and their Recipes ©1995 Dawn O'Brien and Rebecca Schenck, John F. Blair, Publisher, Winston-Salem, MC

A Matter of Taste ©1989 The Junior League of Morristown, NJ

Mennonite Country-Style Recipes ©1987 Herold Press, Esther H. Shank, Scottdale, PA

Mennonite Community Cookbook ©1950, 1957, 1978 Mary Emma Showalte, Herald Press, Scottdale, PA

The Microwave Touch ©1984 The Microwave Touch, Galen N. Hill, Greensboro, NC

Modern Recipes from Historic Wilmington ©2003 Lower Cape Fear Historical Society, Ann Hertzler and Merle Chamberlain, Wilmington, NC

More Richmond Receipts ©1990 Jan Carlton, J&B Editions, Norfolk, VA

More Favorites from the Melting Pot, Church of Saint Athanasius, Baltimore, MD

Mountain Potpourri ©1979 The Haywood County Hospital Auxiliary, Clyde, NC

Mountain Elegance ©1982 The Junior League of Asheville, NC

Mrs. Rowe's Favorite Recipes, Mrs. Rowe's Restaurant and Bakery, Staunton, VA

Mrs. Claus' Favorite Recipes, Janet P. Yarborough, Elon, NC

Mushrooms, Turnip Greens & Pickled Eggs ©1971 Frances Carr Parker, TarPar Ltd., Kernersville, NC

My Favorite Maryland Recipes ©1964 Helen Avalynne Tawes, Tidewater Publishers, Centreville, MD

My Table at Brightwood, April Miller, Brightwood, Chatham, VA

North Carolina and Old Salem Cookery ©1955 Elizabeth Hedgecock Sparks, Beth Tartan, TarPar Ltd., Kernersville, NC

North Carolina's Historic Restaurants and Their Recipes ©1983 Dawn O'Brien, John F. Blair, Publisher, Winston-Salem, NC

Nothing Could Be Finer ©1982 The Junior League of Wilmington, NC

Of Tide & Thyme ©1995 The Junior League of Annapolis, MD

Oh My Stars! Recipes that Shine ©2000 Junior League of Roanoke Valley, VA

The Old Virginia Cook Book, Ladies Auxiliary of the U.M.C.A., Petersburg, VA

The Other Side of the House ©1985 Janie Whitehurst, The Donning Company Publishers, Virginia Beach, VA

Our Favorite Recipes–Book Three, Enterprise Fire Co. Ladies Auxiliary, Mercerville, NJ

Our Best to You!, The Edwards Family of Franklin, VA

Our Favorite Recipes, Damascus United Methodist Women, Damascus, MD

Out of Our League ©1978 Junior League of Greensboro, NC

Pass the Plate ©1984 Pass the Plate, Inc., Alice G. Underhill and Barbara S. Stewart, New Bern, NC

A Pinch of Gold ©2002 Special Olympics North Carolina, Morrisville, NC

Pungo Strawberry Festival Cookbook, Pungo Strawberry Festival, Virginia Beach, VA

Queen Anne's Table, Edenton Historical Commission, Edenton, NC

The Queen Victoria® Cookbook ©1992 Joan and Dane Wells, Cape May, NJ

The Rappahannock Seafood Cookbook ©1984 Rappahannock Community College Educational Foundation, Inc., Warsaw, VA

Recipes from Jeffersonville Woman's Club, Jeffersonville Woman's Club, Tazewell, VA

Recipes from Home, Fontaine Ruritan Club, Fieldale, VA

Recipes for the House that Love Built, Ronald McDonald House of Durham, NC

Recipes from Our Front Porch ©1982 Ella Jo and John Shell, Hemlock Inn, Bryson City, NC

Red Pepper Fudge and Blue Ribbon Biscuits ©1995 Amy Rogers, Down Home Press, Winston-Salem, NC

Restaurant Recipes from the Shore and More..., Calvary Chapel Christian Center, Ocean City, MD

Richmond Receipts ©1987 Jan Carlton, The Donning Company Publishers, Atglen, PA

A River's Course ©2005 Junior Charity League of Shelby, NC

Seaboard to Sideboard ©1988 Junior League of Wilmington, NC

Seafood Sorcery, Junior League of Wilmington, NC

Sealed with a Knish, Loryn S. Lesser, Micahmatt Press, Baltimore, MD

Seasoned Seniors' Specials, Kernodle Seniors, Burlington, NC

A Second Helping, New Egypt Historical Society, New Egypt, NJ

Secret Recipes, Humane Society of Wilkes, North Wilkesboro, NC

Serving with Grace, Wake Forest Baptist Church, Friendship Chapel Baptist Church, and Heritage Baptist Church, Wake Forest, NC

Sharing Our Best ©2001 Antioch Baptist Church Women, Antioch Baptist Church, Dolphin, VA

Ship to Shore I ©1985 Ship to Shore, Inc., Jan Robinson, Charlotte, NC

Ship to Shore II ©1985 Ship to Shore, Inc., Jan Robinson, Charlotte, NC

Sing for Your Supper, Warsaw Presbyterian Church Choir, Warsaw, NC

Sip to Shore ©1986 Ship to Shore, Inc., Jan Robinson, Charlotte, NC

The Smithfield Cookbook ©1978 The Junior Woman's Club of Smithfield, VA

Someone's in the Kitchen with Melanie ©2004 Melanie Reid Soles, Greensboro, NC

South Coastal Cuisine, Friends of the South Coastal Library, Bethany Beach, DE

A Southern Lady's Spirit, Riddick's Folly, Inc., Suffolk, VA

The Special Occasion Cookbook, Avie Lee Huggins, Tabor City, NC

Steppingstone Cookery, Steppingstone Museum Association, Inc., Havre de Grace, MD

Stirring Performances ©1988 The Junior League of Winston-Salem, NC

The Stuffed Cougar, The Patrons Association of the Collegiate Schools, Richmond, VA

Sun-Sational Southern Cuisine, Sun-Sations Tanning Salon and Spa, Inc., Waxhaw, NC

Taste Buds ©1985 Winslow, Woverton, Komegay, Hertford, NC

A Taste of Heaven, Janice Rhodes, Harrisburg, VA

A Taste of the Outer Banks, Bea Basnight and Gail Midgett, B & G Publishing, Manteo, NC

A Taste of Catholicism ©1996 Cathedral Foundation Press, Baltimore, MD

A Taste of Tradition, Sandra Nagler, Georgetown, DE

A Taste of Heaven, Haven of Hope and Healing, Graham, NC

A Taste of Heaven, Ministry of Light Outreach Church, Williamstown, NJ

Taste of the Town ©1969, 1977, 2003 Charity League of Lexington, NC

Taste & See, Philadelphia United Methodist Church, Emporia, VA

A Taste of History ©1982 The North Carolina Museum of History Associates, Inc., Raleigh, NC

Taste of Goodness, United Methodist Women, Farmville, VA

A Taste of the Outer Banks III, Bea Basnight and Gail Midgett, B & G Publishing, Manteo, NC

A Taste of the Outer Banks II, Bea Basnight and Gail Midgett, B & G Publishing, Manteo, NC

A Taste of Virginia History ©2004 Debbie Nunley and Karen Jane Elliott, John F. Balir, Publishers, Winston-Salem, NC

A Taste of GBMC, Greater Baltimore Medical Center Volunteer Auxiliary, Baltimore, MD

Think Healthy, Fairfax County Department of Extension, Fairfax, VA

Thomas Jefferson's Cook Book ©1976 Rector and Visitors of the University of Virginia, Marie Kimball, Charlottesville, VA

Thought for Food, Goodwin House, Alexandria, VA

Tidewater on the Half Shell ©1985 Junior League of Norfolk-Virginia Beach, Inc., Norfolk, VA

Toast to Tidewater ©2004 Junior League of Norfolk-Virginia Beach, Inc., Norfolk, VA

Tried and True Recipes, Joan Dimengo, Centreville, VA

Turnip Greens, Ham Hocks & Granny's Buns ©2001 Dianne C. Evans, EvanCraft, Inc., Charlotte, NC

Vegetarian Masterpieces ©1988 Carol Tracy and Julie Bruton, Charlotte, NC

Very Virginia ©1995 Junior League of Hampton Roads, Inc., Newport News, VA

Vesuvius, Virginia ©2004 The Vesuvius Community Association, Inc., Vesuvius, VA

Vintage Virginia ©2000 Virginia Dietetic Association, Centreville, VA

Virginia Traditions ©1994 Junior Woman's Club of Hopewell, Hopewell, VA

Virginia Hospitality ©1975 Junior League of Hampton Roads, Inc., Newport News, VA

Virginia Fare ©1994 The Junior League of Richmond, VA

Virginia Cook Book ©2001 Golden West Publishers, Janice Therese Mancuso, Phoenix, AZ

The Virginia House-wife ©1984 University of South Carolina, Mary Randolph, Columbia, SC

Virginia Seasons ©1984 Junior League of Richmond, VA

Virginia Wine Country ©1987 Hilde Gabriel Lee and Allan E. Lee, Betterway Publications, Inc., Charlottesville, VA

The Virginia Presidential Homes Cookbook ©1987 Williamsburg Publishing Co., Payne Bouknight Tyler, Charles City, VA

Virginia's Historic Restaurants and Their Recipes ©1984 Dawn O'Brien, John F. Blair, Publisher, Winston-Salem, NC

The Westwood Clubhouse Cookbook, The Westwood Clubhouse of Brain Injury Services, Inc., Fredericksburg, VA

What Can I Bring? ©1999 The Junior League of Northern Virginia, McLean, VA

What in the World Are We Going to Have for Dinner? Cookbook ©1987 Sarah E. Drummond, Richmond, VA

What Is It! What Do I Do with It! ©1978 Beth Tartan and Fran Parker, TarPar Ltd., Kernersville, NC

What's New in Wedding Food ©1985 Marigold P. Sparks and Beth Tartan, TarPar Ltd., Kernersville, NC

What's Cookin' ©1993 Arlene Luskin, MD

Where There's a Will... ©1997 Evelyn Will, Easton, MD

Winterthur's Culinary Collection ©1983 The Henry Francis du Pont Winterthur Museum, Inc., Garden & Library, Winterthur, DE

Words Worth Eating ©1987 Jacquelyn G. Legg, Newport News, VA

WYVE's Cookbook/Photo Album ©1989 WYVE Radio, Wytheville, VA

You're Invited ©1998 The Junior League of Raleigh, NC

Index

PHOTO BY GWEN MCKEE.

Constructed in 1854, the *USS Constellation* was the last all-sail warship built by the United States Navy. It is the only Civil War-era vessel still afloat, and is now preserved as a museum at Baltimore's Inner Harbor in Maryland.

INDEX

INDEX

INDEX

The recipes included in the REGIONAL COOKBOOK SERIES have been collected from the

BEST OF THE BEST STATE COOKBOOK SERIES

Best of the Best from the
East Coast
Cookbook

Selected Recipes from the Favorite Cookbooks of
Maryland, Delaware, New Jersey, Washington DC,
Virginia, and North Carolina